Praise for

NO GOOD DEED

"Basinski chronicles the three-year investigation into one of the country's more bizarre murders with passion, grit, and hard-boiled realism." —*San Diego* magazine

"A fascinating and engaging tale . . . Basinski brings much detailed knowledge of law enforcement techniques and attitude to the book, going to great length to explain to the reader the finer points of crime investigation and preparation for trial common to law enforcement agents. He also conveys the frustration of those agents when pursuing what turns out to be sidetracks on the way to clarity—often caused by the sorts of difficult personalities one finds at a day on the job in a murder investigation. His book is hard to put down." —*The San Diego Espresso*

CROSS-COUNTRY EVIL

TOM BASINSKI

BERKLEY BOOKS, NEW YORK

THE BERKLEY PUBLISHING GROUP
Published by the Penguin Group
Penguin Group (USA) Inc.
375 Hudson Street, New York, New York 10014, USA
Penguin Group (Canada), 90 Eglinton Avenue East, Suite 700, Toronto, Ontario M4P 2Y3, Canada
(a division of Pearson Penguin Canada Inc.)
Penguin Books Ltd., 80 Strand, London WC2R 0RL, England
Penguin Group Ireland, 25 St. Stephen's Green, Dublin 2, Ireland (a division of Penguin Books Ltd.)
Penguin Group (Australia), 250 Camberwell Road, Camberwell, Victoria 3124, Australia
(a division of Pearson Australia Group Pty. Ltd.)
Penguin Books India Pvt. Ltd., 11 Community Centre, Panchsheel Park, New Delhi—110 017, India
Penguin Group (NZ), 67 Apollo Drive, Rosedale, North Shore 0632, New Zealand
(a division of Pearson New Zealand Ltd.)
Penguin Books (South Africa) (Pty.) Ltd., 24 Sturdee Avenue, Rosebank, Johannesburg 2196,
South Africa

Penguin Books Ltd., Registered Offices: 80 Strand, London WC2R 0RL, England

The publisher does not have any control over and does not assume any responsibility for author or third-party websites or their content.

CROSS-COUNTRY EVIL

A Berkley Book / published by arrangement with the author

PRINTING HISTORY
Berkley mass-market edition / January 2009

Copyright © 2009 by Tom Basinski
Cover design by Diana Kolsky
Book design by Laura K. Corless

ISBN: 978-0-425-22489-2

BERKLEY®
Berkley Books are published by The Berkley Publishing Group,
a division of Penguin Group (USA) Inc.,
375 Hudson Street, New York, New York 10014.
BERKLEY is a registered trademark of Penguin Group (USA) Inc.
The "B" design is a trademark belonging to Penguin Group (USA) Inc.

PRINTED IN THE UNITED STATES OF AMERICA

10 9 8 7 6 5 4 3 2 1

For Judy, Nick, and Joe,
my constant reminders of what is important

AUTHOR'S NOTE

This is a true story. The real names of persons were used except for the following:

   1) The names of the prostitute/sexual assault victims were changed.

   2) The names of Mark Elder's wife and son were changed in an attempt to allow them to avoid embarrassment.

   3) The name of Mark Elder's coworker who came forward to assist authorities was changed.

An asterisk* was placed after each fictitious name when the name first appeared.

The information contained in the book was obtained from official police reports, official court transcripts, the document NHI (No Humans Involved), or interviews. If a quotation is used, the quote came from an interview, a report, or a transcript.

Some opinions of the author are contained in this book. These are easily recognizable as opinions.

PART I

San Diego, California

CHAPTER 1

It was just another murder. Or was it? It was merely "another murder" to the people reading the *San Diego Union,* or the San Diego edition of the *Los Angeles Times,* the city's two morning newspapers, on June 12, 1988. A story in the middle of each local section reported that a friend had found twenty-seven-year-old Janet Moore's body in her apartment. The apparent cause of death—stabbing—was listed, but the police spokesman refused to say how many times. The story ran all of a dozen lines and was probably forgotten by the time the reader turned the page or took another sip of coffee. It was, after all, "just another murder."

While San Diego readers skimmed over the story without an afterthought in whatever paper they favored, the homicide team that investigated the killing didn't think of it as "just another murder." Violent death was their business, and the homicide detectives dealt with it every day, even on their days off or when they were on vacation. That was the rub: their cases were with them all the time. Even though she had been killed the night before, the detectives

were still at Janet Moore's homicide scene the next morning while San Diegans perused their papers and planned
the rest of their day.

The night before, June 11, just after 10 p.m., Allen Spies
had knocked on the door of Janet's studio apartment at 914
Seventeenth Street. Janet was supposed to be home in
apartment 8, but no one answered. Spies later told the police that Janet had said she would call him sometime during the evening. They had talked about going to the nearby
Turf Club for a few drinks. Since Janet was usually punc-
tual and dependable, Spies went to her place to see why she
wasn't answering her phone.

From the sidewalk, Spies could see Janet's light on in
her second-story corner apartment. The building has restricted access and one must dial up the resident or know
the entry code before entering. When Janet did not answer,
Spies called the manager, Nathan Smith, who buzzed him
inside. After climbing the stairs, Spies peered through the
small window. He could see a body on the floor in a pool
of blood.

Janet's door was slightly ajar. Spies went in, found the
phone, and tried to call 911. Someone had pulled the phone
from the wall. He ran to Smith's apartment, phoning the police from there.

Patrol Officers Doug Pickett and Roger Owens responded within minutes. This area was the "downtown beat" and
was patrolled by many cars. The Saturday-night spate of
activity, sending cops from call to call, hadn't started yet.

The officers went inside and found the nude girl. Even
though the whitened body looked dead, they checked for
vital signs, verifying that it was too late to render medical
attention. The uniforms backed out while telling Dispatch
to notify the on-call homicide team.

Team III was in the "up" mode, and their pagers started
going off immediately. Sergeant Ed Petrick would head up
this investigation. Detectives Patrick Ruffner and Jaime

Bordine were the "chasers" and would track down leads as they developed. Detective Ron Thill supervised the crime scene. Evidence Technician Randy Gibson would do the actual collecting and document what evidence was collected. Gibson would also snap about a hundred photographs.

The homicide teams for the San Diego Police are "up" for seven days, from 7 a.m. Tuesday until 7 a.m. the following Tuesday. They handle all homicides and suspicious deaths during that time frame. A homicide team consists of a sergeant, three detectives, and one evidence technician. One of the detectives, called a "scene" detective, directs the collection of evidence and photography. San Diego's evidence technicians are so experienced that they perform basically without supervision. The scene detective serves as another pair of eyes, and also keeps "the book" on the case. Every report generated goes into the book. The book is the totality of every effort expended in the case. The other two detectives chase leads and conduct interviews. The sergeant keeps the case coordinated, answers phones, and conducts interviews as needed.

This had been a "helluva" week. Janet Moore's death was their fourth call-out. This being the fourth day of being "up," the cops felt the strain. Team III closed the first three cases in a timely manner. Janet Moore's case would be a bigger challenge.

The homicide team arrived by 11:30 p.m. and stood in the doorway. Most homicide detectives get a strange feeling in the pit of their stomachs when they first arrive at a homicide scene. Questions run through their heads at breakneck speed. Will this one be solved quickly? Will it be solved at all? Will it be a comparatively easy case to solve, or will they have to claw and scratch for each and every lead? Why had this person been killed? And more importantly, who did it? Team III had many years in homicide, but the initial feeling of apprehension was always there. Tonight was no different.

They hadn't approached the body. Peering through the front door, it looked as if someone had dipped a rag mop into a bucket of blood and swung it around the room repeatedly. They couldn't save the young girl, but maybe they could find who had done this to her. It was time to go to work.

CHAPTER 2

Some downtown areas of San Diego are upscale, populated with expensive condominiums. The nine-hundred
block of Seventeenth Street, also called the East Village, is
about a mile removed from the upscale section. While not
a slum, this area was fighting to avoid becoming one. Prostitutes, those involved in the drug trade, the homeless, and
those making a quick buck on whatever scam they could
pull frequented this neighborhood, especially after dark.

Moore's apartment building was two short blocks from
police headquarters at 1401 Broadway. For a diversion, before Janet's killing, Detectives Jaime Bordine and Ron Thill
would sometimes look out the east window of their fourth-
floor office in the afternoon and observe the goings-on in
the neighborhood. At least once a week they would spot a
car burglary in progress. They would pick up the phone, call
Dispatch, and watch while patrol officers converged on the
unsuspecting crook, arresting him, or them. The sport of
"burglar spotting" was a nice change of pace from bloody

crime scenes, grieving families, lying witnesses, and lying suspects.

Among the first jobs on this clear, warm June night was to find out more about who the dead girl was; really was, not just her identity. Finding what she was about would be a key to solving the case, or at least be a big help in doing so. The manager said Janet Moore had moved in by herself about a month ago. She did not work and seemed to have a lot of visitors, mostly black people. The apartment building was a four-story twenty-five-unit complex on the west side of Seventeenth Street. Moore's studio apartment was on the second floor in the southeast corner.

The building itself was of formidable stucco construction with a red tile roof. If one stood on top of the apartment building, one could throw a baseball onto the southbound lanes of Interstate 5, the freeway that continued ten miles south to Tijuana, Mexico.

A security phone with the last names and code numbers for the residents was at the front door. If you were looking for John Smith, but didn't know his apartment number, you could not learn the number by looking at his name on the board. Next to Smith's name was a calling code such as "012" and it did not mean Smith was in apartment 12. The locking mechanism for the entrance was in good working order. The manager attested that the door always closed and locked automatically. He saw to it.

If someone wanted to kill Janet Moore, but didn't know her apartment number, the killer could not find it from the directory at the front door. Was this an earth-shattering revelation? No, but it was a detail that could not go unnoticed. In a homicide investigation, everything needs to be noticed. That is the way of homicide investigation. A seemingly small detail could impact a court case months or years away. The irony was that one never knew what would be important. Sergeant Petrick once said, "We are not judged by what we do in a case. We are judged by what we did NOT do. Everything is important."

Since Moore lived by herself, it was not necessary to obtain a search warrant to process the crime scene. If she had a roommate, the police would have had to wake up a deputy district attorney to assist in composing the script for a telephonic search warrant. After the detective and attorney had assembled all the facts, they would wake up the duty judge and get a telephonic search warrant issued. The final instructions from the judge were always that the detective who presented the verbal affidavit should affix the judge's name at the bottom. Later, a secretary would transcribe the tape recording into an affidavit, and the search warrant would become part of the case file forever. None of that was necessary tonight. They could get to work right away.

Many police homicide teams do a "walk-through" of the scene to get a sense of the crime. Sergeant Ed Petrick did not believe in this method. The nineteen-year veteran believed anyone entering a homicide scene took things in that didn't belong, and usually took things out that should have remained inside. He didn't mean big things. He meant little things like an errant hair, some fabric or piece of thread, anything that might fall off a detective's shirt, coat, or body. A strand of hair from a suspect might attach itself to the sole of a detective's shoe and leave the scene with him or her.

Petrick's method was the ultimate in caution, and it wasn't a bad idea. Petrick had spent many years in Narcotics, both as a detective and as a supervisor. Although he never was a homicide detective, he applied the same investigative principles he had learned over the years. In tonight's case, Petrick's practice was also logical in that there was so much blood on the floor that foot traffic had to be kept minimal, at least in the beginning.

Another difference from many "old-time" homicide sergeants was that Petrick preferred to rely on forensic evidence whenever possible instead of suspect confessions and eyewitness identifications. Petrick had seen so many things go wrong as a result of confessions and identifications that he wanted to make sure everything in every case was wrapped up tight. Almost no one was in prison based on incorrect forensic evidence. The chance for error in forensics was very small compared to the problems associated with confusing and recanted confessions and mistaken identity.

For this reason, Petrick stayed outside waiting to be briefed by Thill and Gibson.

Detectives Ruffner and Bordine started knocking on neighboring doors, while Thill and Gibson remained inside the apartment.

Gibson photographed the cramped living quarters from every angle before anyone could enter and "contaminate" the scene. This photography protocol is a common police practice to ensure that the room is documented exactly as it is before anyone disturbs anything. Defense attorneys pore over crime-scene photographs looking for discrepancies in the placement of objects in much the same way a magazine will have a feature inviting readers to try to "Find What Is Different" in a series of two similar drawings made to test powers of observation.

If something is in a different location, or missing from a previous photograph, the defense attorneys can trumpet how the detectives altered the scene to put blame more easily on their client. Or, if the moved object has no connection to the accused, the attorney can point out the ineptness of the police who altered a crime scene, then didn't even put it back together correctly. Sometimes defense attorneys accuse the police of dishonesty without a trace of evidence. It helps the defense attorneys if there is something concrete to point to like objects that have been moved.

Even though homicide victims can't talk, the crime scene often speaks volumes. And the condition of the body can tell even more. In this case, there was an inordinate amount of blood right inside the front door. It looked like the killer, or killers, had dragged the body away from the front door after death to where it now lay.

From looking at the blood trail throughout the apartment, Thill theorized that the initial attack on Moore started in the dining area of the studio. It appeared that Janet tried to escape and had made it as far as the front door. The fight ended there where she lay, losing most of her blood, until final expiration. Her body probably blocked the exit, not allowing the front door to be opened. Thill and Gibson believed the killer dragged her back to where she now lay so he or she could open the door and leave. A blanket was tossed on the floor. There didn't appear to be a reason for its placement. The presence of the blanket might be a useful piece of information, or it might be nothing.

As Thill took notes, he stole an occasional glance at Janet Moore's nude and hacked body. He kept thinking, *Damn, she's young. What happened?*

When Gibson was done photographing the interior of the apartment, Ron Thill began a careful walk-through. The first thing he noticed was that neither the door nor frame was damaged. The lack of forced entry could mean that Janet let someone in voluntarily, or that someone had knocked, and when she opened the door a few inches, the person forcibly intruded. What was not open to debate was that the door, frame, and lock were intact.

One could not jump to conclusions, especially at this early point in the investigation. There were many possibilities that either could not be ignored or taken as the absolute truth, at least for now. It is a mistake to get locked into a specific scenario too early based solely on speculation. When hard, incontrovertible facts became evident as truth, one could then "take them to the bank." So far, nothing was certain except that a young girl was murdered and there had been no forced entry.

With all the blood scattered throughout, it took a few minutes for Thill to get his bearings and let the crime scene "speak" to him. While not an expert in blood-spatter evidence, Thill, a sixteen-year police veteran, had seen his share of bloody scenes in his two years of homicide investigation and at the many schools he had attended in conjunction with his assignment in Homicide. Thill stood in the living room, slowly taking in everything in the room, the furnishings, their position, the few photos hanging on the wall. He looked at the kitchen, observing everything, looking for something that was out of place or something that would help explain Janet Moore's death.

When Detective Thill went into the bathroom, he paused and whistled softly. "This is something," he said to no one in particular. On the top of the toilet tank was a formerly white washcloth saturated with blood. Next to it was a box of toilet tissue with several bloody tissues. Thill knew damn well that Janet Moore had not come in the bathroom to stop her flow of blood. Thill was certain the killer had cut him- or herself during the attack and had tried to clean up or give self–first aid in the bathroom.

Thill was confident, by the number and location of wounds on Janet Moore, that she had been incapable of trying to clean herself. A good homicide detective never jumps to conclusions, but Thill felt safe in making this assumption. They were dealing with an injured killer.

The washcloth was like Cinderella's slipper. Find the person whose blood was on the washcloth, and you would find the killer, Thill predicted. Later analysis would prove that the blood on the washcloth and toilet tissue was different from Janet Moore's.

Without moving or touching her, Thill ran his flashlight beam up and down Moore's body. He paid particular attention to her hands and her right arm, which bore many gaping wounds. The wounds told Thill that Janet Moore had fought furiously until she could fight no more. The cuts, called "defense wounds," depict the last minutes and seconds of a homicide victim's life and the effort the victim expended to keep on living. The slashes went right through to the bone on her forearm. Tendons were visible on her hand where the blade had cut through. She had fought, but the killer had strength superior to hers.

Janet Moore lay on her back with her right knee bent slightly. Although she was covered in blood, there was an interesting configuration to the blood. It appeared as if someone had dragged fingers along her body. Simply put, it looked like someone had used her blood to fingerpaint her body. In addition to that unusual appearance, there was little blood on her upper torso, stomach, and thighs. Thill speculated that someone had lain on top of Janet after she had bled a lot. Thill didn't want to think about it, but the condition of the body suggested that perhaps the killer had lain on top of her after death. That could be for only one reason, and it sickened the hardened homicide detective.

He had seen many examples of man's inhumanity toward man, but this was way over the top. Killing her was bad enough, but to degrade her further after death was the ultimate in terms of sickness.

Janet's clothing was folded neatly on her bed. Because she was nude, it appeared she had removed her clothes methodically and placed them there. Thill believed it was significant that the clothing had not been ripped off her and tossed about haphazardly.

There were bloody smudges on the partially open drawers, indicating someone with bloody hands had gone through them, possibly looking for something to steal. Because it didn't look like the victim had many possessions in the first place, the detectives safely assumed the minor ransacking was more of an afterthought. That is, they believed the killer thought that since the victim was dead, he might as well look to see if there was anything to take. Her purse had bloody smudges on both the outside and inside.

Thill located a single tooth on the floor near a pair of socks. When they examined the body in detail, he would learn more about the tooth. Continuing his search of the apartment, Thill found two empty Olde English 800 malt liquor cans and three empty Budweiser beer bottles. Did the killer share a few drinks with Moore before killing her, leaving fingerprints on the bottles and cans? Thill knew that would make things too easy for him, and things were never that easy. Thill was not surprised to find a crack-cocaine pipe in the apartment. A picture of the victim's life was starting to form.

Thill had the dispatch center notify the coroner's office that they had a homicide, but the deputy coroner would not be able to enter the apartment for several hours. California law states that the coroner must be notified immediately of an unattended death. The police are not allowed to move or touch the body, but the police are still in charge of the crime scene.

When the police relinquish the scene to the coroner, the deputy coroner collects personal property such as a wallet, jewelry, or keys from the body, and then arranges for the victim to be transported to the office for autopsy. In this case, there were no wallets, jewelry, or keys, just the naked, hacked, and stabbed body of the young girl.

———

In the early days of San Diego, the coroner did not even have to be a medical doctor. Over the years, that concept has changed. Even the name of the office has changed. What used to be called the "coroner" in the 1980s is now the "medical examiner." The county board of supervisors appoints the M.E. and a medical doctor holds the office.

Hours later, when Thill and Gibson had done all they could inside, the deputy coroner came in. He stood by while

Gibson made tape lifts from Moore's body. There were hair and fibers visible on her body in spite of all the blood. Gibson touched a piece of tape to the hair or fiber. He lifted the taped item from the body and placed it onto an index card with an exact description of where on the body it had been obtained. They lifted up Moore's lip and saw a space where a tooth should have been. It was later proved that the killer had knocked out Moore's tooth, and that the tooth Thill found was the missing one. Not only did the killer stab her, the killer beat her, too. There were bruises on her right shin, hip, and thigh.

Thill had Gibson place evidence bags securely over Moore's feet, hands, and head. The bags would be removed at the coroner's office. The "bagging" of a victim prevents possible trace evidence from falling off her body during the transfer to the transport vehicle and at the medical examiner's office. Moore's body would be placed inside a body bag, the inside of which would also be examined when she was put on the autopsy table at the morgue.

Hours before, Janet Moore had been a living, breathing, vivacious woman. Now, sadly enough, she was a piece of evidence. The detectives hoped they would be able to use the evidence to convict whoever had killed her. In spite of the need to view Janet as a piece of evidence, the detectives never forgot that she was a human being who had lived, loved, laughed, cried, and was not deserving of her final fate.

After the deputy coroner ordered the transportation of the body in the early morning hours, the police tried to locate latent fingerprints from inside the apartment. The usual method for lifting fingerprints is to brush fine graphite powder lightly in places where fingerprints might be found, such as near doorknobs, light switches, and on objects that possibly had been moved. The fine powder adheres to oils deposited from fingertips or palms, even lip prints.

This same process involves applying tape to the powder, which by then has the configuration of the finger, palm, or whatever body part has come into contact with the surface. The tape is lifted and placed onto an index card with the exact location of the lift written on the card. An expert trained in latent-print examination steps in to compare the lifted latent-print against the known rolled print if a suspect is located or identified.

One myth perpetuated by Hollywood films and the various *C.S.I.* television shows is that fingerprints can be lifted from almost anything. Truth is, the surface must be conducive to accepting a print. That is, the surface cannot be grainy or rough. It must be smooth enough to accept a transfer of body oil from a finger, palm, lip, or bare foot.

When a suspect has positively been identified through fingerprints at a crime scene, it is difficult to explain how one's fingerprints got there when the suspect has denied ever being in the area. It doesn't cut it for a suspect to say, "Someone must have borrowed my prints, man." Oddly enough, that excuse has been tried more than once.

In this case, there was so much blood around the apartment that the experts elected to use an additional method of latent-fingerprint detection and collection called ninhydrin. The proper term for this chemical is triketohydrindane hydrate, and involves spraying a liquid on areas where fingerprints might have been left. If the ninhydrin comes into contact with oils from the body, the chemical will eventually turn a deep blue. The result is the same as if fingerprint powder had been applied to the print.

Randy Gibson sprayed ninhydrin in the areas where prints might be found. They locked up the apartment, applying a coroner's "Do Not Enter" seal. They would return in a few days to see if they had any good luck.

CHAPTER 3

Part of the purpose for the search of Janet's apartment was to find contact information, both friends and family. A homicide investigation starts with the victim's "inner circle." The statistical reality is that someone very close to the victim is frequently the killer. Often, the closer the relationship, the more likely it is that one relative or acquaintance or friend killed the victim. Why? People who know the victim often have a reason to kill, be it jealousy, money, or anger. Absent other obvious information, the police cannot explore other murder theories until they have cleared those people closest to the victim.

Janet Moore did not have an address book. A pad of paper with many names and numbers sat next to her telephone. The names didn't designate whether the person was a friend or relative. The deputy coroner jotted down the information of those who had the same last name because it was his job to notify the next of kin. A local phone number was written next to the word *Mom*.

Homicide Team III was getting curious about Janet

Moore. People who lived in the area where Janet lived were not "yuppies" who hung out at fashionable San Diego nightspots or those featured in the "City Fair" section of *San Diego* magazine, the "beautiful people" attending society functions. Many who lived in Janet's area were "down-and-outers" who had taken a beating from life. A few had once been successful, but their lives were now slipping downward. Others in the neighborhood struggled to make improvements after having endured life's slings and arrows. The investigators wondered where Janet Moore fit into this picture. Was she struggling to get out of a dangerous lifestyle, or rapidly dropping back into one, or both, at alternate times?

While Thill and Gibson processed the crime scene, Detectives Jaime Bordine and Patrick Ruffner knocked on doors that were near Janet's apartment. Later, during the day, they would contact every resident in the building. But given the late hour, they concentrated on those who might have seen or heard something while it was happening.

The lady in the apartment directly above Janet's told the detectives she heard screaming and banging between 8 and 9 p.m. for about two minutes. She said there was always so much screaming and yelling in the neighborhood she didn't call the police. "If I called you guys every time there was a fight in this neighborhood, we'd have to give you assigned parking."

Another neighbor told Detective Bordine she heard a woman screaming about 5:45 or 6 p.m. "Help me! Someone help me!" the lady reported hearing. Another neighbor heard someone yell, "Help me," around five o'clock. Still another neighbor heard two gunshots. "Was she shot?" the neighbor asked.

The detectives were puzzled. Someone heard cries for help at 5 p.m. Another heard cries at 6 p.m., and someone else heard screaming and fighting at 9 p.m. Another heard a gunshot. If all the neighbors were correct, which screams had been Janet's? She had died too quickly for all the cries for help to be hers. No one had called the police when they heard the screams.

Sergeant Petrick agreed with Ron Thill that because so much blood had saturated the washcloth and tissues in the bathroom, someone besides the victim had been badly injured. Petrick went to the emergency rooms of the hospitals within a few miles to see what he could learn. Some police supervisors believe their only duty is to supervise. Sergeant Petrick made sure that after all his administrative and supervisory duties had been taken care of, he waded in on interviews, reports, and whatever needed to be done.

The nearby Navy Regional Medical Center provided a patient who piqued his interest. The emergency-room staff had administered multiple stitches to a young sailor for a major laceration on his throat. The reason the sailor gave for the injury? He cut himself shaving. He told the attending physician the "boat rocked" while he was shaving, and that caused the cut.

Petrick viewed that story with much skepticism. The sailor expected the medical staff to believe a multiton battleship in calm San Diego Bay rocked enough to cause a man to cut his throat while shaving. Petrick didn't think so. This guy would bear looking at in greater detail. Since he was in the navy, the government had a good hold on him until the police could either clear him or charge him.

Another sailor claimed to have been jumped and stabbed in the city of Coronado across the bay. That little city had almost no violent crime. The small police department usually occupied itself arresting Navy SEALs who had too much to drink or by ticketing elderly retired admirals who ran red lights.

The homicide team would look at these two sailors in greater detail.

Petrick told Detective Jaime Bordine to follow up with the next of kin after the deputy coroner made the notification. Janet's mother, Sarah Sabor, lived only a few miles away. Bordine, ever the gentleman, hated this kind of duty. Yet he had the soothing demeanor and empathetic style to give as much comfort to the family that could be given, considering the circumstances.

Stopping by in the morning, Bordine stayed with Ms. Sabor most of the day, alternately gathering information and providing emotional aid. He confirmed with the mother that Janet did have a drug problem. He also learned she was an accomplished artist. Bordine quizzed the mother to learn all he could about Janet's associates and how Janet lived her life. Unfortunately, Ms. Sabor could not provide much helpful information about the darker side of Janet's life, only that she struggled.

Detective Bordine learned that Janet had one brother and three sisters. The family had lived in many different places over the years. Two sisters lived locally; one sister and the brother lived out of California.

Janet had never been in a formal drug rehabilitation program. Those cost money. Janet had no health insurance, and couldn't have afforded the deductible even if she did. She elected to "kick the habit" by herself in her own way. She would be successful for a while, then slip back into drug use.

Her mother said the company Janet kept was a factor in the addiction. Ms. Sabor had urged Janet to find new friends because the old friends all used drugs. To Janet, this didn't make sense. These were her friends. She was loyal to them. Sadly enough, she did drugs with them too.

Janet could have elected to shoplift, do identity theft, and steal and use credit cards or other illegal things to obtain money to buy drugs. Her mother believed Janet was involved in prostitution, but Janet never admitted as much to her. Detective Bordine did not press the prostitution mat-

ter with Janet's mother. The lady had enough grief to deal
with for now.

———

On Monday, June 13, Detective Thill and Randy Gibson
were at the coroner's office. Beginning at 9 a.m., Dr. John
Eisele performed the postmortem exam on the body of Janet Moore. The assistant removed the bags from her hands,
feet, and head. Gibson took custody of the bags. Gibson
took photographs of the body in the unwashed state. As is
the practice to ensure decency for males and females, a
paper towel is used to cover the genitals while these photographs are taken.

Gibson both snipped and pulled head hair and pubic
hair from Moore's body. He took fingernail scrapings from
all her fingers and carefully deposited them in envelopes.
An earring was caught in her tangled head hair, along with
a small fragment from the broken tooth that was found in
the apartment. The examination of the body revealed Janet
Moore had shoulder-length blondish curly hair and blue
eyes. She had a tattoo of a flower above her left breast.

One never knew what would be important to a case. If
the killer's skin was beneath Janet's fingernails, they
needed to save it. Word from the scientific community was
that experts were making rapid progress with body fluids,
skin, and hair. Someday the authorities would be able to
identify people based on these findings.

The pathologist took anal and vaginal swabs from
Moore's body to see if seminal remains were there. The
results from the vaginal swab showed the presence of semen. In itself, this fact did not prove rape. Semen only
meant Janet Moore had had sexual intercourse. The semen
was evidence; its importance might or might not be revealed in the future.

When the collection of evidence from the corpse was
completed, the assistant washed the body and Dr. Eisele

started the autopsy. He counted and documented twenty-one stab wounds and eighteen incise gashes. The wounds were all over her upper body: the chest, upper arms, shoulder, armpit, and the top of her head. It was "overkill," to be sure. She had fought back, and fought back mightily.

The autopsy revealed no surprises. Dr. Eisele's report listed the cause of death as "multiple stab and incise wounds." Later, toxicology results would show the presence of cocaine in Moore's body. Living where she did, and finding the crack pipe in her residence, the presence of cocaine did not surprise the detectives. While they weren't surprised at this point in the investigation, they would soon be disappointed—again and again.

CHAPTER 4

After the autopsy, Randy Gibson and Thill returned to Janet's apartment. They removed the coroner's seal and entered. Gibson examined the results of the ninhydrin spraying. He made a few fingerprint lifts from places they hoped would yield results, areas around light switches and doorknobs. They hoped at least one of the lifts would help solve the case.

Detectives Ruffner and Bordine began contacting all the people listed in Janet's notebook. They went back to talk to Janet's mother. She had recovered somewhat from the shock of Bordine's first visit. The woman told a tale of a young girl who struggled. Mom said the tentacles of drugs had gripped Janet Moore. Janet's desire for drugs turned her to prostitution, Ms. Sabor was sure, where the money was quick but dangerous.

Photographs of Janet revealed a sweet young blonde one would never suspect of being a prostitute, if it is possible to discern one's profession merely by looks. Many girls who work the streets should be seen from a distance no closer than twenty-five feet, or else seen only in the dark. Many of them have lined, bony faces, cheaply inked tattoos, discolored decaying teeth, and blotchy skin. Someone driving by a bus stop at fifteen miles per hour in search of a brief encounter with a woman might be attracted to one of the hardened girls wearing a cheap discount-store miniskirt. A closer scrutiny, and the smell test, might cause the customer to keep on driving.

This was not the case with Janet. She looked wholesome and generally healthy. Her lifestyle had not left her with facial lines and scars. While she was thin, she was not emaciated and drawn. Janet was a part-time college student studying art. Her mother showed the detectives several of her drawings. The detectives would have told Janet's mother they were good drawings even if they weren't. Ruffner and Bordine were honest in their praise of the young girl's efforts. She had talent.

Janet's mother wrung her hands, her eyes welling up with tears as she told again of Janet's struggles over the years. Janet had been accepted by and attended a prestigious school in Minnesota that specialized in graphic design. The more Ms. Sabor thought about it, the more vocal she became. It was Janet's mother's impression that the fast lifestyle of the artists who attended the school had gotten Janet hooked on drugs. No verification of this was ever made by the police because it was not part of the case.

Janet didn't lack for ambition, just self-control. Her problems were the result of even more than a lack of self-control. Janet's addiction was a vise grip on her life, a real sickness. The grip would loosen occasionally as she struggled to free herself from the drugs. When she was off drugs, she avoided her friends from that unsavory part of her life. But things would happen that would cause her to slip back. A disappointment here, a failed relationship there, a perceived letdown at the hands of friends or family caused her to reach out and embrace the poison of her life—drugs. With drugs came a need for money, and with the need for money came prostitution. The cycle was vicious, unrelenting, and unforgiving.

Janet's mother didn't know much about her friends. Janet avoided her mother when she was using drugs. When she wasn't using, she was busy at school, working a part-time job, or painting. "We all tried to help Janet," her mother said. "It just wasn't enough. No matter what we did. Now look what happened."

Janet's mother could think of no one who would harm Janet. Janet had a husband, but he had a good alibi. He had been in prison for several years. The detectives would verify his incarceration. Stranger things had happened in the world of criminal justice. They would see if the husband was eligible for weekend passes.

Dwight Timothy Scott married Janet Moore on June 11, 1982. Was it a coincidence that someone killed her on their sixth anniversary? Scott robbed a bank, was caught, and went to federal prison in Shelton, Washington, on January 31, 1984, to serve a twenty-five-year term. He had not seen Janet since the day he went to prison. Scott was not eligible for furlough either. His time was accounted for, and several corrections officers could vouch for his presence in the institution. Scott's name never made it to the suspect list. Scott later wrote to the detectives asking for information and inquiring how close they were to solving the case. The detectives also ruled out a "contract hit" ordered by the incarcerated husband.

Scott had no reason to be upset enough with Janet to have someone kill her. The crime scene depicted brutal rage, something a hired killer would not resort to. The person who killed Janet Moore hated her, or hated something about her, the detectives were certain.

Another acquaintance of Janet, Allen Spies, who had

found the body, revealed that he had met Janet when she was sitting on a bus bench, a major hangout for street prostitutes. Vice cops knew a girl was a prostitute because whenever a bus would come by the girl would get up and walk around the corner until the bus was gone. Then she would assume her former position on the bench, cautiously eyeing each car and driver that went by. From more in-depth conversation, the police were certain that Janet was at least a part-time prostitute. They'd thought that initially, but the friend confirmed it.

A thorough check of the neighborhood and the residents of the apartment building revealed nothing. One resident said Janet had had a black female visitor named Tessa a few weeks before who knocked on the neighbor's door asking to use the phone. Janet's phone was not yet installed. When Tessa left after making her phone call, the neighbor noticed a bracelet was missing. She told Janet about the bracelet. Tessa returned a few times and screamed at the neighbor. The bracelet was never returned. Since Tessa was a friend of Janet's, the police would have to talk to her.

Investigation revealed that Janet had romantic relations almost exclusively with black men. While she was multiracial in her prostitution dealing, the men who could be called "boyfriends" were all black, as was her husband.

From a letter found in the apartment, the detectives learned Janet had a boyfriend named Tony Jennings. Finding Jennings was easy because he was in jail, and had been there long enough not to be considered a suspect either. Detective Patrick Ruffner interviewed him right away.

Jennings said Janet had visited him in jail recently. A check of visitor cards revealed that a William Shipman had accompanied Moore to the lockup. Jennings might know who would want Janet Moore dead. Jennings said he had never had sex with Janet even though they were boyfriend and girlfriend. He said Janet liked rock cocaine. She would perform acts of prostitution for money, but not for drugs. She was a prostitute, but not a "crack whore." Ruffner asked about Shipman. Jennings said he was merely a friend of Janet's who drove her places from time to time.

Since Jennings had been in jail for quite a while, he had several letters from Moore. Ruffner looked at them. They were newsy and light. There were no reports of fights with people or threats from others. Janet did not feel her life was in danger. The police were getting nowhere fast.

Jennings said a girl named Patricia Miller* didn't care much for Janet, and she might be capable of killing her. As the interview went on, Jennings admitted that he and Patricia had a child together even though they weren't married. "Let's make sure I have this," said Ruffner. "You and Patricia Miller have a child together, and up until last Saturday you and Janet were boyfriend and girlfriend. Is that correct? And, you think Patricia is capable of killing Janet?"

Jennings said those statements were true. Patricia's name shot onto the list. It inched up higher once the police heard that Patricia was also a prostitute who used drugs. Could it be professional jealousy, a drug debt, or jealousy over the boyfriend?

Privately, the cops believed that a lone woman probably had not killed Janet, unless the woman was some kind of martial-arts expert, and large enough to completely control her victim. If a woman was involved, she probably had help.

Since Janet had lived at the Seventeenth Street address only a short time, Ruffner went to her old apartment several miles away in the four-thousand block of Forty-ninth Street. He spent most of the morning talking to the landlord and former neighbors. They could probably give more definitive information about Janet than her neighbors on Seventeenth Street.

Janet's life while in this apartment had been volatile. She used narcotics a lot during her stay. There were many fights, both verbal and physical, over drugs and drug debts. People had broken Janet's door on one occasion and had broken her window another time.

There would be booming threats to Janet to "GET ME MY GODDAM MONEY AND GET IT NOW!" Residents called the police regarding loud and violent activity more than once. Janet was never a cooperative victim, though. She refused to give statements, so no actual police reports of assault, battery, or vandalism were on file. If a victim refuses to help the police, the beleaguered officers are only too happy to get out without having to write a report. Other calls with victims who actually wanted help were waiting.

The previous landlord said Janet seemed to have a lot of onetime visitors. He suspected she was a prostitute, but wasn't sure. He did say a well-dressed Asian man in a silver Porsche had been a frequent guest. Sometimes the man would stay, and sometimes Janet would go with him. If the man was a customer, he was a regular one. The landlord added the man had a dignified manner. Detective Ruffner wondered if he was a *jealous* regular customer. While a drug debt probably didn't cause such rage in the killer, jealousy might have.

Ruffner learned Janet lived life on the edge, to be sure. Yet, in light of the amount of violence done to her, Ruffner didn't think the death was the result of a drug debt. He had seen a few killings, and this one appeared to be motivated by rage. Why?

A woman named "Monya" notified detectives that Patricia Miller had told a guy named "Doc" that she had killed Janet. After much searching through files, the detectives located the real name of Doc and his most recent address. After they found him, he denied telling anyone that Patricia said she killed Janet. Sometimes people get caught up in rumors. They exaggerate things for unknown reasons, perhaps to make themselves more important. At any rate, Doc denied making the statement to anyone because he said

Patricia never told him about Janet's death. It was a frustrating merry-go-round for the homicide detectives. The people giving them information lacked credibility. The cops lived and died on credibility, both their own and that of their informants and witnesses.

CHAPTER 5

The Team III detectives had a meeting the day after they left the "up" status. They wouldn't be in the hot seat again for another three weeks. This didn't mean they could take long lunches or schedule a manicure.

Detective Ruffner was not actually a homicide detective at the time. His assignment was investigating sex crimes, and he was taking the place of another detective who was attending training out of town. A twelve-year veteran, Ruffner was on the "waiting list" to be assigned to Homicide. He filled in for whatever team lacked a detective.

Ruffner's wait was similar to that of a ballplayer who is a solid team member but not in the starting lineup. You pay attention, make sure you're ready for the next step by doing a good job on the sex-crime cases you work, and you wait. In sports, you wait for someone to go into a slump, get hurt, or traded. In police work, you wait for someone to retire, get promoted from the unit, or get burned out after seeing death over and over in all its different ways.

For this reason, Patrick Ruffner knew he would not be

the lead detective interrogating a suspect if one was discovered in the case of Janet Moore. He would interview peripheral witnesses and track down minor leads. It was a way of life in the world of homicide investigation. If you did a good job taking care of the little things, you eventually got a shot at tackling the big things.

In a conference room, police personnel went over the cases they had accumulated during the "up" period. Even the three cases they'd solved at the scene, or for which they had identified a suspect within days, required a lot of work. Defense attorneys earn their living making sure the police have done their jobs correctly and making sure the prosecution proves every allegation made against the person arrested. Sergeant Petrick repeated his usual statement to his detectives: "We won't be judged by what we did, but by what we DIDN'T do." If the guys grew tired of hearing that, they never let on.

Since a "bird in the hand is worth two in the bush," the police had to concentrate on the in-custody cases they had. Court dates were looming, and if the detectives didn't do their job in a timely manner, a defendant could be released from custody on due-process issues. Therefore, they had to tend to immediate matters. They needed to interview people on the fringe areas of those cases and gift wrap the solved homicides to take to the district attorney. The mystery of Janet Moore had to wait, merely because of logistics.

Janet Moore's case was the final one they discussed at their meeting. Their initial sadness at seeing the life of such a pretty young girl taken away now gave way to anger. The detectives had seen such wastefulness of human life over the years. They knew all about addiction and the hold drugs have on people. They knew it was addiction, not the love of sexual activity, that caused young women to become prostitutes. In fact, most prostitutes actually disliked sex, especially with men. Many of them turned to lesbianism, or bisexuality, if they weren't there already when they began a life of prostitution.

What angered the detectives professionally was that a murder of a prostitute presented a gigantic mystery. A brief, anonymous, onetime encounter with a prostitute was the worst kind of homicide to investigate.

While a street prostitute didn't want or deserve to get hurt, raped, or killed, she greatly increased her chances of having that happen to her by virtue of her way of life. A professional call girl who goes to hotel rooms has a much safer time of it than the girl who gets into a stranger's car and loses her ability to get away. Over the years police discovered many rapists had removed the inside door handles from their vehicles for the very purpose of keeping the girl captive until the rapist was ready to let her go. It was a tough life. If Janet's killer had been a "john," the job of finding him was as difficult as if he had picked her up in a car. Servicing the john in her own apartment increased her potential safety only a little.

Where do you start on such a case? As mentioned before, the detectives started with the "inner circle" of family and friends. Yet they always had to consider that a stranger picked up Janet, probably didn't even know her real name, and killed her, without giving his own name. Trying to solve such a case was a frustrating experience. It was like stepping into the batter's box with two strikes against you while keeping one eye closed. Doom was present everywhere. Failure seemed a real possibility. Team III didn't like to think about failure.

If Janet had been an expensive call girl, they could have raided her madam's home and obtained her customer list. If she'd been a self-employed call girl, they could have checked her Rolodex and grilled all the men whose names it contained. But she mainly worked the streets, getting into the cars of man she had never seen before and probably would never see again. It was maddening.

Homicide teams look at solving a case in a couple of different ways. One way is that it's *your* case. *Your* name goes on the bottom of the reports. If the case doesn't get solved immediately and leads develop later, maybe after you retire, someone else will look at the case. The new detective will see *your* name at the bottom of the reports. Others will judge your work. Others will comment on and criticize your work. Pride is a powerful motivator to do a good job, maybe not egotistical pride, but professional pride.

Detectives are motivated to solve a homicide in hopes of delivering justice. No one should be allowed to kill another and get away with it. Homicide detectives believe killers should answer for what they have done, no matter whom they harmed. Homicide detectives all over the world believe unproductive members of society, such as those in gangs, dope dealers, prostitutes, and the homeless, still deserve to have their homicides solved and the perpetrators prosecuted. As one veteran homicide detective said many years ago over a glass of bourbon, "I am their [the homicide victim's] voice. They can't talk anymore. They're dead. I now speak for them, and I'm gonna make damn sure people hear them. I don't care what they've done and what they haven't done in their lives. I am now their voice." The detective wasn't being overly dramatic. Good homicide detectives actually feel that way.

If the prospect of solving a prostitute's murder wasn't remote enough, San Diego was experiencing a rash of hooker killings. So many of them had been murdered that the San Diego police and the sheriff's department, along with the district attorney's office, eventually combined to form a task force in 1990. The murder of Janet Moore was different from the other hooker deaths the task force had looked at because the other victims were "body dumps"; the girls were strewn along Interstate 8, the east–west artery between San Diego and Arizona. Or, in some cases, the girls were tossed in Dumpsters in alleyways in the inner city.

Maybe Janet was a victim of the hooker killer, or killers, and the only reason she was killed at home was that she had taken the guy home instead of performing the sex act inside his car in some dark alley. Maybe the killer thought, *I don't need to dump her body. I've already given her what she deserves. I'll just leave her here.* The possibilities were nearly limitless, and the situation wasn't good.

Maybe the killer didn't have a car and that's why they had to go to her room. Maybe he was a homeless person who slept in doorways the cops passed each and every day. The unknowns began to pile up.

But what to do now, this minute, on this case? They had to keep working on Janet's inner circle. She had a sister who was an emergency medical technician for an ambulance company in San Diego. She rarely saw Janet. Other than her mother, most of the family was out of state, or out of touch. Janet had some cousins in the county, but since her tailspin into drugs and prostitution, she rarely saw them.

A good place to start the search was with the people listed on Janet's notepad. They also wanted to speak with Patricia Miller, the woman who'd had the child with Janet's boyfriend, Tony Jennings. Tessa, the woman who stole Janet's neighbor's piece of jewelry, would be another one.

CHAPTER 6

The next week, when things slowed down on the "in custody" cases, the police spoke with William Shipman, the friend who accompanied Janet on her visit to the county jail to see Tony Jennings. Shipman was a white guy. He explained that he met Janet one day when he drove past a bus bench where she was sitting. Shipman gave her a ride because "she seemed like a nice person." Even though Pat Ruffner believed there might have been more to the encounter than merely giving her a ride, he proceeded with the interview in a low-key manner. Ruffner looked closely at Shipman's hands. There were no injuries, such as a large cut.

Shipman said he developed a friendship with Moore. The friendship consisted mostly of Shipman's driving her places. He denied having a sexual relationship with her. "Your semen wouldn't be inside her at the time of her death?" Ruffner asked.

"No, sir."

"Would you mind if we took a blood sample to check for typing and stuff like that?"

"Nope. You can have anything you want."

It was not exactly the reaction one would expect from a killer. They took Shipman's blood and compared it against the type from the washcloth. They rolled his fingerprints to compare with the lifts taken from her apartment. Weeks later, Shipman was not a suspect.

The day after dealing with Shipman, they checked out a "Henry," whose phone number was listed on Janet's notepad. A call to his number revealed his full name was Henry Tan. After speaking briefly with him on the phone, Ruffner met him at his apartment. A silver Porsche was parked outside. When Tan answered the door, the detective noted that he was Asian. This had to be the "dignified older guy" who was a regular visitor to her former address on Forty-ninth Street.

Tan shocked the detective when he told him he was a medical doctor, a pathologist to be exact. He was currently practicing medicine and teaching mathematics at a local university.

Tan was going through a divorce. His medical practice and former home were both located in La Jolla, one of the most upscale areas of San Diego.

Henry Tan proved initially to be a mystery to the police. They didn't know if he had been involved in drugs himself, as some people in the medical profession are. They did know that someone who was a medical doctor didn't generally live as modestly as Tan was living. Of course the impending divorce and usual split of community property could explain this.

Tan didn't use the term *sugar daddy* when describing his relationship with Janet Moore. He seemed too refined to say such a thing. The detectives did use the term when discussing him out of his presence. Tan explained that he really liked Janet. He skirted admission of a physical relationship with her in exchange for money. He termed himself as more of a "benefactor" to Janet. He gave her money and provided transportation for her on a regular basis. Yes, they did have sex, he eventually said, but it was because they both wanted to have sex. While discussing the case later, the detectives privately doubted that, but kept it to themselves.

Tan even financed a trip to Hawaii for Janet and a boyfriend. He didn't seem disturbed that she was a prostitute. He said he cared deeply for Janet, that she was a sweet, caring, vulnerable, artistic soul. They worked together to get her off drugs, he said. When the police asked how this "work" went, Tan said it was mostly him counseling her, and being available to her when she felt herself slipping. He had no training in substance-abuse treatment. He said, "She always knew I was there for her."

Tan admitted visiting Janet at her former residence and at the one where she was killed. He admitted being affectionate with her. He seemed to care so much for her that he would excuse her dalliances with other men, as long as she would leave some time for him. The term *love-struck* came up in conversations the police had among themselves regarding Henry Tan.

At times Tan became emotional during the interview. It was obvious that this man had deep feelings for Janet. He said he would do whatever the police asked of him. Tan knew a few of Janet's friends. Of the names he mentioned, the police already had them on their list. Tan could not think of any of Janet's circle of friends who would do harm to her. "She was fun and funny. She made me feel good to be around her. When I felt bad about my marriage doing poorly, Janet would perk me up," he said.

These detectives had been around the block a few times, and strange relationships among people didn't perplex them. They had seen weird marriage arrangements, living arrangements, and tastes and preferences. They didn't judge. They would have to check out Henry Tan in more detail, though. During the interview Ruffner took note that Tan didn't have any injuries on his hands.

Because hair fibers had been lifted from Moore's body, Ruffner asked Tan to give blood and hair samples and have his fingerprints rolled. Tan, of course, was aware of the value of forensic evidence. Their initial assessment was that he was truly upset about Janet's death, and he wasn't their guy. Nothing ever happened to change that attitude. Weeks later, when the forensic-evidence analyses returned regarding Henry Tan, the police took him off their list.

The days and weeks went by. June turned into July. As each lead came in, Sergeant Petrick assigned it to be checked out either by someone on the team or did it himself. It depended on what the others were doing on the other cases. Nothing was working successfully toward solving Janet's murder. Team III members knew they couldn't move on until they had thoroughly exhausted Janet's "inner circle" of friends, a wily, transient group of people.

If a homicide victim had a steady job, the detectives could go to the workplace, get a list of coworkers from Human Resources, and interview all business associates within and outside of the company. With a street prostitute, part-time sporadic worker, and part-time student, they couldn't operate that way. It was frustrating.

Several fingerprints were lifted from the area near the light switch in Janet's apartment. They came back to a guy named David Mark, whose prints were already in the automated database. The police had spoken with him previously because his name was on Janet's phone list. Mark cooperated with the police, telling them he had helped Janet move into her apartment. He had no wounds on him. When he voluntarily provided blood and hair, they too checked negative. Another possible lead that went nowhere.

The days piled up without significant progress on the murder of Janet Moore despite the detectives' effort. Sometimes several weeks would go by without Team III doing anything on the case because there was nothing left to do.

A homicide team operates on a triage priority similar to the emergency room of a hospital. If a doctor is working on a broken arm and a bleeder comes in, the person with the broken arm has to wait until the doctor stops the bleeding.

The same thing happened with all of the homicide teams in the San Diego Police Department. The year 1988 was a banner one for murders, as were '89 and '90. The homicide teams were stretched so thin that the police administration finally added a fifth investigative team, then a sixth and seventh. This disrupted the regular makeup of the teams because experienced detectives were taken from existing teams and put with the new teams. New detectives, although experienced in police work and investigation, had to undergo training in the latest homicide procedures.

In recent years forensic science had advanced by leaps and bounds. Methods of DNA (deoxyribonucleic acid) detection were improving regularly. At the time of Janet's murder, the examination of blood yielded only the ABO blood type. Janet's was type O and the mystery blood was type A, which belonged to 40 percent of the population. Scientists continually worked to develop a genetic fingerprint of the blood and body fluids. Once the so-called genetic fingerprint was developed, blood and semen would be as unique to a single person as is the fingerprint. But, as with the fingerprint, there had to be someone to compare the sample to. Science wasn't quite there to fully utilize DNA in 1988.

CHAPTER 7

Once things settled down and Team III had completed all the urgent tasks, they focused on revisiting each aspect of the case, making sure every step in the Janet Moore investigation had been done correctly. In early August 1988, they sent fifty-one letters to various San Diego hospitals and medical facilities inquiring about laceration patients who came in to be treated during the twenty-four-hour period after Janet's death. Thirteen positive responses had come in, including the two that Ed Petrick found that first night. It took time to write the letters to the hospitals, have the letters sent out, and wait for a response. Those leads had to be tracked down and closed out one way or the other. All thirteen possibilities were eliminated.

While not ruling out anyone, the detectives from Team III believed that a black person was probably responsible for the murder. Janet had hung out predominately with black people, both men and women, and had a black husband and a black boyfriend. She had had hellacious verbal and physical fights at her former apartment with black men and women. She bought her drugs from blacks and, more often than not, ingested the drugs in the company of blacks. The cops weren't being racist. They were being logical. Eliminate the inner circle first, and then go on to more elaborate, exotic theories. That's the way a homicide investigation is done.

Locating Janet's friends proved to be a bigger job than expected. The police didn't find Patricia Miller until November. She was the one who frequently hung around with Janet. She was high on the list because she had a child with Tony, Janet's boyfriend, who was in county jail at the time of Moore's murder. Sources had told the police that Patricia told Doc she had killed Janet.

Witnesses had said Janet and Patricia had argued over drugs in the past. She might have been jealous of Moore's relationship with the father of her baby. Other people told the police that Janet and Patricia had worked as a prostitute team if someone wanted to do a "salt-and-pepper" threesome.

Patricia was a hardened woman. While tough on the exterior, she was cooperative during the investigation. It was not her nature to be empathetic regarding the fate of Janet. Nonetheless, she gave a blood sample and fingerprints willingly when police interviewed her on November 2, 1988. Miller had no wounds on her hands either. Detective Ruffner noticed a soft side of Miller, which she resisted revealing to others. Miller remained on the suspect list, but Ruffner lost his enthusiasm for her. If she did it, his homicide instincts were off.

Witnesses even gave the first name of a possible client of the Janet-and-Patricia prostitution duo. "James" was rumored to be the manager of an insurance company in the Mission Valley section of San Diego. The detectives spoke with Patricia about him. She said she had never heard of a john named James who worked in Mission Valley. She denied ever doing tandem sex with Janet. Witnesses even told the police they suspected Patricia and Janet of having a lesbian relationship. Patricia denied this too. There was no immediate way to disprove any of her denials at this time. It was later determined that the type-A blood on the washcloth was not hers. Was the blood from someone who helped her kill Janet?

The detectives questioned many street prostitutes in the area where Janet formerly operated. Finding the girls was difficult because they didn't keep regular hours. They often had unofficial "territories" where they stood or sat, waiting to be picked up.

Their level of cooperation was dubious, to say the least. The prostitutes believed that every time they said something that might be helpful to the police, they became eligible for a return "favor."

The homicide detectives tried to be tactful. "If Vice gives you a break now and then for some information you turn over to them, then it's between you and Vice. We're trying to solve a homicide," they said. If a prostitute gave one of the homicide detectives some information regarding Janet Moore, she expected to receive a "Get Out of Jail Free" card for an arrest for solicitation or shoplifting. Sadly, but in keeping with Team III's bad luck, no prostitutes gave any useful information on Janet Moore.

Patrol cops heard this familiar refrain every time they processed paperwork on a shoplifter: "Officer, check with Detective [supply name]. I'm working a deal with him, giving him info on a dope house. You need to cut me some slack so I can continue to give him information." Sometimes the girls were telling the truth. More often than not, when the patrol officer would call the named narcotics or vice detective, the detective would say, "I know her, but I haven't talked to her in a year. Book her. Oh, and tell her to call me when she gets out." Life was tough on the street. Tough for everyone, cops and prostitutes alike.

When they tried to locate Tessa, the girl who allegedly

stole the watch from Janet's neighbor, they discovered she had vanished. Innocent people usually do not vanish. Finding Tessa was now a priority.

———————

In late November, Laurie Rawlinson, a forensic serologist from the Southern Research Institute, officially informed the detectives that the blood on the washcloth did not come from a black person. The cops said, "Oh well," and accepted her analysis. That is another reality of homicide investigation. Certain informational items are put together in a case to help form an opinion. This opinion is not hard-and-fast. It is merely a tentative conclusion based on gathered information. When solid scientific evidence invalidates this opinion, the detectives have to go with the solid evidence. It did not mean they categorically eliminated a black person as a suspect. It just meant that a white person was the source of the blood, and a white person probably killed Janet Moore. The blood evidence also meant that only one person was involved.

The blood analysis also made it look more like a prostitution customer had killed Janet instead of one of her black friends. Again, this opinion was not set in stone. It only meant the probability was higher that the killer was white.

The police knew that if a prostitution customer killed Janet, the odds of solving the killing dropped drastically.

———————

Homicide detectives are not biographers. While it is true they need to know who the victims are, and with whom they associate, the knowledge the police need is limited to helping solve the case.

In the case of Janet Moore, the detectives learned she was a decent person with only a limited number of enemies, who had had some minor drug-debt disputes. She was not a major drug trafficker. Her failures to pay drug bills resulted

in broken doors, windows, and shouting matches, not death.
Janet did not appear to be a target of anyone.

If the detectives had the time to delve deeper into the life
of Janet Moore, they would have discovered she was the
daughter of Sarah (called "Rusty" by family and friends)
and Gerrell "Gerry" Moore. Her father had passed away
the year before, in 1987. His passing may have contributed
to a downward spiral in Janet's life, but that wasn't a known
fact. In the world of homicide investigation, her father's
death and any resulting changes in Janet's life weren't really relevant to solving the crime. Janet was frequently es-
tranged from everyone meaningful to her when she was
using drugs or working as a prostitute.

Gerry had worked as a mover of heavy construction
equipment. He drove the big trucks everyone sees with
the WIDE LOAD sign on the back, slowly lumbering along
the highway. His work carried him to several places in the
United States over the years. Much of the family's living
was done in Arizona, Indiana, and eastern San Diego
County. The family moved with him wherever work took
him. Janet, as we've said, had three sisters and one brother.

Janet graduated from high school in Fort Wayne, Indiana. She moved to Ohio shortly thereafter, and settled in
San Diego in 1980 when she was twenty.

Janet's family described her as a "people person" who
made friends easily. She got along with everyone, and
considered everyone she met a friend. She liked to travel,
going to Boston and Hawaii on occasion.

If the detectives had the time, they would have discovered that Janet had been a sweet child. Her family called her
"Little Miss Muffet." For some reason there was tension
between Janet and her mother, Rusty. No one in the family
knew the reason for this.

Janet developed a strain of strong-willed independence,
if not subtle defiance, over the years. No one could say how
her sometimes confrontational demeanor related to the

relationship with her parents. Nonetheless, there was nothing in Janet's early family background that helped explain why she was brutally murdered at her young age. The drug involvement and prostitution were the most telling forms of explanation.

Bob Moore, Gerry's brother, who was affectionately known to everyone as "Uncle Bob," lived with the family for several years when Janet was very young. He recounted how headstrong were both Janet and her mother. Rusty wouldn't allow the toddler Janet to get out of her high chair until she had eaten all her vegetables. Janet wasn't about to eat them. A standoff would develop. Uncle Bob would sit with Janet while Rusty was clearing the table. When Rusty left the room, Janet would hold the vegetables out for Uncle Bob to eat. Sometimes Bob would tease her and shake his head no. When that happened, both Janet and Bob would laugh. Bob would then take a vegetable. It was fun, but it showed an independent streak that would last a lifetime, albeit a short lifetime.

Neither Janet nor Rusty would give in when they had an area of disagreement. That contentiousness between them lasted forever.

The San Diego of the late eighties was a different city from the one Janet moved to in 1980, and would become even more different later.

When she arrived, many of the streets south of Broadway were havens for the homeless. Eventually, the wrecking ball hit the area. Entire blocks of peep shows, bars, tattoo parlors, and twenty-four-hour movie theaters where drunks and bums slept all night were leveled to make room for urban renewal. The San Diego city fathers wanted to bring people back downtown, a place the populace had abandoned in favor of suburban malls. Plans were hatched to fix up the area. Construction began in the Gaslamp Quarter, a historical area that had gone to seed over the years. By the mid eighties, trendy restaurants and hotels were starting to get a toehold in downtown.

Once the Gaslamp Quarter (some now call it the Gaslamp district) started to get established, the city and the San Diego Padres baseball team wanted to move from Mission Valley to downtown. This project took many years and involved much civic wrangling. The stadium became a reality in 2004 when the Padres moved downtown to Petco Park, so named because of sponsorship from the pet-supply company.

Right in the middle of the downtown district was Horton Plaza, a landmark named after the late Alonzo Horton, one of San Diego's founders. A modest entrepreneur, Horton would have turned over in his grave in 1980 to see what had become of the small grass-and-flowers park bearing his name. The one-block section on Broadway between Third and Fourth avenues was a haven for sleeping derelicts, small-quantity dope pushers, and seedy-looking guys who hung around the men's room in the park in search of furtive male companionship. There was an occasional impromptu preacher, or a musician with a dilapidated guitar and a coffee can or cigar box on the ground for donations.

By 1982, two years after Janet's arrival, the city fathers had had enough of Horton Plaza's occupants. Several blocks were condemned and a huge shopping center eventually became a reality. In 1985, the Horton Plaza Shopping Center (today run by the Westfield Corporation) opened with a variety of upscale stores and good restaurants. Today, the park still exists in front of the shopping center. Gone is the public restroom, a constant headache for the police. Most of the people one sees in the park are waiting for a bus.

In 1986, Maureen O'Connor became the first female mayor of San Diego. One other woman, Susan Golding, has held the mayoral position since then. The city expanded at a rapid rate. Lofts and businesses sprang up in the Gaslamp and East Village. The San Diego Trolley put down tracks to service travelers from the northern, eastern, and southern parts of the county. Prostitution, homelessness, and the small-time drug trade still exist in San Diego. They simply moved away from where they were in 1980.

The morning newspapers that reported Janet's murder, the *San Diego Union* and the San Diego edition of the *Los Angeles Times,* would undergo changes too. In 1992, the *Union* merged with its afternoon sister paper, the *San Diego Tribune,* to become a morning paper, the *San Diego Union-Tribune.* The *L.A. Times* packed its bags in the mid nineties and left San Diego completely. Today, the *Union-Tribune* is undergoing even more changes. Veteran reporters, columnists, and editors are being bought out for early retirement or laid off. A once-healthy rivalry to get the news first and best is gone. Very little in-depth reporting is done in the local paper today. It was not that way when Janet Moore first called San Diego her home.

CHAPTER 8

In November 1988, five months after Janet's murder, the detectives still wanted to locate Tessa Rayburn*, the woman Janet's neighbor suspected of stealing the bracelet. They didn't have enough evidence to get an arrest warrant. In July, they notified other agencies, and the local crime computer system, that if anyone in law enforcement stopped Rayburn they should call Sergeant Petrick or one of his detectives, day or night. It was a slow, uphill battle. Nobody called. Where was Rayburn? Janet Moore had been dead almost half of a year and they needed to find Rayburn.

In January 1989, the detectives located "James," who managed the insurance company in Mission Valley. He was a retired army officer. Rumor on the street said Janet and Patricia had done a threesome with James, a rumor Patricia denied.

The detectives were straightforward with James. When

shown a picture of her, he said he knew Janet, but hadn't seen her for a long time. Detective Jaime Bordine asked if his semen would be in her. James laughed. "I'm almost ashamed to tell you guys this, but my semen won't be anywhere. I'm impotent. When Janet came by I used a 'strap-on.'"

While they didn't exactly take his word for it, the detectives thought it took a lot of guts for James to admit he couldn't get an erection, or have an emission. It wasn't something that a guy normally lied about. Nonetheless, since homicide detectives don't take anything at face value, they arranged for a blood draw and fingerprint comparison. The detectives noted James had no old injuries on his fingers or hands.

Weeks later the results from the blood draw removed James from the suspect list. Sometimes the detectives sat in the Team III cubicle and discussed James and his use of the strap-on. It was strange, to be sure. James derived nothing from that activity in the way of pleasure. A prostitute rarely derives any kind of pleasure or satisfaction from a sexual encounter with a customer. It boiled down to Janet participating in the sex act only for the money and James performing his part possibly for the physical intimacy, even if it didn't result in any kind of sexual satisfaction. The detectives agreed that sometimes they knew too much about people and their habits.

Years later James passed away of natural causes.

———

The average person in San Diego didn't care that Team III was working the Janet Moore case. To the citizens, it was just another murder of a hooker, something most law-abiding people couldn't relate to. The case of Janet Moore was never mentioned in the newspapers again.

San Diegans continued to kill one another at an alarming rate. When 1988 ended, the homicide total for the year was a whopping 144. Each of the four homicide teams averaged thirty-six killings that year. Since each team was "up" for only approximately twelve weeks, it meant they handled nearly three homicides every week. And, the detectives were called out to other suspicious deaths that were eventually ruled not to be homicides.

In addition to the crime duties, the homicide teams also responded to industrial deaths. If a trench caved in while a worker was in an underground excavation site, the homicide team responded along with a district-attorney investigator and a representative from the California Occupational Safety and Health Administration. If the district attorney and Cal-OSHA determined that a company was trying to save money by cutting corners on safety procedures, or not providing mandated training, that company would be fined civilly and prosecuted criminally.

Along with becoming conversant in blood spatter, gunshot residue, fingerprints, and other things associated with homicide investigations, the cops also learned a lot about the requirements of shoring up a trench, proper safety harnessing of workers who worked above the ground, and proper safety tailgate meetings of construction crews.

Eventually, the practice of sending a homicide team to the site of an industrial fatality was scrapped. But, in 1988, responding to a worker's death was the practice. It was a drain on the officers' time.

———

Numerous unsolved murders of females caught the attention of the media. The San Diego Police Department knew the sheriff's department was investigating several body dumps in the eastern portion of the county. The San Diego cops had a few murders of prostitutes in areas of high hooker activity.

The local newspaper and a well-known magazine began looking into the killings. The large number of murders, and the publicity the murders generated, were enough in early

1990 for District Attorney Edwin Miller Jr. to form a task force, calling it the Metropolitan Homicide Task Force.

The task force feared that the Green River Killer from Washington State was now in San Diego plying his deadly trade against hookers. Communication was set up between the San Diego police and the agencies involved in the Green River investigation. They talked and they talked. They shared and compared information. The agencies from both states traveled back and forth to each other's offices. Nothing was accomplished, not yet anyway.

The San Diego headquarters for this elite group of thirty-two investigators, a few attorneys, and support staff was at an "undisclosed location in Mission Valley." Mission Valley is about five miles from downtown San Diego. Interstate 8 runs through the valley. Most of the bodies of the various women had been dumped in an area about ten miles east of the site of the Metro Homicide Task Force offices.

Former cop and current deputy district attorney Dick Lewis headed up the contingent. Lewis was a no-nonsense, tell-it-like-it-is kind of guy. He had made his bones in a patrol car, later becoming a crack investigator dealing with organized-crime figures. Lewis went to law school at night, passed the bar, and became an equally accomplished deputy district attorney. Now an attorney, Lewis had the square jaw, penetrating stare, authoritative voice, and mental makeup of a cop.

Lewis was "old school" in every sense of the term. He was tough, crusty, and direct. He made no secret of his dislike and distrust of the media. He believed that no good could come from standing in front of a news camera telling everything you knew about a case. He had seen a number of cops and attorneys get burned by giving too much information to a reporter, both print and film. Therefore, Lewis tried his best to keep the Metropolitan Homicide Task Force secret, and outgoing information to a minimum.

Meanwhile, back at San Diego Police Headquarters, Sergeant Ed Petrick and the rest of Homicide Team III did not believe Janet Moore was a victim of whoever was killing the women and dumping them along the interstate. In fact, not all of the women found in the wild were even hookers. Some were housewives and professional women who happened to be out there for legitimate reasons.

Petrick allowed the task force to look at Janet Moore's case, but he refused to relinquish the investigative tasks. That would have been too easy. Petrick thought his team could solve her murder, and he didn't think Janet Moore had been the victim of a serial killer. Petrick believed she had brought some kind of psycho back to her place and the guy killed her in a rage. If the task force found something different, more power to them. Petrick would gladly give the case to the "hotshot" specialists. He didn't think Janet's case belonged in the task force's jurisdiction. No one challenged his opinion. Team III kept the case.

CHAPTER 9

Murders in the city of San Diego dropped off slightly from 144 in 1988 to 121 in 1989. That was still a lot of killing. Team III never forgot Janet Moore. It is easier to forget a killing solved quickly by your team. A man shoots his wife and calls the police to confess. The man claims there is a reason he did her in. The district attorney presents evidence that the man had no good reason to kill her, that divorce would have been a better alternative. At trial, the man's defense attorney tries to present evidence of many reasons why he killed her, if he did in fact kill her, because the attorney will make the D.A. prove everything anyway, even though there is ample evidence of guilt. Unless the defense attorney can conjure up a self-defense issue, or evidence of insanity, the man will go to prison for either a few, or many years.

Those cases are forgettable, at least for many cops, because they never had to invest extraordinary effort to solve them. Those domestic homicides are "paint-by-numbers" exercises. Process the crime scene. Interview the suspect. Talk to friends, family members, and acquaintances. Check bank accounts and insurance policies if applicable. Present the case to the district attorney. Attend the trial. There is nothing spectacular attached to these investigations.

Sergeant Ed Petrick said he "remembered every case" he'd worked on, even the so-called easy ones. Maybe he did, or maybe he didn't, but it's a safe bet that he remembered the case of Janet Moore. All the detectives did. It was a senseless, brutal killing of a young, apparently sweet girl. They remembered Janet's case because investigating the murder of a prostitute by a stranger was so frustrating.

The detectives followed up on every lead in the Janet Moore case no matter where it came from or how dubious it seemed when received. About eight months later, in February 1989, reality began to set in. There were no new leads. There was nowhere to go and nothing to do.

While Team III didn't wave the white flag of surrender, they accepted the facts for what they were: barring some unforeseen circumstances of a new lead, the case was over. Sergeant Ed Petrick would never admit it publicly, nor would the individual detectives, but in their hearts they knew something extraordinary had to happen in order to solve Janet Moore's murder.

———

Detective Ron Thill reluctantly put Janet Moore's "Murder Book" on the shelves when he went to the Metro Homicide Task Force in 1991. The various assigned detectives thought about her frequently, but there wasn't much they could actually do except look at the case, cross off a name if that person was cleared, and put the book back. Janet's murder was a particular challenge because of the lack of leads. The case also represented a challenge that saddened the team members because Janet was so young. To give up trying to solve the case meant they were admitting defeat. They refused to admit this. They hoped they would solve it. Some days they weren't so sure.

———————

On January 12, 1990, twenty-one-year old Tiffany Schultz was murdered in the apartment she shared with two roommates in the Clairemont area of San Diego, near the beach. Another homicide team handled that case. Petrick was mildly curious about the killing. Along with being a student, Schultz was a nude dancer, pretty and white. The sex angle was similar to Janet Moore in that both women made money by enticing men. Was Schultz's killing connected to her occupation? Was Schultz's killer the same as Janet Moore's? Petrick looked at Tiffany Schultz's case with the permission of the other team sergeant.

There was forced entry to Schultz's apartment, a different scenario from Janet Moore. The killer stabbed her forty-seven times, some of the wounds so deep that the point of the knife exited her back. While Janet Moore's killer thrashed, slashed, and hacked her, Tiffany Schultz's killer was more methodical. The wounds inflicted were in her upper torso, with a tight pattern of twenty wounds in the right breast area. While both women were dead, Janet Moore's killing was more a "destruction" than a murder.

While Janet Moore's body lay in a haphazard fashion, dragged back from her doorway, Tiffany Schultz's body seemed to be posed, with her legs spread apart. She was wearing only bikini bottoms. Petrick believed Janet Moore's assailant killed her, tended to his own bleeding wound, probably incurred when his hand slipped off of the knife, and made a hasty exit. It looked like Schultz's killer took his time, positioned the body, and even rubbed her body in certain places. Petrick believed different people killed Schultz and Moore, but he wouldn't rule anything out, not yet anyway.

Five weeks later, on February 16, 1990, in an area very near where Tiffany Schultz lived, Ed Petrick's homicide team caught a case. Janene Weinhold's roommate found her body in their apartment. Weinhold, also twenty-one, white, and pretty, had suffered multiple stab wounds. She was wearing only a bra. Sergeant Petrick and his crew handled the crime scene the way they always did, thoroughly and methodically. There was no evidence of drug use at either Schultz's or Weinhold's apartment.

The investigation revealed that at 9 a.m. Janene drove her roommate to work. Both girls were students at the University of California San Diego. Janene would spend the day doing laundry and studying. There was no class that day. Janene was supposed to pick up the roommate at two o'clock that afternoon. Janene never picked her up, a rare event for the ever-dependable Weinhold.

The crime scene was the apartment. There was no forced entry. Weinhold had been stabbed twenty-two times, with a cluster of eight wounds in a tight pattern above the right breast. Weinhold's legs were spread in a position that suggested the killer had posed her that way. Bloody smudges were on the doorknob. The print pattern on the door indicated the killer had worn a glove, or some kind of covering over the hand in an attempt to conceal fingerprints. The attempt was successful. No identifiable loops, ridges, or whorls showed up.

Sergeant Petrick examined the case, noting that this victim and Tiffany Schultz had no involvement in drugs or prostitution. Both had clean arrest records. Although Tiffany Schultz worked in the sex trade, it was a legal sex trade. There was no evidence she "moonlighted" by going with customers after hours, as some dancers were rumored to do. Also, the autopsy revealed no evidence of recent sexual activity.

Petrick examined the notes of the team handling the Schultz homicide. He looked at everything, including the cause and manner of death, how entry was made into the apartment, and the ritualistic position of the victim's body. He concluded that the same killer who murdered Tiffany Schultz murdered Janene Weinhold.

When he presented his findings to the San Diego Police administration, the brass agreed with him. The decision makers decided Team III would now get all homicides apparently committed by the person who was now a confirmed serial killer. The suits that run the department believed the two similar killings, five weeks apart, close in geographic proximity, showed that a serial killer was on the loose. Rather than have any of the teams on the regular rotation handle future cases as they came in, they hoped the continuity of one collective set of investigative eyes would make for a more fruitful investigation.

Within a few weeks the lab report came back on vaginal swabs taken from Janene Weinhold. The semen was almost certainly from a man of African-American descent. Petrick remembered that the semen from Janet Moore was from a Caucasian. Okay, probably a different killer. Team III put their respective heads down and dug into the killings of Schultz and Weinhold. They also held their breaths, hoping there would be no new killings.

———

They didn't have to hold their breath too long because on April 3, just two and a half weeks later, eighteen-year-old Holly Tarr was brutally murdered in a relative's apartment. Tarr and a girlfriend, both high school seniors on spring break, were visiting from Okemos, Michigan. Holly and the girlfriend had finished playing tennis and were sitting by the pool of the apartment complex. Holly went upstairs to take a shower, leaving her friend at the pool.

When she did not return in the expected amount of

time, the girlfriend went upstairs to the apartment. The door was locked. The friend could hear loud talking, and perhaps a scream and some banging. The friend left to look for a maintenance man. When they returned a few minutes later, the maintenance man unlocked the door. The chain bolt was in place.

The friend explained to the apartment employee that something bad was going on inside. The maintenance man forced the door open, ripping the safety chain from the doorjamb. As they proceeded down the hall a short, stocky, muscular black man holding a cloth over his face met them in the hallway. He was carrying a knife. The man bolted from the apartment.

Holly Tarr was on the floor in the bedroom clad only in a bra and panties. She had a single stab wound that eventually measured seven inches deep, almost exiting through her shoulder blade.

When the patrol officers noted the similarities, they notified the on-call homicide team. The on-call team notified Team III, as they had been instructed to do. Once again, Ed Petrick and his team assembled outside. The crime scene revealed no forced entry, except for what the maintenance man had done. They did find a bloody shoe print. Also, a ring was missing from Holly Tarr's finger.

The girlfriend was questioned extensively. She remembered a short, muscular black man in the workout room when they were in there briefly. She thought he might be the one she saw running from the apartment, but couldn't be sure because he had covered his face in the one-second time frame it took for him to run past her.

The killer didn't have time to pose the victim, nor did he have time to play in her blood, as was evidenced by the Tiffany Schultz and Janene Weinhold crime scenes. But Petrick was positive the same killer had struck again. This was number three, and there was no letup in sight.

CHAPTER 10

Sergeant Ed Petrick knew the police had a potential publicity powder keg on their hands. The media was adding things up. Seeing Petrick and his crew at both crime scenes, and knowing Team III was not "up," the news reporters familiar with the comings and goings of the homicide teams started asking about the possibility of a serial killer. Three young girls stabbed to death. The same homicide team handling the young girls' killings out of sequence. It was too much of a coincidence.

Was a serial killer operating? Why else would one homicide team be handling a murder when it wasn't their turn? Such are the stories that kick off the evening news to ensure that viewers stay tuned. "A killer is on the loose in the Clairemont area. Hear the full story and what the police are doing on our six-thirty broadcast."

Shortly thereafter the San Diego Police Department announced the formation of a task force to catch the "Clairemont Killer." The SDPD spokesman was careful to reveal only what he was told by the administration. Yes, a suspected serial killer had stabbed three young women to death. The police were searching for common threads between the three victims and the cases. Holly Tarr's thread was weakened because she was from out of state and had been in San Diego only a very short time. The police did not want to inspire full-blown panic on the part of Clairemont residents, but felt the need to warn them.

Sergeant Petrick was temporarily shorthanded in his own team again because one of his top detectives, Greg Walton, had been promoted to sergeant and left the unit to work Western Division Patrol.

The killer hit again on May 20, some six weeks after Holly Tarr's death. Elissa Keller, thirty-eight, lived with her eighteen-year-old daughter in Clairemont. The young girl discovered her mom's body. When the daughter arrived home, she discovered the door unlocked and the safety chain not in the clasp, precautions usually taken by Elissa. The daughter warily made her way down the hallway. Calling to her mother all the way in a voice starting to reflect fear and concern, the daughter looked in the bedroom. There she saw Elissa, a blanket covering her upper torso, lying on the floor.

She wore only a tank top. Her legs were wide apart. Bloody underwear lay inside-out as if hastily removed, next to her body. Keller's chest bore nine tight cluster stab wounds. The autopsy would reveal that she had been punched in the mouth, choked, and blood smeared on her body.

Ed Petrick and Team III responded to the crime scene. Sergeant Petrick is always conservative in his assessments. There was a slight nagging doubt about whether or not the killing of Keller was the handiwork of the Clairemont Killer. For one thing, Keller, although athletic and attractive, was older than the other victims. It appeared that entry to Keller's residence was gained through an open window instead of through the doorway, as was the case with Tiffany Schultz, Janene Weinhold, and Holly Tarr.

Petrick didn't want to go out on a limb, so he elected to give the case to the on-call team. The homicide sergeant reasoned that if it was later confirmed that Elissa Keller was a victim of the serial killer, Team III could always take over. If Team III started out with the case, investing many hours of investigation only to learn later that it was not the Clairemont Killer, they would have devoted too much time to a case that should have been given to another team. Nonetheless, Petrick vowed to keep a close eye on the investigation of the murder of Elissa Keller.

After the hectic rush of four stabbing murders of women in a five-month period, things slowed down. Petrick was able to go over the cases in greater detail. Even though Team III didn't officially have the Elissa Keller case, the homicide sergeant increasingly became more convinced that she was the fourth victim. Keller's crime scene spoke volumes to the experienced detective.

Petrick used his time wisely. June, July, and August went by without incident. Had the killer moved? Was he in jail on other charges? Did he realize the evil of his ways and reform? Not likely. The detectives were happy that no one else was getting killed, but where was he? Was he killing women in another state?

The investigators believed they were looking for a black man. Bulletins circulated across the state and within the county of San Diego. Patrol officers generated hundreds of "field-interrogation" slips. These "FIs," as the cops refer to them, document a brief detention of someone by a patrol officer. The FI memorializes the name; date of birth; physical description; clothing worn; and date, time, and location of the encounter. Of course the police must have a reason to fill out a field-interrogation form. They couldn't grab any black person walking down the street or coming out of a grocery store. The reason for the brief detention had to be included in the details of the stop.

The detectives checked out the people listed on the field-interrogation slips once the slips made their way back to the detective bureau. Sometimes the detectives contacted the subject for further information. If nothing jumped out at the detectives screening the slip, they made a note of the detention and filed it away.

———————

September 13, 1990, four months after Elissa Keller's death, marked the resumption of killing, and in a big way. This time there were two victims, a mother and her daughter, both fit and attractive white women. The mother, Pamela Clark, forty-two, and her eighteen-year-old daughter, Amber, were murdered inside their residence, in University City, an area not exactly in Clairemont, but close enough to fit within the profile. Sergeant Petrick knew from the initial call that this case was his, and that the Clairemont Killer was back in business, possibly making up for lost time.

He knew that with every killing, the chances of catching the killer increased. But the cost was human life.

Attendance records verified that Pamela Clark had been at the Family Fitness workout center on Miramar Road, where she was a member. Neighbors later reported hearing Amber, Pamela's daughter, hollering. Although the loud voice was uncharacteristic of the household, no one called police or inquired further. When Pamela did not show up for an appointment, and no one answered Pamela's phone, coworkers went to her house.

Pamela was just inside the door. She was lying on her back, nude, her arms spread at a ninety-degree angle and her legs together. She suffered eleven cluster stab wounds in her upper left chest.

Down the hallway Amber lay, fully clothed, but with her

blouse pulled up, exposing her breasts. She too had several deep cluster stab wounds to the chest. Crime-scene investigators believed that the assailant gained entry through the dining-room window. Sergeant Petrick knew this was the handiwork of the Clairemont Killer. He was frustrated and angry.

The Pamela/Amber Clark investigation went nowhere. The detectives examined all leads thoroughly. A killer was lurking out there. The news crews went into high gear, pressing everyone in a position of authority for details. Panic didn't exactly grip San Diego, but a strong sense of watchfulness and awareness prevailed.

Because leads in the Janet Moore case were nonexistent, Sergeant Petrick and the rest of his crew devoted their time to cases that had actual leads, such as the Clairemont Killer cases. They might not have been able to bring justice to Janet Moore, but they would do their best to find this serial killer.

One bit of information surfaced three months later on December 19, 1990. A woman returned to her apartment during the midmorning from a workout at the Family Fitness Center on Miramar Road. Within minutes there was a knock on her door. She opened it to find a short, muscular black man. The woman stared at the man, who stared back. Just then, the woman's neighbor across the hall opened her door. The young man turned around, obviously noticing the presence of the neighbor.

The man stammered, "Is, uh, Terry here?"

"No Terry lives here," the woman said. Her neighbor remained behind the man, covering him with a watchful glare. With that, the man hurried away.

On January 22, and January 24, 1991, women reported being followed home from the Family Fitness Center on Miramar Road. A short, muscular black man followed them. It had been more than three months since the Clairemont Killer had last struck. Petrick immediately keyed on the

Family Fitness Center connection. Fortunately, one of the women had had the wherewithal to follow the man and get his car description.

Detectives went to the Family Fitness Center, alerting the staff to be on the lookout for such a man and the vehicle the woman had described. On February 4, a staff member phoned the police that a man fitting the description was sitting in the parking lot in a car that also fit the description the police had given.

Patrol officers converged on the area and made contact with a young man named Cleophus Prince Jr. The officers took Prince to the police station for an interview. They took blood, photos, and fingerprints. Since there wasn't enough evidence to book him, Prince was released.

In going over all of the documents in the various cases, Petrick noted the police had already talked to Prince several months earlier. In fact, he had lived in the same apartment complex as one of the victims, and within blocks of others. Petrick's heart started to beat a little faster and a little harder. Could this nightmare finally be over?

CHAPTER 11

Although he was normally under control, at least on the outside, the pressure of multiple murders and heavy supervision tasks had been getting to Sergeant Petrick. He continued his regimen of running five miles a day. His sleep was fitful, and he could count on some form of interruption from the police department every night. Later he joked, "I thought there was a microswitch located under my pillow. Every time my head hit the pillow, the phone would ring. At least it seemed that way." He noticed he was breaking out in hives. The 135 San Diego homicides in 1990 and his assumption of the Clairemont Killer task-force duties were getting to him.

If Prince was their man, they couldn't let him slip away. Yet he almost did. The more the police investigated, the stronger the case became. Investigation and countless interviews connected Prince to more than twenty other burglaries in the area. The detectives learned he had redeemed a large sum of Italian currency at a local money exchange. The exact amount Prince exchanged had been taken in a burglary the day before the redemption. Given the small amount of Italian currency floating around San Diego, this was more than a coincidence.

Prince had pawned several items of jewelry and given rings to friends. These rings had been taken in burglaries in the Clairemont area. Prince had given one ring to his then girlfriend. The ring came from the finger of one of the murder victims.

Deputy District Attorney Dan Lamborn swung into action, preparing an arrest warrant for Prince. In the meantime, police learned he had left town suddenly. The detectives turned up the heat on Prince's friends. Someone gave the police an address in Birmingham, Alabama. Things started happening rapidly. After a few tense phone calls, Alabama authorities took Prince into custody on the murder warrant. He sat in a cell awaiting extradition to California.

One minute Sergeant Greg Walton was driving his patrol car in San Diego's Western division. An hour later he was packing his suitcase. One more hour after that and he was on a plane to Alabama. They had their man. They knew it in their investigative bones. The case was over. San Diego could rest easy.

The case wasn't over, though, as cops, district attorneys, and defense attorneys well knew. The work—the *real* work—was just starting.

———————

Some people are against the death penalty at all costs, no matter what the convicted person has done. Others believe the death penalty should be reserved for the very worst segments of society, those who kill and enjoy it, those who taunt and torture their victims and desecrate their bodies after death, those who kill again and again. For these multiple killers there is no real reform. Opponents of the death penalty, if they concede the guilt of a defendant, will ask that he be imprisoned for the rest of his life. This debate will go on as long as there are people who can talk. A handful of inmates continue to kill even in prison.

The San Diego District Attorney's Office believed Cleophus Prince Jr. had earned his place on Death Row at San Quentin Prison, and they aimed to do their best to make sure he ended up there. The district attorney's death-penalty review committee consisted of several experienced prosecutors, many of whom had worked on death-penalty cases before. They were unanimous in their vote: Cleophus Prince's crimes merited the death penalty.

Even though Prince was safely in jail, Sergeant Petrick, because of the complexity of the investigation, had to continue to commit himself full-time to the case. There was so much more work to do to ensure a successful prosecution.

Prince's seminal fluid could be connected only to to Janene Weinhold. Search warrants had to be served to find the numerous souvenirs he had taken from the homicide victims and the "regular" burglary victims. Many items taken during the murders turned up around town. These recovered valuables made the case against Prince stronger.

A profiler from the Federal Bureau of Investigation was brought in to compare evidence at the homicide scenes and help make a determination that one person had done all the killings. The work was exhaustive and extensive.

All the while Sergeant Petrick was working on the Cleophus Prince case, he continued to follow and update his other cases, including that of Janet Moore. The prostitute Tessa Rayburn was still out there. Notifications had been made to other agencies asking if anyone detained Rayburn to let the San Diego homicide cops know.

Sergeant Petrick thought December 1991 would be his lucky month. Tessa Rayburn turned up in the Metropolitan Corrections Center, courtesy of federal law enforcement authorities. Detective Jaime Bordine hurried over for an interview. Rayburn was cooperative. She gave blood, fingerprints, saliva, and handwriting. Now the San Diego guys were getting somewhere.

In spite of his earlier thoughts, December proved *not* to be Sergeant Petrick's lucky month. It was a devastating month, as were several months to follow. It was in December 1991 that Petrick learned his wife, Officer Michelle Petrick, had cancer. He altered his work schedule, making time for consultations, treatments, and time with Michelle. He still managed to continue coordinating the Cleophus Prince Jr. investigation. Because the district attorney had elected to seek the death penalty, a bare-knuckled street fight in the courtroom was coming.

Defense attorneys fight with all they have to spare the life of a killer, even if the evidence of guilt is overwhelming. Every single aspect of the case is challenged. In the case of Prince, there was much to consider. Every recovered piece of stolen property was checked to make sure the police had seized the property legally.

Even though physical evidence would play a major role in the prosecution, eyewitness identification would also be important.

Detective Jaime Bordine conducted a live lineup of five similarly appearing black men, along with Cleophus Prince Jr., for witnesses to view. Ever the gentleman, but still a tough cop, Bordine asked the defense attorney if the makeup of the lineup was acceptable to the defense attorney. After viewing the five who had been selected from a pool of approximately twelve, the attorney agreed. Bordine allowed the defense attorney to place Prince wherever he wanted in the line of six.

According to case law, a lineup only has to be "fair." It doesn't have to be "perfect." Some defense attorneys would prefer to have sextuplets in a lineup. When a lineup is ordered, the lineup deputy at the county jail takes a booking photo of the suspect. The deputy looks around the jail population for similar-appearing inmates, in size, age, color, and hue. The participants must have the same facial hair as the accused. All are dressed alike, usually in jail garb. If one of the participants, including the defendant, has visible tattoos, steps are taken to cover up the artwork, such as wearing long sleeves, or keeping the hands concealed in the waistband of the trousers.

Some defendants do strange things like grow or shave beards and mustaches. If the booking photo is taken of a black suspect with hair in cornrows, often an inmate will fluff the hair into an Afro. It goes on like that.

If a suspect said something to the victim like, "This is a holdup. Give me all your money," all participants in the lineup must say the same thing. Everyone in the lineup must do the same walking and turning motions so as not to call undue attention to the suspect.

For their efforts, the participants are given an extra lunch, or an extra visit from the outside. Some of the participants in the lineup act like the whole process is a joke. In the end, they do a disservice to their fellow inmate who is the suspect. Inmates have been known to laugh, scratch, elbow one another, and make comments under their breath during the lineup, while one participant (the accused) is dead serious. Guess which participant the witnesses will focus on? Which participant stands out?

According to case law, defense attorneys are allowed at lineups as observers only. They are not legally entitled to provide input. Some police officers will not acknowledge the attorney's presence except to note they were there on an attendance sheet. If defense attorneys object, some officers will say, "This ain't a courtroom. I'm running this lineup. If you don't like it, file an appeal."

This was not Bordine's way. He knew from experience that to avoid a problem before it arose was the best way for a case to proceed. Sometimes defense attorneys will try to take over and actually engage the officer running the lineup in a confrontation. Experienced detectives handle those problems with finesse and aplomb. In the case of Cleophus Prince Jr., Bordine was gracious and accommodating. Nonetheless, many years later the lineup issue and the defense attorney's agreement of the makeup of the lineup would be brought up on appeal. The state supreme court would deny that appeal.

Sergeant Petrick knew that leaving the lineup in the hands of Detective Bordine was one less thing he had to worry about. He had enough to worry about because Michelle's cancer was the kind that was aggressive, rapid, and usually fatal. Both Ed and Michelle gave their all to fight it, and then, in the end, to ensure that Michelle was comfortable. By July 1992, her fight was over.

After tending to Michelle's final arrangements, Ed Petrick took some time to compose himself. Then he threw himself back into his work, as good a method of grieving as any, experts say. He thought of Michelle often, spoke of her a lot, and moved on with his professional duties, mainly making sure that Cleophus Prince Jr. received the fate he deserved.

In spite of all the other cases they had and would have, the team members never forgot Janet Moore. Jaime Bordine had bonded with Janet's mother in a big way when he relayed the death message to her. He could have said, "Your daughter has been murdered. Here is my business card. Call if you hear anything, or suspect anyone." He didn't. He stayed with Janet's mother and talked with her. He had learned about Janet's artistic talent, even though it didn't appear to have anything to do with the case. As a parent himself, Bordine couldn't help but put himself in her mother's place. The loss of a child just isn't right.

Ed Petrick was haunted by the fact that Janet's case was still open. They had good crime-scene evidence and that evidence should damn well contribute to an arrest. It didn't, though. Petrick was a "by the book" cop. Even though he had a sense of humor, he was mostly all business. Rather, it was "business first, fun later." Bordine was more emotional. He felt the "humanity" of the case more deeply than the others. It was his nature to be helpful and solicitous of other people's feelings. When a detective from another agency came to SDPD headquarters to get information on possible related crimes, Bordine would go out of his way to make sure the stranger was well taken care of. Sometimes detectives from smaller departments held the San Diego cops in awe because SDPD was where the "big boys" hung out. Some SDPD detectives were abrupt to strangers. Not so with Bordine. This human quality was also present in the way he looked at Janet Moore's case. Janet's mother would never forget his kindness.

Ron Thill was a combination of Bordine and Petrick. Thill didn't have the soothing "bedside manner" of Bordine, but he had a softer approach than Petrick. Being the "scene detective," he was well aware of all of the evidence and the reports that went into the murder book. But he too was concerned about the human side of the case and the senseless loss of life of one so young.

CHAPTER 12

The physical evidence taken from Tessa Rayburn at the federal jail, along with her extensive interview by Detective Bordine, removed her from the list of suspects in December 1991. Authorities had looked for her for a long time. They had hoped evidence would prove she was the one, or could lead them to the killer, because they were running out of suspects. She was not the one. So far, everyone except the sailor who had been stabbed in the peaceful city of Coronado had been cleared. When you clear every possible suspect in a case and you haven't made an arrest, have you failed? The detectives believed they might be on the path to failure. They wouldn't give up, though. It wasn't over yet.

The situation of the police was similar to being in a football game in which your team is behind by two touchdowns with four minutes left. You say, "C'mon, guys, we're going to win this thing! Don't give up!" Yet, at the same time, the players know the odds of scoring twice in four minutes are definitely against them. The good ones never give up, and that is how Homicide Team III felt.

In the years before Ron Thill temporarily left the San Diego Police homicide unit to participate in the Metropolitan Homicide Task Force, both he and Bordine often looked out their window on the east side of the police building. Before Janet Moore's murder the two detectives watched for car burglaries in progress. After her murder, when Thill would drop by the police station in the afternoon from task-force headquarters, they would merely look at her building and shake their heads. They wanted to find Janet's killer. That four-story building where Janet was killed was a constant reminder that yet another killer lurked out there.

Forces within the community were beginning to question the San Diego Police Department's motivation to catch the killers of prostitutes and certain other women. Before it was over, a local group not only accused the San Diego police of incompetence and indifference, they also accused them of corruption.

Five members of the local arts community, Deborah Small, Elizabeth Sisco, Carla Kirkwood, Scott Kessler, and Louis Hock, believed the San Diego Police Department did not care that women were being killed.

The artists' first foray into educating the public by aesthetic means was not about murder, though. The first project happened back in 1988, an effort entitled *Welcome to America's Finest Tourist Plantation*. The title for the art project was a variation on San Diego's official slogan, "America's Finest City."

The "Plantation" project consisted of pictorial displays on the backs of a hundred city buses. It consisted of three side-by-side photos of:

1. A pair of hands washing dishes
2. A pair of hands being handcuffed
3. A pair of hands delivering clean towels to a hotel room

The artists hoped it would be evident that the pictured hands belonged to undocumented immigrant workers in the San Diego area.

This project, funded by the National Endowment for the Arts, was meant to depict how hard undocumented workers performed their labors in San Diego. It was put in place in time for the Super Bowl held in San Diego in order to show tourists the exploitation of undocumented workers and how the workers were forced to cater to the fat cats who came to town for the Super Bowl for a festival of debauchery.

The city of San Diego was the target in the "America's Finest Tourist Plantation" project. The public greeted it with a collective yawn. The tourists who left over a million dollars in San Diego during the Super Bowl did not appear to notice the artwork. The undocumented illegals who flocked to San Diego to make more money than they could in their native countries didn't say anything about the project either.

The NEA funded another project by the same artists in 1990 called "America's Finest?," with the question mark being the focus of attention. This project sought to demonstrate the brutality of the San Diego Police Department. Bus benches all over town displayed human silhouette targets, the kind used for shooting practice. The purpose of this outdoor exhibit was to critique the use of deadly force by the San Diego police and the city's apparent refusal to hold the police accountable for their brutality.

While a few people who had been injured during confrontations with the police successfully sued the city in brutality cases, no officers were prosecuted. Both the local department where a shooting happens and the district attorney's office scrutinize every police shooting in the county. None of the recent cases was deemed "criminal"; no member of the police force committed a crime.

"America's Finest?" did not seem to register with the public either. Most people believed if they were holding a knife, shovel, gun, or club and a uniformed officer instructed them to "drop it" or "freeze," they would, and should, comply. The populace believed that armed people who don't do what the police say get what they deserve. The artists' art project elicited another "so what?" from the public.

―――――――

Between 1985 and 1992, there were forty-five unsolved murders of women in the San Diego area. The sheriff's department handled some of the cases and the San Diego police handled the rest. Many of the women were prostitutes.

The same five artists, all with ties to local institutions of higher learning, believed the cases were not solved because the police thought no humans were involved. The artists believed the police performed less than thorough investigations because the lives of these homicide-victim women were somehow worth less than the lives of the rest of the population.

The five artists, again with funding from the National Endowment for the Arts, titled their exhibit "No Humans Involved." The title of the thin book they collaborated on was *NHI*. The exhibit was presented in several ways. The first part was the display of two large commercial billboards. One was placed directly across the street from the San Diego Police Department at Fourteenth and G streets. The other was an equally large billboard across from the county administration offices at Cedar Street and Pacific Highway. The picture showed the face of Donna Gentile and the letters *NHI*.

Donna Gentile was a local prostitute who had testified against some police officers. She had had a physically intimate relationship with at least two officers. They had taken her to the Colorado River, near the Arizona border, a favorite recreation spot for many San Diegans. While there, they water-skied, partied, and, well, partied some more. In return for sexual favors, some officers allegedly tipped her off about where certain vice cops would be lurking when she returned to the streets of San Diego.

The police conducted an internal investigation in which Gentile participated and testified. One officer was fired and another was demoted.

Months later, Gentile was murdered in the rural eastern part of the county. She had been strangled. Dirt and gravel were allegedly stuffed into her mouth. Neither the police nor the sheriff's department solved the case.

On the "NHI" project, the group of artists tried to show that there was a problem with an uncaring justice system. They attempted to speak with Dick Lewis, the deputy district attorney who headed up the Metropolitan Homicide Task Force. Lewis did not trust the press, and certainly felt he was under no obligation to discuss ongoing homicide investigations with any group of artists.

Lewis was aware of the bus ads depicting the undocumented workers. While he didn't care one way or another if the artists were outraged about the treatment of undocumented workers, he was not enthralled with the depiction of San Diego police as brutal. Lewis had walked a beat, driven a patrol car, and prosecuted many criminals during his career. He knew the streets were tough. He also knew that when people were scared and threatened and in danger, they did not pick up the phone and call the local artists' colony. They called the police.

Getting nowhere with Lewis, the artists tried to obtain information from the homicide divisions of both the sheriff's department and the San Diego police. The authorities did not share information on the investigations.

The artists asked for photos of some of the victims for the display. They were able to obtain fewer than ten pictures. The project was now in full swing. In addition to the two large billboards, the artists rented a storefront at 622 Fifth Avenue in the heart of downtown San Diego and turned it into a gallery. The billboards would be on display for one month starting on February 19, 1992.

Because the artists could only get photos of a few of the homicide victims, they solicited other women in the community to have their pictures in the display to somehow give faces to the rest of the victims. They asked San Diego mayor Maureen O'Connor for her picture. O'Connor declined. They were able to get enough pictures to show that forty-five women had been killed.

Along with the photos, the book called *NHI* was for sale. It detailed what was known about the death of Donna Gentile and police involvement with her before her death. It also detailed how the sheriff's department, which handled Gentile's death, investigated the San Diego police officers that Gentile testified against in their administrative hearings. The implication was that San Diego cops were responsible for Gentile's death. The fact that none of them was ever actually accused, or even considered as a viable suspect after the investigation, only solidified the artists' claim that corruption was involved and the sheriff's department was giving a "wink" at the San Diego cops.

Dick Lewis, the prosecutor from the Metro Homicide Task Force, did comment on the term *no humans involved.* Lewis said he remembered it as a term he'd heard old-timers from back East use. He said he first heard the term when he was a young kid reading detective magazines. Lewis said local police officers did not use the term in reference to the murders under investigation by the task force. The artists at "NHI" said that was not true, that cops routinely referred to murders of prostitutes in that way.

In a publication called *Critical Condition—Women on the Edge of Violence,* edited by Amy Scholder, published by City Lights Books in 1993, Elizabeth Sisco, one of the artistic five, detailed many events of the NHI project. Local law enforcement took a sound bashing from Ms. Sisco.

She said the local police "mishandled" the murder

investigations. Sisco cited a quote from an unnamed San
Diego police officer in the *Sacramento Bee* who said,
"These were misdemeanor murders, biker women and
hookers. We'd call them NHI's, no humans involved."

Sisco also wrote that the San Diego officials, from the
mayor to the district attorney to the police chief, "did little
to refute the idea that these forty-five women deserved to
die because of how they lived."

The article even took a potshot at the police for solving
the murder of college coed Cara Knott in 1986. The implication was that the police solved the murder only because
Cara was pretty, white, and a college girl. The article didn't
mention police corruption, possibly because the police arrested a California highway patrolman, Craig Peyer, for
the on-duty strangulation of Knott. The artists took a brief
holiday from logic in their disingenuous reasoning. How
could there be a police cover-up if they arrested a cop? The
probable answer was that Cara Knott was not a prostitute.
Peyer was convicted of murder and is currently serving a
prison sentence. The parole board has denied him freedom
each time he has appeared before them, most recently in
January 31, 2008.

Elizabeth Sisco also did a one-woman dramatic presentation on February 22, March 7, and March 14, for a show
entitled "Many Women Involved." This production, held at
the gallery at 622 Fifth Avenue, showed the many ways
violence is perpetrated on women by people even within
their own families, and by the public at large.

The group held a panel discussion on Sunday, March 8,
1992. The topic was the series of murders and gender violence in San Diego. The police took a beating on that one
too.

The people behind the project seemed to pick and choose
what they wanted to discuss. Elizabeth Sisco's article mentioned, without mentioning the killer's name, the six murders committed by Cleophus Prince Jr. On the one hand, the

project said violence against women was ignored. On the other hand, the police were chided for working so hard to solve the Cleophus Prince murders. The article by Sisco said the police held daily press briefings on Prince's murders, and ignored the others, as if that was something bad.

During those turbulent, murder-filled years, if the San Diego police held press briefings on all their homicide cases, they would have had to start their own twenty-four-hour network called the "San Diego Murder Channel."

The difference between the Cleophus Prince murders and the murders of the forty-five was simple: Prince's victims were killed inside the safety of their own locked homes. Many of the forty-five featured in the "NHI" project were prostitutes who climbed into the cars of strangers. While not asking to be killed, the prostitutes put themselves in a position where death or injury could happen.

The local press devoted little space to the "NHI" project in the news sections. Arts-and-entertainment sections of the local paper and several out-of-town publications gave some publicity to the project, however. They were getting noticed, not especially by people interested in hard news, but by people in the arts.

The five artists were able to claim victim status after all when the National Endowment for the Arts canceled further funding for their projects. They could cry "censorship" because the government was now involved in silencing them.

Louis Hock, the only artist who would cooperate with a writer doing a project on the Janet Moore case years later, said the group of five came under criticism from the public and possibly the police themselves. Hock remembers getting anonymous threats over the telephone. He said the group received an eerie invitation from an unidentified caller to attend a party at the J Street Marina in Chula Vista at midnight. (The park closed at 10 p.m.) Hock said, "Un-marked police cars were in front of our houses." While the artists never made any reports to the police department of the threatening calls, midnight invitations to the pier, or the possibility of unauthorized police surveillance, the group was still unnerved but undaunted. Why make a report to the police when the police were most likely the ominous, anonymous callers?

CHAPTER 13

The police did not notice the criticism by the artists, or at least when interviewed years later they would not admit they noticed. Maybe a few talked about it over coffee or in casual conversations. The criticism never influenced the way the police performed their duties.

The artists said the police "mishandled" murder investigations. They said authorities "botched" the cases. They said the police "covered up" police involvement with a number of murdered women. Because the artists' claims were largely ignored by the police administration and the police themselves, no one ever asked the artists to back up or explain their claims. And the artists never attempted to prove them. They just made them.

In the gallery where the victims' photos were displayed, there was a guest book for patrons to sign. Elizabeth Sisco's article quoted an unnamed "homicide investigator" who wrote in the book of being "trained to disregard the humanity of victims from the 'darker side' of life." Years later a writer asked Louis Hock if the writer's occupation was ever verified. He said no. The writer then asked, "Could anyone who attended the exhibit have written that statement and labeled him or herself a homicide investigator?" The answer was, "Well, yes, possibly."

The project attempted to raise public awareness of the multiple murders by criticizing the callous attitude of the police. It accused the police of not caring if the victim was a prostitute, or even caring about any woman killed and dumped along the side of the road.

Were the police guilty of an unfeeling attitude? Police departments are made up of human beings. Police officers undergo extensive pre-employment screenings and submit to a battery of psychological tests, including standardized personality evaluations and polygraphs. Some officers steal, rob, beat, rape, and even murder after they are hired. There are no guarantees as to how a particular police officer will perform or react once employment is gained.

Years ago, at Assumption Roman Catholic Seminary in San Antonio, Texas, the rector, Father Roy Rihn, told an assembly of prospective priests, "We are men, not angels. Unfortunately, we have to pick our people [priests] from the human race."

The same is true for police departments. Did a particular police officer say of a prostitute murder that no human was involved? Maybe. Is this concept taught in any police academy in the United States? Highly unlikely.

Mark Fuhrman was castigated during the O. J. Simpson case for saying he had never uttered the word *nigger*. After that lie was exposed, everyone expected a parade of black people the detective had mistreated over the years to come forward with details of beatings, tainted convictions, confessions that never happened, or worse. None were produced, and it was not for lack of trying on the part of the defense team. In short, Fuhrman's words were one thing and his deeds were another.

Words are truly one thing and deeds are another. Even

if a detective callously said that no human was involved, the collective deeds of the police showed a more dedicated, professional level of effort.

Sometimes, if one career criminal killer kills another street thug over a dope debt or other illegal activity, the cops will label the death an "ecology killing." It is called that because the streets are rid of one open sore (the deceased), and probably another festering sore (the killer) because the killer is going to prison. Thus the ecology is maintained because two bad apples are gone. Is that callous and unfeeling? Maybe. Even though the characterization of the two parties involved may be harsh, it is still true that the police arrested the killer and put him or her in prison. They didn't look the other way because the victim was not a productive member of society. They may have said things they wouldn't repeat at a society cocktail party, but they still solved the case.

The dark humor of cops, reporters, doctors, and nurses is another thing to consider. One reporter said, "We laugh at some strange things, but it [the laughter] is to keep from crying."

Instead of taking aim at the police, should the artists have blamed the citizens and the mainstream media? The murder of Janet Moore vanished from the newspapers in a matter of days after the killing. If a story is not on television or in the papers, the public tends to forget quickly. Yet the police quietly continued to investigate Janet's murder without the scrutiny of the media.

Average citizens are concerned when someone like Cleophus Prince Jr. is breaking into locked homes to kill women he has stalked from a health club. The public is still concerned, but not nearly as much, when a woman gets in a stranger's car, offers to perform a sex act for a few dollars, and rides away with him. People don't like it when the woman later ends up dead. A citizen's natural reaction to the death of a street hooker is, "I am very sorry this happened. The poor girl, but what did she expect?" Is a citizen who obeys the law, keeps the doors locked, and does not get into the cars of strangers to perform sex for money not entitled to this reaction?

The prostitute-victim didn't expect, or deserve, to die. But she put herself in a position where it was very likely to happen.

Several years later, Detectives Ron Thill and Ed Petrick were asked specifically and pointedly about the "NHI" project and how it affected their work. The two were interviewed separately. Using different words, both said essentially, " 'NHI?' I never heard of it." Maybe they did know about the project and weren't telling the truth. Maybe they were so busy trying to solve the plethora of homicides that they weren't concerned with an art project that pilloried the police. Maybe the two cops were actually telling the truth when they said the "NHI" project was unknown to them.

Five years had passed since the June 1988 death of Janet Moore. Sergeant Ed Petrick was mourning the loss of his wife, Michelle. After Cleophus Prince Jr. was safely on the prison bus to San Quentin's Death Row, Petrick transferred out of Homicide. He returned to narcotics enforcement in September 1993.

The Metropolitan Homicide Task Force disbanded in 1993. Their statistics indicate that they solved twenty-six of the forty-five murders. They didn't hit their mark of forty-five. They worked with what they had. Their success would not satisfy the five artists who did the "No Humans Involved" project, even though the project was over. The closure figures did not satisfy the task force either. But they did the best they could. Dick Lewis, chief of the task force, returned to his duties at the district attorney's office.

Detective Ron Thill, who started with the San Diego police in 1972, opted to go to the district attorney's office as an investigator in 1994. While Thill lost his seniority and went to the bottom of the list for vacation preference, the D.A. job was a step up. District-attorney investigators, for the most part, work regular hours. Unless one is assigned to the gang prosecution unit or the officer-involved shooting assignment, there are seldom any call-outs in the middle of the night.

Thill spent his time in what was then called the pretrial unit. Prosecuting attorneys assigned the pretrial investigators cases that have already been issued for prosecution. Even though these cases have met the standard for being issued, most were not "courtroom ready." The D.A. investigators "fine-tune" the cases. Some witnesses have to be reinterviewed. Live lineups have to be conducted. Often surprise witness would emerge, either of their own volition or at the behest of defense attorneys.

The D.A. investigators interview the witnesses and prepare reports. The D.A. investigator's job was not nearly as stressful as rolling out of bed at 2 a.m. and being gone for forty-eight hours on a fresh homicide. Thill liked his new job.

———

The number of homicides in San Diego began a downward turn in the mid nineties. From an original four investigative teams, the unit ballooned to seven working groups at the peak in 1991 when the killing total was 167. When things slowed down, the police administration cut back on the homicide sleuths. San Diego homicide detectives no longer responded to the scene of industrial work-related deaths. Promotions and transfers accounted for attrition. The administration decided to return to four teams, with one minor alteration.

San Diego Homicide added a fifth team in August 1995, one that would investigate old murders. How old? As old as they happened to be. It didn't matter. The first point of order was to give a name to the fledgling unit. Creative minds decided "cold-case unit" was too common and everyday. Every department that had a cold-case unit called it just that, the "cold-case unit." More than one television program shared that name. The San Diego cops tried to be clever and accurate at the same time.

Because old, forgotten homicide cases are often solved due to advances in technology and the examination of physical evidence, they elected to call the new unit the "Homicide Evidence Assessment Team," or HEAT, the exact opposite of "cold." The announcement of the HEAT group didn't exactly arrive with a star-studded "open house" featuring coffee, cookies, and a ribbon-cutting ceremony. The team didn't have a special office with an engraved "HEAT" sign either. They were quartered in, of all places, a file room surrounded by stacks of old homicide cases. No ambience there.

They had spartan metal tables and sturdy, straight-backed steel chairs. One concession to the twenty-first century was computers and telephones. When people gave tours of the homicide unit, they would stumble into the cramped HEAT area and say, "Uh, and this is, uh, where the detectives investigate old homicides." The tour takers would look around the cluttered file room, usually with wide-eyed, puzzled silence, before the guide hurriedly moved them on.

Eventually, the HEAT fell in step with the rest of law enforcement and changed its name to the cold-case homicide unit. They now have their own office on the seventh floor of San Diego Police Headquarters. Their cubicles are small and they are jammed together. But they now have a real office with a real name on the door.

The assigned detectives pored over old cases as rapidly as they could while still remaining thorough. They looked for a glimmer of an opening that might help solve a murder. Many of the cases listed suspects who had never been arrested. It is very frustrating to suspect a possible killer but be unable to prove anything. Sometimes the suspicion is stronger than that. Sometimes the cops *know* someone did a killing, but they just can't prove it.

The members of HEAT reinterviewed witnesses who had been interviewed years before. Often the suspect would be in prison on another charge. The detectives would remind the witness that the person of interest was safely locked away and could not harm them. Many old cases were solved in this manner. No longer afraid, the witnesses would sometimes admit they saw a certain person kill someone else.

At the eventual trial these witnesses had to undergo vigorous cross-examination at the hands of defense attorneys because of their "new and improved" memory. Years before, they told the police they hadn't seen anything. Now they suddenly remembered that the defense attorney's client actually did pull the trigger. How would the district attorney combat that?

The straightforward approach worked best. The witness would tell the truth on the witness stand, saying something along the lines of, "I lied to the cops because I was afraid of [supply name of defendant]. He said he would kill me if I told anyone. I believed he would kill me. Now that he's in prison, I'm not so afraid." Most of the time it worked. Jurors tended to believe the tortured souls who got up on the witness stand and laid themselves bare before the court, defense attorney, and the often menacing eyes of the accused. The convictions piled up.

By 1995, scientific advances also helped solve crimes. Machines and microscopes became stronger and more sensitive. Research strengthened the examination of bodily fluids and other human evidence left at a homicide scene. Advances in DNA were announced regularly.

The HEAT wanted to add someone to their team from the United States Marshal's Office, and someone from the district attorney. Having personnel with connections at these other offices made for smoother investigations. Even though he was at the district attorney's office, the San Diego Police Department and the district attorney's office believed Ron Thill would be the perfect investigator to liaison with the team. While his paycheck would come from the county of San Diego, his body would be in both places, the San Diego police station and the Hall of Justice, which housed the district attorney's office. Thill had the best of both worlds. He could get back to doing what he loved and did best, solving homicides. And he wouldn't have to put up with the pager and telephone at all hours of the night.

He could take a case and examine it thoroughly without being on a strict timetable. This didn't mean he could lollygag. It meant he could do his job in a thorough, painstaking manner.

Over the years Thill became an expert in the extradition laws from other states. If a suspect in an old San Diego murder was identified, and the suspect wasn't already in prison, the suspect had often relocated to another state. It would be Thill's job to learn where the suspect was, get him into custody, and then get him legally back to San Diego.

The team solved cold cases at an impressive rate. The news media found HEAT to be a catchy story. The local press lapped up the statistics put forth by the police administration. The public was impressed too.

———————

Still, the murder case of Janet Moore stood neatly filed away, with no one to look at it. Terry Torgersen, one of the charter members of the HEAT unit, did look at it once. After careful analysis, Torgersen determined that only one possible suspect remained. The sailor who claimed to have been stabbed in the peaceful city of Coronado was still out there. They needed his blood. As Torgersen pored over the case he noted that the sailor was white, the race to which the serologist had connected the blood in Moore's apartment. A white person was most likely the killer.

Torgersen noted that a "locate" had been placed in the nationwide system to notify the San Diego Police Department if the now-discharged sailor was found. There was nothing else to do. Team III, under Sergeant Petrick, had done everything they could. Petrick's initial catchphrase to his troops—"We will not be judged on what we did, but on what we did NOT do"—would not be an issue in Janet Moore's case. There was nothing they had not done.

The case went back on the shelf.

CHAPTER 14

By the mid-1990s, DNA was an established evidentiary tool in law enforcement. While it was a mystery at first, people, including the media, were getting attuned to DNA evidence in criminal cases. Scientists explained DNA in simple terms to juries. Because DNA was science, defense attorneys could only attack DNA evidence in a narrow range, such as collection methods and contamination of samples. While DNA was making its presence felt, most police departments were overloading testing laboratories with DNA requests. Evidence that could be tested for DNA was sitting in locked evidence areas. The evidence in Janet Moore's murder was in the category of "waiting for someone to test it."

Scientists and prosecuting attorneys experienced some tense moments in 1995 after the O. J. Simpson verdict because the verdict related to DNA and other scientific evidence. While experts remained solidly convinced of DNA's reliability, the public who watched the fiasco of a trial on television wondered.

Through obfuscation, confusion, and some "razzle-dazzle," defense attorneys from the Innocence Project, who normally used DNA evidence found at a crime scene from someone other than their client to show their client *didn't* do it, did an about-face and helped free someone (Simpson) whose DNA actually was at the crime scene. Other physical evidence—a glove and imprints from a rare imported shoe—implicated Simpson too. In the opinion of many, the Innocence Project suffered a credibility hit after their representatives appeared at the O.J. fiasco. Some thought the staff from the project was not really interested in freeing the innocent. They were interested in freeing EVERYBODY.

Eventually most thinking people came to the realization that the strange jury would have acquitted Simpson even if there had been a videotape of him committing the double murders. Well, maybe not that drastic, but the experts decided that it was the faulty jury, some questionable investigative efforts, and debatable prosecution strategy, but not improper DNA collection that caused Simpson's subsequent freedom. DNA was here to stay. If anything, the national exposure and explanation of DNA during the Simpson case may even have strengthened its evidentiary credibility with the public and future jury pools.

Criminalists and police officers learned from the Simpson circus too. All law enforcement personnel at a crime scene now took extreme care to ensure serological evidence was handled correctly and not carried around in a detective's coat pocket. Procedures were implemented to make sure that trace evidence on clothing would not contaminate a crime scene.

Allowing O. J. Simpson to be a free man in society was an expensive price to pay for lovers of justice. But improved methods of handling evidence assisted crime fighters everywhere. Possibly because only about one hundred miles separated Los Angeles and San Diego, San Diego beefed up its DNA testing facilities. Authorities didn't want their lab referred to as a "cesspool of contamination" like their neighbor to the north, Los Angeles.

When DNA was in its infant stage, evidence-wise, the San Diego district attorney sought training for Deputy District Attorney George "Woody" Clarke in cases involving DNA. Eventually Clarke became well versed enough in DNA that he was called upon to train deputy district attorneys in the art of questioning witnesses regarding DNA. Because of his impressive scientific and legal credentials, the Los Angeles district attorney asked Clarke's superiors in San Diego to let Clarke assist with the Simpson case. During the trial, Clarke did his best to present the DNA evidence. Clarke went through each exhibit that had DNA, examining and interpreting the results. He questioned the experts for the prosecution, and he cross-examined the experts of the defense. Clarke was satisfied with his efforts. But his work was to no avail. The jury acquitted Simpson.

Before and after the trial, Clark traveled all over the country giving training and assisting in trials where DNA was an issue. Clarke wrote a book, *Justice and Science: Trials and Triumphs of DNA Evidence* (Rutgers University Press, January 2008). He is now a superior-court judge in San Diego.

———————

The San Diego cold-case team went about their business, working hard to bring their investigations to a close. Of Team III, as it originally existed, only Detective Jaime Bordine remained. Sergeant Petrick went to Narcotics. Ron Thill went to the Homicide Task Force, then to the D.A.'s office. Patrick Ruffner, the substitute detective who assisted the original members, was on another team.

Work proceeded as usual, but none of it was connected to Janet Moore's case. There was nothing more to do.

———————

While life went on for everyone, the hand of fate touched a member of Team III. Way back in 1977, when he was thirty-three, Jaime Bordine had been diagnosed with a brain tumor. After its removal, he felt fine and returned to work. In 1984, the tumor grew back and he had to have a second surgery. This surgery was more difficult to bounce back from. He endured uncomfortable radiation treatment, but continued to work.

In 1991, three years into the Janet Moore investigation, a problem in the form of small tumors showed up in Bordine's lung. The doctors always said the tumors were benign, but they were tumors nonetheless. He had a lobe of a lung removed in yet another very difficult surgery. Medical personnel went through his ribs to get to his lung to complete the removal. Once this was over, Bordine, ever the trooper, went back to the work he loved.

In 1995, Jaime's back started to hurt and he couldn't figure out why. He continued working, but this time had to walk with the assistance of a cane. He never complained and carried a caseload like everyone else. He was in such pain at the end of the day that his wife, Marcie, had to help him get undressed. Bordine kept quiet publicly, but the pain was taking a toll on him and his family.

Bordine's oncologist sent him to a physical therapist, who treated him for a slipped disk. Finally, the therapist phoned the physician to tell him there was something more wrong than a slipped disk, that the therapy was hurting Detective Bordine more than it was helping.

The doctor ordered a Magnetic Resonance Image. The procedure revealed a tumor on Bordine's spine. He was told he needed radiation and more surgery or the tumor would go through his spine and paralyze him. The radiation made him very sick, but Detective Bordine did as he was told. A team of three doctors, made up of a general surgeon, a thoracic surgeon, and a neurosurgeon, performed the operation. They had to remove a rib and disk to get to the tumor. The doctors used cadaver parts and metal inserts to put Bordine back together. He had to wear a "tortoiseshell" protective apparatus. By now, he was on disability because he couldn't perform at work any longer.

Marcie quit her job to care for him. The family bought Jaime a hospital bed and a big-screen television. He made camp in the living room. The doctors finally admitted that Bordine had cancer. Further tests showed the cancer was everywhere, including his liver.

Bordine faced the inevitable. He knew he was dying. Although he did not want to retire, the other detectives convinced him he had to so Marcie could get benefits.

Finally, in 1997, after a productive life and an excellent police career, Jaime Bordine passed away at age fifty-three. He never got to see his first grandchild, who was born one year after his death, or the others who followed in succeeding years. Ron Thill took Bordine's death as hard as anyone in Bordine's family. They had been inseparable on the job for years. Bordine had served as best man at Thill's wedding. To this day, Thill speaks fondly and reverently about Bordine. In actuality, Thill is not too reverent about many things.

So yet another member of Team III was touched by tragedy. All the original voices in the Janet Moore case were gone from the original team. Who would speak for her now?

The forensic-science unit is housed upstairs in the police station at 1401 Broadway. Patrick O'Donnell, a Ph.D. from San Diego State University, who joined the police department in 1990, heads up the unit. O'Donnell did not originally work in the criminal-justice field.

Among other things, he worked with insects. After laboring in the late 1980s studying the "defects in muscles of fruit flies," O'Donnell decided the study "was so esoteric and uninteresting to the general population" that he asked himself, "What contribution [to society] am I making?"

After working at the SDPD crime lab helping to solve crimes, O'Donnell knows with certainty that everything he and his workers do in the lab touches people in many positive ways. However, there are a few people residing in the California prison system who don't care for Patrick O'Donnell or his work.

After the O. J. Simpson case, crime laboratories around the country improved their facilities. Politicians located formerly elusive money to upgrade and maintain the scientific arm of law enforcement. The San Diego Police Department developed a full-service crime lab that could analyze physical evidence collected at crime scenes. The SDPD lab does this without sending the work out to be handled by another agency.

Smaller departments have to rely on other overworked facilities like the sheriff's lab or the state department of justice to get their lab work done. While the sheriff's people do a very good job, they are overworked. And it is a fact of life that if a deputy sheriff who personally knows the sheriff's scientist walks in and asks to have his evidence looked at right away, that evidence is likely to go to the top of the pile. On the other hand, if there is a package from a smaller department with a regular lab-analysis request in the pile, it very well might remain there until the analyst gets to it.

The San Diego Police Department has its own forensic-biology department. Within this department the DNA unit analyzes physiological fluids, bone tissue, and hair. The most commonly examined materials are blood, semen, and saliva. The San Diego administrators are proud to point out that the American Society of Crime Laboratory Directors has accredited their operation.

Patrick O'Donnell's crime lab had been awarded a grant to examine evidence in old cases. In keeping with his scientist's demeanor, O'Donnell systematically had police interns go over old cases, usually sex crimes and homicides that had possible DNA evidence. The intern would then make a one-paragraph summary of the case, including the potential evidence.

The process of going through cases, reducing the "meat" of the facts to a few short sentences and getting the casebook to a scientist, took a long time, given the large number of outstanding cases.

If the volumes detailing Janet Moore's murder had a human voice, one can envision the binders standing on the shelf in the HEAT area emitting a tiny cry of, "Me! Look at me! Try me! I have evidence for you!" That was not the situation. Janet's case languished in the stacks for many months, waiting its turn.

David Cornacchia was one of the Patrick O'Donnell's forensic scientists. Born in Warren, Michigan, near Detroit, and educated at Michigan State University with a Bachelor of Science degree in forensic science earned in 1993, Cornacchia had worked for a few law enforcement agencies before landing with the San Diego police.

He was a forensic-science intern for the Wisconsin Crime Lab Bureau shortly after graduation. His undergraduate degree convinced David he needed more training. Cornacchia took basic serology training with the Oklahoma State Bureau of Investigation in early 1994 in Oklahoma City.

Cornacchia stayed in Oklahoma to continue his training in basic and advanced bloodstain-pattern analysis. Not wanting to be a one-trick pony, he became familiar with basic crime-scene photography. He learned microbiology and statistics at Oklahoma State University in early 1997 and genetics at the University of Central Oklahoma that same year.

The year 1998 found Cornacchia studying molecular biology and biochemistry at two different universities in Oklahoma while still working for the Oklahoma State Bureau of Investigation.

Heeding Horace Greeley's advice to "go west, young man," Cornacchia moved to California in November 1998 to work for the San Diego County Sheriff's Department. Here, he discovered that blood was, well, in his blood. He helped establish the DNA laboratory for the Sheriff's Department while gaining expertise in DNA-PCR poly-marker typing. He also learned forensic and paternity data analysis.

In 2000, Cornacchia moved over to the San Diego Police Department, where he continued to labor in the forensic-biology unit. David sharpened his expertise even more, and became an expert witness in the fields of forensics in which he had been trained. Defense attorneys pored over Cornacchia's curriculum vitae in an attempt to find a weak spot. Over the years Cornacchia has responded to hundreds of crime scenes. He has examined biological evidence for thousands of cases and testified in hundreds of criminal cases. Cornacchia is a member of the California Association of Criminalists.

Defense attorneys go through the motions of trying to trip Cornacchia up both for his investigative procedures and his court testimony. So far, they haven't succeeded.

———

In December 2002, the tall, lean Cornacchia looked at a one-paragraph summary of a cold case. His brow furrowed. It looked like a young girl had been slashed and stabbed in her apartment in 1988. Two things jumped out at him. The first was the presence of crime-scene blood different from that of the victim. A washcloth saturated with blood was found at the crime scene. The second item was a vaginal swab of semen recovered from the victim. Her name: Janet Moore.

Cornacchia went to the Homicide Evidence Assessment Team and asked Terry Torgersen about the case. Torgersen located the book in the stacks. He confirmed to Cornacchia the existence of the case and that it was still unsolved. Torgersen supplied the correct lab numbers of the bloody washcloth and vaginal swab.

A few days later Cornacchia checked the items from evidence and carefully transported them from the refrigerated section of the property room to the sterile confines of his domain, the crime lab. He took the vaginal swab and made a slide for examination purposes. Looking under the microscope, he was happy to learn that the slide bore evidence of sperm. From the slide, Cornacchia made a full DNA profile. He performed similar actions with the bloody washcloth, making a similar DNA profile.

Once Cornacchia had the DNA reading, he went about putting the findings in a database called the Combined DNA Index System, or CODIS. This didn't happen overnight. Cornacchia had picked up the evidence in late December 2002. He made the CODIS entry on March 13, 2003. This type of crime-lab work doesn't happen with the speed it does on television, especially when there are no viable suspects.

The first database checked for a DNA match was the San Diego Police Department's own. The DNA reading from Janet Moore's case was not in the SDPD base. The profile was then sent through the State of California's database. Finally, they ran the results through the Federal Bureau of Investigation's national database. When no hits happened, Janet Moore became a cold case once again.

The computerized results are checked through the same search process once a week, every week.

Janet Moore, sadly enough, was "just another murder" once again.

PART II

Volusia County, Florida
January 2004

CHAPTER 15

Volusia County, on the Atlantic coast of Florida, is home to several small cities. The most well known is Daytona Beach, with a listed population of about sixty-five thousand. Depending on what event is happening, the numbers often swell to over five hundred thousand during the legendary Daytona car races, Bike Week in March, and the Motorcycle BiketoberFest in October.

Volusia County itself, home to more than 445,000 residents, is larger than the state of Rhode Island. There are sixteen municipalities across 1,207 square miles of territory. Four bridges connect the "mainland" of the county to the beach portion. Miles and miles of beautiful shoreline are dotted with hotels and motels, some of which are four-star-rated, and some without any stars at all. On the beaches a tourist may rent a beach chair and umbrella. For the more adventurous, there is a half-hour ride on a parasail, a parachute that is pulled over the water by a motorized watercraft. People can rent all kinds of fun beach things during the day. After dark, one may even rent a woman.

Like any modern warm-weather area, Volusia County has its share of transients and those committed to making a buck outside the law. A short strip along Atlantic Avenue, called A1A by the regulars, is known for its prostitution and narcotics trade after the tourist families settle down for the night.

People who watch Fox television's reality show *Cops* have never seen a segment filmed in Volusia County. Daytona Beach police officers say the reason is that police administrators and city fathers do not want the nation to view Volusia's seedy underbelly. It is a tourist area and they want families to spend their money on taxable things like hotels, dinners, souvenir T-shirts, postcards, and parasail rides. Prostitution is not taxable and is often accompanied by many other crimes.

———————

Abbe Smith[*] and her husband, Slim, lived in several places and frequently spent time along the Atlantic coast of Florida. On a cool January night in 2004, they were on a mission in Volusia County to buy drugs. Life had been tough for them. Unemployed, undereducated, and desperate, they were near New Smyrna Beach trying to look up old friends who might sell them drugs on credit. Abbe and Slim were staying in a low-class motel on the mainland side. If being out of drugs and out of money was not bad enough, the manager was getting ready to evict them for being several days delinquent in their rent. Even though the motel catered to lowlifes, druggies, and prostitutes, the manager hoped something good would happen and he would get his money.

If Abbe and Slim hadn't had enough bad luck already, their truck ran out of gas. Slim elected to stay with the vehicle to guard the few meager valuables they hadn't left in their room. Another reason he stayed behind was that his work tools were in the truck. Even though he had not worked in a long time, he still had his tools—those he had not pawned, that is. If he had left them in the motel room, there was a good chance they'd be gone when he and Abbe returned. Also, if they got evicted, the manager would hold the tools ransom until their back rent was paid. Life really was tough. For Abbe, it was about to get tougher.

Walking north, along Ridgewood, near Orange Avenue, on the mainland side, carrying an empty plastic half-gallon milk container, Abbe looked at cars that drove past her. She would worry about the legality of putting gasoline in an unapproved container later. Hopefully, the clerk would not even notice that she did not have a red can, as required by law.

A dark blue van stopped in front of her and pulled to the curb. As Abbe slowly made her way toward the vehicle she hoped she would get enough money for a couple of cheeseburgers for her and Slim and a few gallons of gas. She hoped she could give the motel manager ten dollars to keep him at bay on the back rent. She knew what she would have to do to get the money. Her husband wouldn't mind. In the past Slim had even vacated their motel room while Abbe "took care of business" with another male.

The driver of the blue van was in his late forties. He was stocky, had dark greasy hair and a paunch. The man smiled pleasantly and asked Abbe if she needed a ride. He talked like a gentleman.

"To the gas station, if you don't mind." Abbe was equally polite.

"Not at all," he said with a grin that Abbe thought was pleasant, but might be lecherous too. She had seen that kind of grin before. The man was totally unappealing physically. She knew he was not a Good Samaritan offering help to a stranded woman. Something else was on his mind. Why else would he be out here after midnight?

On the short drive to the gas station Abbe sized up the man while she looked around the unkempt van. Tools lay all over the inside, possibly for carpet installation. The man didn't look like a cop. His gut seemed too big. He needed a shave. That didn't matter. Fat men who needed a shave had arrested her before, and they really were cops. Most cops had an air about them, an all-encompassing, alert look in their eyes. This guy didn't. She was still cautious. He could be a good actor.

The condition of the dirty van didn't give her any comfort either. The man, if he was a cop, could have borrowed the vehicle. One time a cop had arrested her for solicitation while he was driving a ratty van with paint spattered all over the interior. The young man was wearing white pants, a white T-shirt, and a white paper painter's hat. Dried paint drops adorned his clothes and he even had paint spatter on his face and arms. She should have known a professional painter didn't get that much paint on himself.

Abbe fell for the "paint man" act and agreed to give the painter oral sex for thirty dollars. Her heart sank when he produced a badge and told her to keep her hands in plain sight. She asked, "Where did you get this damn van and this damn equipment?"

"My brother-in-law," said the undercover vice officer, almost apologetically.

After that episode Abbe tried to take a really close look at the men she propositioned, not just their clothes, but their demeanor too.

When they pulled into a cut-rate station Abbe bought a half gallon of gas. As she climbed back into the man's van she said, "Can you take me back to my truck? It's only a mile away."

The man gave her another grin that made Abbe feel even more uncomfortable. They drove along the main boulevard in silence for a short distance. Finally the man asked her, "Do you date?"

Had it been Abbe's lucky day, she would have said, "No thanks. I'm married, but I'll take your interest as a compliment."

Instead she said, "Yes, I date, but I do it for money." The man smiled at her. He raised his eyebrows rapidly a couple of times to show they were on the same wavelength. His grin unsettled her even more. She and Slim needed the money. Abbe reminded herself not to make a statement to the man about what she would do to him and how much it would cost. The girls in county jail had told her many times to "make the man say the price, and the act." If the man was the one to say those things, it was entrapment and the arrest wouldn't stick in court.

That is, if the cop told the truth in his report and in court. In the past, when her court-appointed defense attorney read her arrest report to her in the holding tank, the statements in the report had been transposed. The report had Abbe saying the things the undercover cop had said.

It was frustrating. Abbe told her appointed attorney, "I never said that. The cop did. He was the one who talked about the money and the sex. I just agreed."

The lawyer said, "Look, you were out there turning tricks. The cop knew it, and you knew it, and everyone driving down the street knew it. I believe you're telling me the truth and the cop is fudging on the statements. But given a choice, who is the judge going to believe? It won't be you, guaranteed. I suggest you take a plea, get credit for time served, some probation, and be on your way. I'll get you enrolled in a job-training program and this'll impress the judge. And for God's sake, get out of the street life."

That's how it went. Abbe would agree. Silently, she would vow to be more careful next time. Damned lying cops anyway.

In spite of Abbe's unsettling feeling tonight, the man continued to be polite. He actually returned her to Slim and the truck. When she gave the gas to Slim, she told him she and the man were going for a "little drive." Slim knew what that meant. It also meant Abbe would return with more money than she had when she left. Slim could almost taste that cheeseburger.

Abbe and the man drove along the coast, taking a few turns. In Abbe's opinion they passed several good spots for a "quickie." "I know a great spot up the road," the man said." They ended up in a cemetery on Bellevue Road, back near the Veterans' Memorial. "It's nice and secluded here," the man said, not grinning quite as much.

They agreed on oral sex for forty dollars. Abbe liked doing that better than many of the things she had to do to get money. It was quick and she could probably leave most of her clothing on. She had developed a method of blocking the man's view of his penis while she did more to him with her hand than she did with her mouth. It was less disgusting than actually doing it with her mouth and the man was none the wiser.

Once they parked, the man motioned for her to climb to the back of the van. She did. The man followed. He said, "Let me see your pretty titties." He reached to touch her left breast.

Abbe pulled back. She had been a street girl for a while. Even though she didn't know anything about this guy, she knew she had to keep her "street face" on. Abbe's eyes narrowed, her jaw set firmly.

"Not until I see the forty dollars."

"I left it in front of the van."

"Climb up there and get it. I'll wait for you."

The look on the man's face changed from merely unsettling to downright scary. He grabbed her by the hair and spat, "Look, bitch, you're going to do what I want." His hands were strong and rough. His look was menacing. Abbe was scared. Men had beaten her before, and she didn't like it. She had to go along with this guy. Maybe, when he was done with her, he would give her the forty dollars, or at least most of it. For a minute she almost wished he was a cop, or that a cop would drive back into the secluded cemetery.

The man continued to berate her with a litany of profanity, calling her many horrible names. When Abbe saw that the inevitable was coming, she asked him to please put a condom on. "Fuck you, bitch. I ain't got nothin' you need to be afraid of. I probably oughta be afraid of what your sorry ass is carrying."

He made her perform oral sex, then straight sexual intercourse. He ejaculated inside her. Then he gave her the most sickening grin she had ever seen. "Now, that wasn't too bad, was it?"

The man never took his eyes off Abbe while he was putting his pants back on. He grabbed her by the hair again and pulled her to the front of the van. "Get the fuck out, bitch."

The man drove away. Abbe had to walk all the way back to where Slim was waiting by his truck. She told Slim what had happened. Abbe and her husband had some drug paraphernalia in the motel room. Fearing a search by the police, she did not make a report.

―――――――――

Approximately six months later, in June 2004, Kelly White* was walking in an area on North Street in Daytona Beach in Volusia County. A male pulled his dark blue van next to the curb and asked her if she wanted a ride. Being slightly fatigued from the summer Florida heat, Kelly accepted. In a statement made several months later, she said there was no talk about a "date" or sex.

The driver was a white male in his mid forties. He had greasy black hair, a potbelly, and needed a shave. Kelly's recollection was that he was polite and soft-spoken. They drove a long way to a secluded spot on Williamson Street near Interstate 95 on the mainland side. When the man pulled the van over to park, Kelly did not say anything, or ask why they were stopping. She had an idea it was to make a deal for sex. She was damn sure going to make him say the words of an offer. Then, without warning, the man grabbed her by the head and pushed her to the back of the van, with him right behind.

The man climbed on top of Kelly and held her by the throat. It is believed that Kelly took out one of two pocket-knives she carried. The man immediately grabbed the knife and threw it to the floor of the van. She had another knife, with a red handle, in her pocket. In spite of being held down, Kelly attempted to open the second knife. They struggled over the now-opened knife. Kelly believes she cut the man's hand during the melee. She fought fiercely before climbing out the front door. Kelly ran from the van and headed for the interstate. She lost one shoe, a crisscross size 6, during the struggle, believing the shoe remained in the van.

Two Port Orange police officers approached her while the blue van was speeding away. They asked her if there was a problem. Because she was afraid of the police (even though she later said nothing was ever said to the man in the van about a "date" or sex), she did not say anything about the attack. The police officers believed something was not quite right. How could a woman wearing one shoe and running from a van speeding away not be in trouble? But if the one person in the world who could make a complaint would only say that everything was okay, they had no choice but to do nothing except give her a ride back to Daytona Beach. No report was filed.

The scoreboard now read:

Violent Man in Blue Van: 2
Ladies Who Accept Rides from Strangers: 0

———————

Carrie Bell* was sitting at a bus stop on South Ridgewood Avenue in Daytona Beach in approximately October 2004. She didn't want to ride the bus. She wanted to ride in a car with a man who would give her money. When a bus approached, Carrie would get up from the bench and walk in a circle with her back to the bus so the driver wouldn't think she was a prospective passenger. If the bus stopped for a rider to get off, Carrie would not make eye contact with the driver. She wouldn't turn around until the bus pulled away. Then she returned to the bench and watched the cars as they drove by.

Carrie was tall and slim with light brown hair that came just past her shoulders. She wore denim short shorts and platform sandals that called attention to her long, tanned legs. A deep blue tattoo of a barbed-wire strand at midthigh on her left leg brought more attention to her model's legs.

Shortly before midnight a dark blue van pulled next to the curb in front of the bus bench. The driver eyed Carrie and she eyed the driver. He seemed to be in his late forties with dark, shiny hair and needing a shave. The white T-shirt he wore had a blue-gray tinge to it, a garment badly in need of bleach. The T-shirt was probably a cotton-polyester blend. It had been washed so many times that the cotton was worn away and the polyester was nearly see-through. The driver had a protruding gut.

Carrie had been arrested for solicitation for prostitution before. She knew you couldn't be too careful sizing up your prospective customers. She decided right away that this creepy-looking guy couldn't possibly be a cop. Sometimes the guys in Vice used disguises. If this guy was a Vice cop, he had the best disguise she had ever seen. She couldn't imagine this slob as a detective on any assignment. Because of his gut, he couldn't be a patrol cop on loan to Vice either. She had seen a few cops in her day. If this guy was the law, she was losing her touch for detecting cops.

If he wasn't a cop, and she was *almost* sure he wasn't, was he a weirdo? On the subject of weirdos she wasn't so confident of her detecting skills. Still leaning on the van's passenger door, she continued to look him over while they talked.

"Are you dating?" he asked.

"Yeah. Whadda you want?" She knew enough to play the "word game" with this guy. He had to mention the act and the price. If he mentioned those two things and he was a cop, it was entrapment. If she mentioned the price and the act and he was a cop, it was criminal solicitation for prostitution on her part. Carrie had no intention of mentioning the particulars. If he hemmed and hawed and stumbled over his words, he probably was a cop just trying to act dumb and she would move on down the street. She didn't think he was a cop, though.

He said, "How about head?"

"Okay."

"Well, get in."

"There's sumthin' else we gotta talk about," Carrie said.

"How's thirty?"

"Make it forty."

"Get in."

With the negotiations out of the way, and the strong probability that he wasn't a cop almost confirmed, she now had to worry about the man himself. Carrie had been beaten, burned with cigarettes, and cut with a knife by prospective customers. She didn't have a good feeling about this guy. The interior of his van was as unkempt as he was. It looked like there were carpet remnants and tools in the back. She thought to herself that forty dollars was forty dollars that she didn't have, and forty dollars that she needed. She decided to go through with it. Maybe he would be okay.

They drove a few miles, going farther from the inhabited areas than she wanted, finally pulling into a cemetery on Bellevue Avenue. It was dark and no one else was around. The blue van stopped in the very back of the property near the Veterans' Memorial. The man backed the van into a corner, affording a view of any cars coming toward them.

"Okay, in the back." The man motioned to her. "Get naked. I wanna see them jugs."

She crawled to the back. Since the agreement was for oral sex, she had not planned on disrobing. Nudity would cost extra, she decided. The man followed her back. He started to unzip.

"I always get my money first," Carrie said.

"I never pay first," he said.

"Then it ain't gonna happen. No pay, no play." Who did this asshole think he was?

"No, baby. We do it first," he said.

"Bullshit." She climbed back to the front of the van to the passenger seat. "If I don't get my money I'm gettin' outta here." He made no attempt to pay, so she opened the door and began walking.

The man followed her out the passenger door. When Carrie saw him coming she began to run. He was too close and her platform shoes weren't built for speed, so he caught her. The night air was punctuated with his angry curses and name-calling. He grabbed her by the back collar and ripped her white cotton blouse down the back, popping all of the buttons on the front. He grabbed her by the back of the bra and swung her around. The fabric wouldn't tear, so she went in circles with him holding on, the bra digging into the front of her chest.

When she went down on her front, he straddled her back and undid the bra fastener, bending the tiny metal hooks in the process. He flipper her over, grabbing her short shorts, ripping them open and down. After yanking the shorts, he ripped her peach-colored thong like it was made of tissue paper.

She lay on the ground, naked except for one of her platform sandals. Now she was really scared. The man pulled his pants down quickly. He had a wide-eyed, purposeful, committed look on his face, the likes of which she had never seen on anyone. Now she wasn't worried about money, or about being arrested. She just didn't want to get hurt.

Carrie, trying to do anything to get this guy to stop, told him she was pregnant, even though she was not.

"So?" the man said. "I done it that way before. It's all good."

The man mounted her and gained penetration. Within seconds he ejaculated and got up off the ground, leaving Carrie trembling on her back, the moist dirt and grass sticking to her perspiring back, causing her to itch.

He walked back to his van as if nothing had happened. "Are you leaving me here?" she cried after him.

"That's not my problem," he said. His calm was even more alarming. "You should have thought of that before you started getting all shitty with me, fucking bitch."

He drove away. She was too upset to get his license number.

She assembled her clothes the best she could. Carrie walked out of the cemetery. And, no, she did not report the incident to the police.

CHAPTER 16

About one month later, in November 2004, Debbie Farris*
walked quickly down Atlantic Avenue in the beach area of
Volusia County, eyeing each vehicle as it went by. Debbie
was twenty-four years old, slim, single, cute, and no stranger
to the criminal-justice system. A high school dropout who
thought she "knew it all" a few years before, she was rapidly coming to the realization that there was a whole lot she
had to learn.

Tonight Debbie kept telling herself to "slow down." The
crack cocaine she smoked two hours before was beginning
to wear off, but her mind was still bombing away at record
speed. Her legs were pumping too. Her head was on a
swivel looking at all the vehicles. She and her friends had
used the last of the drugs and it was time to get more. More
drugs meant she needed to get money. She couldn't go to
the automated teller machine and withdraw money because
she didn't have an ATM card. There was only one way to
get money. She didn't like it, but she had done it many times
in the past.

Debbie couldn't approach her boss for an advance because she didn't have a boss, or a job. It was too late to go back to school, in her mind anyway, and Debbie's aim was now to get enough money to get through each day. Her dependence on drugs didn't help either.

Debbie Farris started out the way countless others do: drinking alcohol and smoking marijuana in high school and laughing at those who said drugs and booze were bad for you. Debbie was very pretty. She thought her good looks would help her out in the world. The good looks only took her so far. The good looks could not take a history or English test for her. Good looks did not know how to type or use correct grammar. Debbie gave up on academics and concentrated on pleasing her friends and herself.

When booze and marijuana became too tame, she moved on up, taking whatever her friends did, a little crystal methamphetamine and crack cocaine for fun. Soon the casual meth and coke for fun became necessities. Debbie always said she could quit drugs and booze whenever she wanted. The truth was that she was hooked.

Those drugs didn't come cheap. Since her earning skills were minimal, Debbie sold her body for money. Nothing very bad had happened to her. She didn't like the guys. They were creepy for the most part. Why would the guys have to pay for sex if they weren't creepy? Some were downright ugly. While she performed the sex the man paid for, Debbie tried to put her mind somewhere else.

There were a couple of arrests. She cleaned up quite nicely for court and her public defender convinced the judge that if only Debbie Farris had another chance she could turn her life around. The defense attorney enrolled her in a drug diversion program and an educational track at the local skills center. When cleaned up, Debbie presented a promising figure in court. The judge admitted he was taking a gamble, but granted probation. Debbie went to one session each of a drug class and a high school extension course before dropping out. The probation department was too busy to follow up on her lack of commitment.

On November 6, Debbie had finished smoking crack cocaine at a friend's house. The friend was out of coke and Debbie was out of money, so she hit the street. A dark blue van driven by a white guy drove past her once, made a U-turn, and eventually pulled up next to the curb. Most cops pulled right to the curb. Customers usually drove past her once, looking her over. So far, this vehicle didn't seem like a cop's. The driver was in his forties and weighed about 190. He sported a noticeable paunch.

"Need a ride?"

"Sure, why not?" said Debbie. This guy didn't look like a cop. She decided to talk with him a little before saying anything that could get her into trouble.

"Where to?" the man asked.

"Oh, anywhere up there, I guess." Debbie pointed north.

"What do you think about getting a room?" the man asked.

"Yeah, that'd be all right." She hadn't said anything about sex or money that would get her in trouble. It wasn't against the law to get a room. Besides, Debbie was getting even surer that this guy wasn't the law.

They left the mainland, crossing the bridge on Seabreeze Avenue. They passed a motel where Debbie had turned some tricks before. She pointed to it and told him to go there; it was a good place for them. The clerk often gave her a five-dollar kickback after the trick left because he had overcharged the trick ten bucks to begin with. The man kept driving, saying he knew of a better one. Debbie started to feel uneasy. She looked around the van. It had bucket seats. There were no side windows. The back was full of carpet remnants and what looked like tools for installing carpet.

They passed another motel that Debbie told him would be a good one. The man shook his head, saying he knew an even better one. Soon they passed the commercial section of town and were rapidly going north on Ridgeview to where there were no houses or businesses. Debbie, at first only alarmed, was now getting scared.

"Are you married?" she asked. Because of her growing apprehension, she thought if she could get him talking, it might make him feel more personal toward her. If she got him talking about himself, maybe he wouldn't be so creepy.

"Getting a divorce."

Debbie tried to get the man to make more small talk. She thought he said his first name was Mike. But he mumbled, so she wasn't sure.

At Turnbull Bay Road and Pioneer Trail the man pulled the van into a secluded area and turned off the engine. Debbie didn't like this one bit. They were in the middle of nowhere. They hadn't discussed money or sex, and they had passed several motels. Yet she knew they were there for sex. She hoped that was all.

He reached over to her in the passenger seat, pulling up her blouse. Debbie swatted away his hand. "Hey," she said. "Not so fast. I get paid first."

"The hell you do," he said. With surprising agility the man pounced over the middle console onto Debbie's seat. He grabbed her by the shoulders and wrestled her to the back of the van. Debbie was overpowered from the start. The man straddled her while unzipping his own pants. By now Debbie didn't care about the money. She only wanted to get the hell away from this psycho idiot.

He forced his midsection toward her mouth. Debbie clenched her jaws tightly and turned her head rapidly from one side to the next. After a struggle that left both of them breathless, the man slid himself down toward her feet. He grabbed the waistband of her pants and jerked them down past her knees in one rapid move.

He fondled himself for a very brief time and then threw himself on top of her, causing her to lose her breath. "Wait!" Debbie said. "A condom!"

"Too late." He grinned at her. The smell of stale tobacco hit her in the face like a baseball bat.

Moments later it was over. Debbie was hurt and scared and angry. She cowered in the back corner of the van, looking around, taking note of the carpet tools, strips of carpet, and smaller rolls of different patterns of carpet. She saw a utility work knife she could use to slash him, but was too scared to use it. If she didn't kill him, her attempt might make him madder and he would carve up her face. Debbie wasn't sure she could kill anyone, even this animal. She was scared for what might happen next, but still hated him.

"Thanks, bitch, for the pussy, but you've got to go."

"No. I don't know where I am."

"You're right here, stupid bitch." That evil smile took the place of the original polite one once again.

"No, I'm not getting out."

"The hell you ain't." He dragged her to the front, reached across her, and opened the passenger door. "See ya." He pushed her out onto the sandy soil.

"How am I going to get home? I don't know where I am."

"Not my problem. I already told you you're right here." He laughed. "Okay," he said. "Just walk back that way. When you get to the corner, turn right. Town ain't too far away. You'll be okay."

He drove away. Debbie was too upset and hurt to look at his license plate.

When she got to town she was not too upset and hurt to call the police.

───────────

As soon as the patrol deputy rolled up to the pay phone outside the convenience store, he knew who had called. The disheveled, crying woman in the torn T-shirt waved at him when he drove around the corner.

Despite being only twenty-four years old, Debbie was a

woman of the streets. She knew her way around. She knew how to cope in county jail. She knew how to con a public defender and probation officer. She wasn't always successful, but she knew how to con people, and she tried. She knew how to look sincere in front of a judge, hoping for probation instead of jail time.

She didn't like cops, and she didn't like crying in front of one. So Debbie composed herself and told the story to the uniformed officer without so much as a sob.

In keeping with Volusia County sexual-assault protocol, the deputy gathered just enough information to make sure the elements of the crime of rape were there. He did not interview Debbie at length. He did ask if there was talk of sex in exchange for money. When Debbie said no, he didn't argue. He knew she was a prostitute because he worked the streets every night and wasn't stupid.

To his credit, the patrol deputy did not make a judgment about the fact that Debbie was a prostitute. He had learned in the academy that hookers could get raped too. Over the years one of the complaints of sexual-assault victims was that they had to tell their story too many times—to patrol cops, detectives, victim advocates, emergency-room nurses and doctors. There were reinterviews later with the cops. If the rapist was captured, there were court preparation interviews with the prosecuting attorney and the preliminary hearing itself.

If the case was bound over for trial, there was the trial at which she had to tell the story yet one more time. This grueling experience was followed up by a blistering cross-examination by the defense attorney, who actually put the rape victim on trial instead of the rapist himself.

For this reason, the deputy kept his questions of Debbie to a minimum. He transported her to the Sexual Assault Recovery Center. Investigator James Day, the on-call sexual-assault deputy, met them there. Day obtained a more thorough set of facts from Debbie Farris.

In the meantime, Day called the state's attorney victim advocate, Joy Allen, into the process. Allen was an advocate who had Farris's best interests at heart. While those in the social-service field are enthusiastic protectors of victims, Allen also had an eye on the prosecution aspect of the case. That is, she wanted to make sure Farris was treated well by everyone, that she was kept aware of what was going on, and that her injuries were addressed. She also made sure pregnancy-avoidance and disease-control measures were offered to the victim. She provided information for follow-up counseling. Lastly, she gave her phone number to Farris to make sure she had someone to talk with whenever she needed, if she needed. The prosecution needed to keep Debbie "on their side" in case a suspect was eventually arrested.

Allen also explained that physical evidence needed to be obtained from Debbie's body. Even though it was horrible that the monster who raped her did not wear a condom, the monster probably left valuable evidence in her body, evidence that might lead to a criminal conviction. The specially trained nurse at the center took vaginal, anal, and oral swabs from Ferris, as required in the sexual-assault protocol.

During the process, Debbie was a model patient, and a model client for Joy Allen and James Day. She cooperated, was polite, and not demanding. She gave Allen and Day her home address and phone. She provided a cell phone number.

When the physical examination and probing interview were over, Detective Day gave Debbie a ride back to the motel where she was staying. The next day Allen and Day compared notes. They thought Debbie Farris, in spite of being a prostitute who was probably addicted to drugs, was a good person. Impressed with her spirit of cooperation so far, they were confident she would follow up on any additional help they might ask of her. If a perpetrator was ever arrested, they were sure Debbie would assist.

Two days later, on November 8, Volusia County sex-crimes detective Cynthia Gambrell looked at the Debbie Farris crime report.

Gambrell was nobody's fool. She knew the rape report of a prostitute victim was loaded with problems from the outset. Over the years she had received acquittals on righteous rapists who showed up in court wearing a suit, with recently groomed hair, carrying a Bible, and accompanied by an adoring wife hanging on their arm. After being sworn, the accused rapist would get on the stand and testify that he had met a woman in a bar and then "made a terrible, terrible mistake" by leaving the bar with the woman and going to her apartment.

The usual story was that one thing led to another and this awful woman convinced him to have sex with her. Later, after the act, upon learning the man was married, the woman, obviously overcome with remorse and shame, cried "rape." While the man had made a mistake in judgment, he was no rapist. He was merely a weak man who had succumbed to the wiles of this woman who changed her mind. Invariably the jury would ignore the bruises on the face where the rapist had hit her, the torn undergarments, and the frightened demeanor of the woman. And, the woman in that scenario was not even a prostitute. She was a lonely woman who left a bar with a man who had lied to her and told her he was single. When he let it slip that he was married, she said no and he raped her.

Gambrell often thought the only way to get a rape conviction was to have a woman wearing a housedress and apron, baking cookies, have a stranger kick in her back door, and rape her. If a woman left a bar with a man she didn't know, the woman was automatically labeled as "loose" or "easy" and was consequently fair game for the unscrupulous defendant.

By the time slick defense attorneys and lying defendants

were done dragging a woman's name and reputation through the mud, it seemed criminal convictions were hard to come by.

Nonetheless, Detective Gambrell looked at the Debbie Farris case as a challenge. She had seen similar circumstances before. A man picks up a prostitute. They agree on an act and a price. When it comes time to pay, the man says no and forcibly performs the sex act on the unwilling prostitute.

The woman would have agreed to have sex if he had paid beforehand. But he didn't pay, so she said, "Stop!" and he used force and/or fear to finish the act. That, according to the law, and logic, was rape. It wasn't the most "appealing" rape in the eyes of the criminal-justice system, but it was still rape and no woman deserved it.

Detective Gambrell called the listed phone number on the crime report. There was no answer, and no answering machine. Later that afternoon the detective drove to the listed address. It was a shabby motel. The surly clerk barely changed his attitude when Gambrell showed him a badge.

"Nah, she's gone."

"When?"

"Don't know."

"How about looking it up. It's important."

"Yeah, they're all important," he mumbled as he thumbed through a shoe box with a bunch of handwritten receipts. Apparently this dump had not gone the way of computers. Why should they? No one probably ever made reservations.

The clerk said it looked like she had moved a few days ago. Detective Gambrell noted to herself that Farris moved the day after the rape. She owed for two days rent anyway. "Did she leave anything behind?"

"Nah. Took everything she had. We cleaned the place out. Wasn't nothing left."

They exchanged insincere "thank yous" and "you're welcomes" and Gambrell went back to the office.

She called the cell phone number listed for Debbie Farris. A man answered. He didn't know any Debbie Farris. "Wait a minute. Was she a cute chick in her early twenties? If she was, I loaned her my phone a while ago. She gave it back. I had a bunch of long-distance calls on it. Tell her to call me. She owes me."

So Detective Gambrell read the report again. The description of the rape suspect and his dark van didn't ring any bells with her on other cases she was investigating. She put the case aside, opting to investigate cases where the victims could be located and would cooperate. It looked like another case of the stereotypical rape of a prostitute. Gambrell remembered what she had learned working patrol: sometimes you couldn't save people from themselves. The system wanted to help a prostitute who had been raped, but the victim made it impossible.

Detective Gambrell notified victim advocate Joy Allen that, due to her inability to contact Debbie Farris after repeated attempts, the investigation of the case would be suspended.

CHAPTER 17

Two months later, in January 2005, Ellen Graham* meandered along a street in Daytona Beach, Florida. "Meander" is how prostitutes walk when they are trolling for prospective customers, or johns, or "tricks." Even though Ellen thought she knew all of the undercover cars the Vice cops used, she did not have a false sense of security about the cops. She also knew they often used their private vehicles when on a prostitution abatement detail.

Several months before, in the afternoon, a guy in a dress shirt and tie pulled over to talk with Ellen. The guy had a magnetic sign on his car door indicating his affiliation with an independent real-estate company. Later, Ellen knew she should have asked the guy some real-estate questions. The only problem was that she didn't know anything about the real-estate business. If she had been able to ask specific questions, she would have learned the guy didn't know anything about the business either. He was a Vice cop. It was the first time she had been arrested by a clean-cut guy wearing a dress shirt and tie in the middle of the afternoon. Live and learn.

Shortly after midnight a dark van with no side windows pulled up next to the curb. The driver, a white guy in work clothes, asked Ellen if she wanted a ride. She was used to the usual rap of the Vice cops, trying to act cool. All this clown was asking her was if she wanted a ride. No harm in just accepting a ride. She looked him over. He looked goofy, but he didn't look like a cop. Along with looking goofy, he had a "goofy" air about him. He was polite, almost overly polite. Most cops, except for the really good actors, no matter how hard they tried, could not shake the authoritative air they eventually pick up on the job. This guy wasn't authoritative.

He looked about forty-five years old. He was clean-shaven. His body looked like he needed to hire a personal trainer to get rid of his gut. The inside of his van smelled like tobacco and marijuana. This guy couldn't be all bad.

Since there was no law against accepting a ride from a stranger, she got in. If he tried to get her to mention a sex act or a price, she would get out at the next stop sign, even if he hadn't stopped the van completely. Ellen was not about to get arrested tonight.

They drove a few blocks. The man looked over at her occasionally, smiling from time to time. She thought he was a creep, but probably a harmless creep. He better have thirty or forty dollars he was willing to part with.

Ellen looked around the interior of the van. She saw handsaws, hammers, and other tools associated with the building industry.

The man pulled in the back of a closed library, near the courthouse on City Island. So far no mention of sex or money had taken place. Ellen could be patient too. Both she and the man knew why they were there. They just hadn't said anything about it yet. Maybe the waiting game was part of this jerk's program. If he didn't speak up soon, Ellen was getting out and going someplace where she could earn money.

"Well?" she asked.

"Well, what?" he asked in return.

Before Ellen could say anything, the man's goofy demeanor vanished. It was replaced by pure menace. "Bitch, you're going to suck my dick. That's what." Before she could reply, or react, the man reached over the console and grabbed her around the neck with both hands. He choked her. The man threatened to kill her. Ellen fought back, scratching him on the face.

Within seconds it became apparent to Ellen that she was no match for this guy's strength. She was winded and weak and he was still strangling her. She gave up. "Okay, okay," she managed to gasp.

Unzipping his pants, the man fondled himself for a few seconds, then put his penis in her mouth. She did not resist anymore. The grip of his callused hands tight around her neck was too much for her. She gave in.

After he ejaculated, she spit the contents of her mouth in the back of the van. With as little emotion as one might have telling someone the correct time, the man said, "Get out, bitch, I'm done." She climbed out the front door and watched him drive away. The flood of anger, pain, and frustration was so great that Ellen did not think to get his license number. Her neck was tightening up and she was still very afraid.

Ellen walked out from behind the library. After getting her bearings, she walked toward a commercial section of Daytona Beach, where she called the Daytona Beach Police Department. While waiting for the patrol officer to arrive, she bought a bottle of water to rinse her mouth out, removing any possible physical evidence in the rinsing process. Ellen made a formal police report. Authorities could not locate any biological evidence linking a suspect to the crime. The patrol officer said a detective would call her.

No detective from the Daytona Beach Police Department ever contacted Graham for a follow-up investigation.

In early March 2005, a forensic chemist from the Volusia County Sheriff's Department performed an analysis of the semen retrieved from the vaginal cavity of Debbie Farris back in November at the Sexual Assault Recovery Center. This analysis was one of thousands of chemical analytical procedures the sheriff's office conducted every year. There was no suspect listed on the request for analysis, and therefore no urgency.

Because the crime was sexual assault, the Volusia County chemist obtained a DNA profile in much the same way David Cornacchia of the San Diego Police Department had done approximately one year before, thousands of miles away in California. The chemist from Florida entered the profile in the Combined DNA Index System.

On March 5, 2005, two months after Ellen Graham's sexual assault behind the library, Frances Hellmann* was walking her "route" on North Street near Ridgewood Avenue in Volusia County. Just before dusk a dark blue van without side windows pulled up next to the curb. Frances peered inside the rolled-down passenger window. She thought she recognized the guy, a guy she'd done business with before—sex business, to be exact. She couldn't remember his pleasure of choice. He did look familiar, though. Tonight he was wearing a New York Yankees baseball cap.

"Hey, do you date?" he asked.

Frances smiled and got in. This guy knew the routine. In a half hour she would be back at the hamburger shop getting a double-burger combo with cheese and a large vanilla shake. "I think I know you," she said. "What's your name?" Many months later she told a police officer she thought he had said his name was Mark.

They drove along the beachside boulevard. Frances

eyed him. He appeared to be slightly intoxicated. This might be a problem. Drunken guys often couldn't get or keep an erection. This could take longer than she'd anticipated. He found a strip mall near Third Avenue and pulled behind it. Most of the stores were closed. It would be private. Frances only hoped that some nosy patrol cop wouldn't drive by. After the man parked, he reached over and started fondling her breasts and tugging at her blouse. He mumbled and grunted in a primitive manner while fingering her clothing.

"Not so fast, Romeo. There's a matter of money. Do you remember how this works?"

"I don't got no money," he said.

"I seen money on the visor over the driver's seat, asshole. Take me back to where you got me. I ain't no nonprofit organization or nothin' like that," she said.

"You bitch. You'll do what I say." With surprising speed he climbed over the console, grabbed her by the hair, and wrestled her to the back of the van. Frances could see carpet remnants and a wooden box with various tools. The man rolled onto his back, pulling Frances on top of him. He had Frances's hair just above both ears in his hands. He pulled her toward his groin. "Don't get no ideas," he said. He let go briefly to unsnap his pants and pull down his undershorts. By now Frances accepted that this brute had overpowered her. Her best option was to give in and never forget this bastard's face or vehicle.

He grabbed her again and pulled her toward his groin, eventually entering her mouth. After a few minutes he gave her the directive to "Swallow! Swallow! Dammit!" Frances did.

The man grinned. "That wasn't so bad, was it?" Frances looked at him with a combination of fear and hatred.

When he finished zipping up, he said, "If I ever see you again, I'll make sure you'll never be seen again. Get out."

Frances got out. The monster drove rapidly away.

Frances found another trick within a few minutes. She overcharged him for oral sex, because she had just given a freebie and she didn't like freebies. And, no, Frances didn't report this incident to the police.

CHAPTER 18

April 29, 2005, was a significant date in the annals of the Volusia County Sheriff's Crime Laboratory. Investigator James Day sent word to Detective Gambrell that they had a positive CODIS match on the semen from the vaginal swab of Debbie Farris taken on November 6, 2004. It had been so long since Gambrell had handled the case, and so many sexual assaults since then, that she had no independent recollection of Farris. She reviewed her notes, remembering that Farris had moved, leaving no forwarding address. Farris's cell phone number was no good either. Several of Gambrell's attempts to contact her had not been successful. So last November, she had decided to pursue cases in which the victim was more cooperative, and actually wanted help.

Often the notification of a positive DNA hit will provide the name of the donor. This information usually causes a hubbub of anticipation and activity among the chemists. Even though the chemists aren't the ones to go out and put handcuffs on the suspect, they know they did their part to make the arrest happen. And, they would be a part of the court process to ensure that justice would be done.

Instead of providing the name of the DNA donor, they learned the match was only to that of another DNA submission. This is called an "evidence-to-evidence match" because only unknowns are matched. The submission was from San Diego, California. That crime happened June 11, 1988, a murder nearly eighteen years old. The San Diego victim: twenty-seven-year-old Janet Moore. The provider of the DNA in that case was unknown as well. The California murder was so old that the Volusia County chemists double-checked the information to make sure there was no typographical error. There was not. Matching DNAs, especially from so far away, without a named donor was not the kind of thing that happened every day.

The Volusia authorities were now convinced that the California killer of seventeen years ago was more than likely the Florida rapist. The question for the ages was: Who is he?

A Volusia County forensics expert phoned the San Diego Police Department with the news.

Back in San Diego, forensic chemist David Cornacchia was very happy to learn a CODIS hit was made on the work he had done in the Janet Moore case. He was not happy to learn that no DNA donor had been identified. But since the donor had committed a rape in Florida, at least they had someplace to look.

Cornacchia called Terry Torgersen, telling him the good news. Information on a cold case, especially one that old, was always welcome news. Since the inception of the unit, the San Diego Police Department had fallen in step with the rest of the world, and with Hollywood. They now called their unit the "cold-case homicide unit."

Torgersen notified Ron Thill, the district attorney's liaison with the San Diego cold-case team, and one of the original investigators on the Moore killing. Thill was over-joyed on the one hand but anxious on the other. He remembered well the case of the young artist caught up in the throes of drugs and prostitution and the bloodbath crime scene. He also remembered the amount of work his team had put into the case, only to come up with nothing.

The killer was still out there actively committing rapes, apparently in Florida. Thill knew they had to get him before he raped and maybe killed again. As he dialed the number of his former boss, Ed Petrick, Thill wondered how many more women the rapist had killed across the country in the last seventeen years. Hopefully he had been in prison and had not killed anyone.

Petrick was retired now, involved in his own life and supervising a home-remodel project. Even though the homicide had happened a long time ago, Petrick remembered it, and was very happy at the news. He knew Ron Thill would see the case through to the end.

In 2002, there was a bitter election for the office of San Diego's district attorney. The incumbent, Paul Pfingst, in spite of some impressive courtroom victories by his deputies, was coming under fire for a variety of unsavory activities within his office. Allegations of favoritism and vindictiveness surfaced, putting blemishes on Pfingst's reputation. The deputies who didn't like him (80 percent) voted no confidence in him because of his unchecked arrogance and his ignoring of rules that did not suit him.

One of the division chiefs was accused of running a real-estate business from his seventh-floor office within the Hall of Justice at the same time as he was a deputy district attorney. When Pfingst learned of the alleged transgression, he took no formal action, but said he warned the transgressor.

The attorney continued his unethical activity unfettered.

The public was not aware of the discord within the office because news of the unrest never went beyond the walls of the office. Yet when the same division chief was accused of hiding exculpatory evidence against a murder suspect, the "news" hit the fan, so to speak.

Clerical staff came forward to say the division chief who was running the real-estate enterprise never slowed a business beat after being "warned" by Pfingst. That, and other troubles within the office, caused a four-way fight for the office of district attorney. The murder defendant who claimed the D.A.'s office was hiding evidence that would have mitigated his guilt was able to get out of prison several years early as a result of the official misconduct. The press played that episode up big, as did the candidates running against Pfingst.

One of the candidates for Pfingst's office was superior-court judge Bonnie Dumanis. In a kind of Cinderella story, Dumanis had started at the D.A.'s office many years before as a clerk typist. She worked herself up to "investigative specialist." The duties of this job included assisting prosecutors in getting cases ready for court. Documents had to be retrieved, subpoenas issued, witnesses contacted, and their court appearances finalized.

Eventually, Dumanis enrolled in law school and earned her law degree at night. District Attorney Edwin L. Miller Jr. hired her as a deputy district attorney. Several years later Dumanis was appointed a municipal-court judge. California subsequently elevated all judges to the superior court, and she labored at that job, apparently content. Many people in the community, and within the office, pleaded with her to try to unseat the incumbent.

Running for district attorney had its downside. Dumanis had to take an unpaid leave of absence in order to campaign. She wasn't a politician at heart. Giving the same speeches over and over to civic groups and engaging in repeated debates were not what she wanted to do.

During the campaign, one of Dumanis's opponents was Mark Pettine, himself a deputy district attorney. Dumanis and Pettine, along with being former colleagues, were friends, and friendly rivals. One of Pettine's campaign promises was to form a cold-case unit. Several of the local police departments had cold-case investigative units. When they brought the cases to the D.A.'s office, the police were shuttled to whoever was up next to get a murder.

Bonnie Dumanis won the election by the smallest of margins, but she won. Pfingst went back to private practice. Dumanis made good on her promises. She embraced the few employees who had backed Pfingst, even giving some of them more prestigious jobs than they'd enjoyed under Pfingst. She urged those who supported her during the campaign to forget old battles and concentrate on the job at hand, working for justice. She also made Mark Pettine a deputy chief and adopted his campaign promise by forming the cold-case unit. Ron Thill was taken from the pretrial unit and put into cold case. He served as the liaison to the San Diego Police homicide unit.

Thill contacted his superiors at the district attorney's office. He was happy to learn they assigned the Janet Moore case to Andrea Freshwater, a fifteen-year veteran prosecutor with over a half-dozen murder convictions to her credit. Freshwater was new to the cold-case prosecution unit. The young prosecutor pulled the case and spent hours going over the particulars. The crime-scene photos were particularly gruesome.

Ever a stickler for detail, Freshwater noticed the bloody marks on Janet Moore's dresser drawers and inside her purse. The prosecutor cross-checked the evidence list and learned the blood on the drawers was not Janet's. This meant the killer had taken took the time to go through the victim's apartment before leaving.

Andrea Freshwater phoned Cindy Gambrell to make sure the
Florida detective knew what kind of a killer they were dealing with. Secure in the idea that Gambrell knew the seriousness of the situation, Freshwater left the Florida police to do
their jobs. She started familiarizing herself with the case,
which she hoped would be seeing the inside of a courtroom
soon.

After learning that Debbie Farris's rapist was most likely
a killer, Detective Gambrell went over the crime report
again in an attempt to figure out how to locate the itinerant
woman. A potential publicity pipe bomb was in Gambrell's
hands. She had to make sure it did not detonate. A guy who
picked up a prostitute and raped her was the same person
who had killed a prostitute in California seventeen years
before. He had probably raped that girl in San Diego before
killing her. The heat was on. Maybe the homicide detectives
in Florida would soon be investigating a prostitute murder.
Gambrell swung into high gear. She hoped she wasn't too
late, and he hadn't killed again. They just didn't know.

The first order of business was to find Debbie Farris
and get even more familiar with the details of the case, a
task easier said than done. Gambrell checked Farris's
criminal history, learning she had been in and out of jail
since the initial report of rape. Her booking sheet contained different reference information on where she could
be found. Even though Detective Gambrell couldn't find
Farris at the time of the initial rape, it was imperative she
locate the young prostitute now, for Farris's safety, and for
the safety of every hooker in Volusia County.

Detective Gambrell hit the streets once more, tracking
down information on the young girl. Again she hit a dead
end. Nothing Farris said at the time of her most recent arrest was valid now. Gambrell had to find Debbie Farris. The
game clock was ticking, with each tick louder than the last.

The sheriff's department initiated a countywide notification directing any police officer who stopped Farris to

notify Detective Gambrell immediately—day, night, weekend, or holiday. Cindy Gambrell waited, first patiently, and then with heightened apprehension.

A week later, on May 12, the jail called Detective Gambrell to inform her that Debbie Farris was now a guest of Volusia County, having been arrested for a failure to appear on a previous prostitution warrant.

Gambrell sped to the jail to begin the interview. Her first two questions were, "Why did you give bad information, and why did you disappear?"

Farris did not seem to be impressed with the urgency in Detective Gambrell's approach. The jailed young woman said the information she gave at the time of her detention was correct. It was just that she moved around a lot, and by the time Gambrell tried to find her, things in her life had changed. Farris didn't exactly disappear. She just wasn't where she said she would be.

What was the big deal? And, Farris said she didn't think anyone would believe a prostitute could be a rape victim anyway. "I know what you guys think of us," Farris said, referring to her belief that the police considered prostitutes second-class citizens. Farris did say Investigator James Day and the victim advocate, Joy Allen, were "real nice," though. Farris acted like this situation were Detective Gambrell's problem instead of a problem that could affect many people.

Without hitting the panic button, Gambrell told Debbie that it looked like the man who had raped her had committed some serious crimes in the past and they needed to take a closer look at the case and try to find him before he did something equally bad, or worse, to another girl. Oddly enough, Farris still didn't seem that impressed. She acted like she would avoid any future tricks in a blue van with no windows. As for the other prostitutes, "Oh well." Farris promised to keep in contact with Gambrell.

Gambrell took Debbie to Captain Tim Cunningham,

the forensic composite artist who, using an Identikit, made a drawing of the man. The drawing was cast as a "Wanted" poster. "Yeah, that looks kinda like him," Farris said.

Gambrell and Farris went over the case report line by line to narrow down what had happened, what the man in the blue van said, how he said it, and what he did. They reviewed his physical description from the top of his head to what Farris could remember about the shoes he wore. It was a necessary exercise in detail that sometimes seemed to bore Farris. Gambrell wasn't bored. Even though Farris didn't know much about makes and models, they hammered out a good description of the vehicle, including the fact that the van was used in some kind of building trade, possibly carpet installation. She thought hard and said maybe there was a *J* in the license plate. One letter wasn't much information, but at least it was something.

Then Debbie went back to jail to wait for adjudication of her case.

———

Cynthia Gambrell spoke with another female inmate who now said she'd been raped. Abbe Smith, who had spoken with Debbie Farris about Farris's rape, came forward to give details of what had happened to her back in January 2004. Smith provided even more specific details on the interior of the van. She was positive her assailant was a carpet installer because he told her he was. Also, she remembered seeing a large carpet roll in the back. When Smith viewed the drawing, she said she thought the guy was older than the one in the drawing.

Abbe told her husband what had happened and gave him the description of the van. She said she had seen the van several times after the rape. One time she saw the vehicle on Palmetto Avenue. She wrote down the license number and gave it to her husband, Slim. Abbe couldn't remember the number.

This caused Detective Gambrell's heart to accelerate noticeably. Without sounding too eager, Gambrell asked what Abbe's husband might have done with the license number. "Dunno. Probably put it in his wallet."

"Where is your husband now?"

"Dunno. I been in here two weeks. He ain't visited me none."

Detective Gambrell quizzed Smith in the hope of finding out how to locate the husband. Abbe still didn't know. She seemed annoyed that she had already told Detective Gambrell she didn't know and Gambrell was persisting. Abbe and her husband were completely homeless now, and even had to sell the truck and all her husband's tools.

How about friends, relatives, or places where the husband might be? Abbe had not even one hopeful idea. Damn. Gambrell delicately asked why Abbe hadn't notified the police at the time of the rape. Abbe said they had some drugs in their motel room, and she thought her husband might have had a warrant. The less they saw of the police, the better. Besides, Abbe was a prostitute and she didn't think anyone would believe her.

Along with circulating the countywide law enforcement bulletin, Detective Gambrell altered her work shift, hitting the streets at night in kind of a rolling surveillance. She stopped patrol cops all along Atlantic Avenue, even going into other jurisdictions to show the composite drawing and remind the patrol officers that a dangerous rapist lurked among them.

———

Carrie Bell happened to be in the Volusia County Jail now. After talking with the other girls, Bell asked to meet with Detective Gambrell. While in the interview room, Bell recounted the tale of being raped in the cemetery on Bellevue Avenue back in the autumn of 2004. She said she did not think she could assist with a composite drawing of the rapist. But if shown a photograph of him, she was sure she could identify him.

More women in jail came forward to look at the composite. They told similar stories of being raped. Detective Gambrell thought the women were being truthful. Although a defense attorney a long way down the line would probably accuse them of mass hysteria if this ever got to court, Gambrell went forward collecting the information. The credibility of the women would be an issue. A defense attorney would say they assembled for a gabfest in the jail's recreation room, collecting details and making up stories of rapes and beatings just for fun. A defense attorney could say the women were playing a game of "Can You Top This?"

———————

Two months went by with nothing. Had the rapist learned of the surveillance and bulletins and stopped his nefarious activity? No press notices went out. How did he know enough to stop? Was he still raping, but the women were still not reporting the assaults? Was the rapist a cop and slowing down until things cooled off? Stranger things had happened.

Shortly after the sheriff's department learned that a rapist in their area was possibly a murderer in California, Gemma Johnson* was out on Atlantic Avenue near Shark's Lounge in Volusia County arguing with a so-called male friend nicknamed "B-Dog." As usual, they were arguing over money, money Gemma said she had earned and money B said belonged to him, a common activity between the two.

B hadn't gotten physical with Gemma, and probably wouldn't, because the last time that happened it cost him three days in jail until he could convince her to drop the domestic-violence charges. B did not want to travel down that road again. Tonight he did call Gemma several varieties of "bitch," "whore," and other sweet nothings of the street.

He never touched her, though. B-Dog had things to do, and jail was a definite inconvenience.

A man pulled up next to the arguing couple. Gemma hoped he would be her knight in shining armor. Her knight would do two things: he would get her away from B and he would provide her with some money. The man, in his mid to late forties, was driving a white Lincoln. He had dark hair and a protruding gut.

As they drove along the boulevard the man said, "It looked like you needed to get away from that guy. Your boy-friend?"

"Nah, jus' a friend. Mm-hmm."

"Do you date?"

Gemma was sure this guy wasn't a cop. She looked him over again to make sure. She looked around the interior of the Lincoln. She looked on top of the sun visors for a min-iature clip-on microphone that would transmit to a police radio. She looked on the floor of the driver's side for a foot-activated button that would begin the transmission. Not seeing anything that aroused her street instincts, Gemma figured she'd go along and get some money.

"Yeah. What you want?"

"How about thirty dollars for head? I'll pay fifty if we go to a room and take our time. That way we can relax and I can enjoy those pretty titties."

Thirty dollars sounded good. Fifty sounded better, al-though if they got a room she would be off the street lon-ger. On the other hand, she could keep the key and bring other guys there until noon the next day and make even more money. Gemma agreed.

Gemma happened to be coming down from a crack-cocaine high when the man interrupted the argument she and B were having. She began to get sleepy in the front seat when she was finally able to sit comfortably and rest her legs. She actually fell asleep during the drive.

When Gemma awoke she was not at a motel. The man

had driven the car somewhere into the woods off of Shell Road near State Route 95. It was dark. Trees were all around. What the hell was going on? The man got out, taking the keys with him. He walked around to the passenger side. Opening the door, he told Gemma to get out. His friendly tone was gone. The man unzipped his pants. "How about sucking some dick?" he said.

"How about paying me fifty dollars, and where is the damned motel?" Gemma was fully awake now.

"I ain't payin', bitch, and you're suckin' my dick, you worthless cunt." The man grabbed her by the shoulders and neck, yanking her in a circle, throwing her to the ground. As he moved toward her, she pulled a pocketknife and waved it at him. The man grabbed her forearm with strong, callused hands while she tried to slash at him with the knife. Even though she did not strike him with the knife blade, he let go of her arm. She ran into the woods. He delayed chasing her while he zipped up his pants.

Gemma ran and ran until she came to a barbed-wire fence. She climbed over, catching her jeans on the barbs, and waited. He had not pursued her. Not knowing where she was, she blindly ran until she came to a busy street.

A man stopped to offer help. She asked the man to call the police. When officers showed up, Gemma told them the story. She later said she did not think the officers believed her. Citing their perceived indifference, Gemma refused to make a formal police report. Damned cops, anyway. To their discredit, the cops didn't insist on taking a report, just for the record. Hookers were a pain in the ass anyway.

For three consecutive nights from 8 p.m. until 2 a.m., shortly after learning of the DNA matches, Detective Gambrell and Detective Larry Meeks were out on Atlantic Avenue looking for a blue van. They stopped by a convenience store at

Shady and Ridgewood, where they saw two Daytona Beach patrol cops. Jason Kilker and Robert Carter were leaning against their patrol cars having a cold drink. It was after midnight.

Gambrell flashed her badge, even though she didn't need to. Any patrol cop could spot the plain, stripped-down ride of any detective bureau in the state. Gambrell explained the situation to them. She showed them the composite drawing. She told them about the van and the tools within it. She said the rapist was possibly a carpet layer or some kind of contractor. The young cops seemed genuinely interested. They remembered hearing about such a character. Now, with the personal contact from Gambrell, they said they would look more closely for him.

"Please do," Gambrell said. "This guy's gonna kill someone. Again."

———

A few weeks later, in the latter part of June, Heather King* was out on Atlantic Avenue for a stroll, or maybe one could call it a "troll." King was a prostitute and made no secret of it as she swung her hips down the street. She looked at each car with the expertise of someone who had been arrested before and did not plan to be arrested again. If a Vice cop pulled up, so what? It wasn't against the law to walk on a public sidewalk in a provocative manner. If a cop questioned her, she would say she was out "doing errands." No one could prove otherwise. Despite a few arrests for solicitation in her past, Heather believed she could now spot an undercover cop.

A white guy in a dark blue van drove past her slowly, looking her over, top to bottom. The van went to the corner, then made a U-turn. The man drove past her the other way, making another U-turn before pulling up next to the curb. Heather looked inside, taking note that if the driver was a Vice cop she was the Queen of England. The talk was quick, but the price wasn't cheap. Commercial labor negotiations should go so rapidly. Forty dollars for oral sex, climb in, and off they went.

Heather suggested a public park near the bridge where she often plied her trade. It was secluded and no one such as a nosy patrol cop could sneak up and hang her with the cheap-ass charge of "committing a lewd act in public." The public-lewdness arrest was better than solicitation for prostitution, but was still a major inconvenience, what with court appearances and lying to the public defender, probation officer, and judge. She didn't have the time for that kind of nonsense. Forty bucks for a quickie blow job sounded just fine to her.

When they passed the park Heather had suggested, she said, "Hey, that's where I want to go. It's cool there. No cops or nothin'."

"I know a better place," he said. The man continued driving to Nova Road.

They drove a mile or so to a shopping center. It was past closing time for the stores, but the lot was still well lit. "I like it here," he said. "I can see if anyone's coming. We blend in." Heather shrugged. This would be over in no time, and she would have forty bucks she didn't have before.

Both Heather and the man climbed into the back of the van. She told him she needed the money before they started.

"I don't pay first."

"You do with me. What the hell you pullin'?"

"It looks like I'm pullin' your neck, bitch." The man grabbed Heather by the neck and began choking her.

Heather now realized getting in the van with this psycho had been a mistake. He was too overpowering for her. They struggled. She had no leverage, and not enough strength. She knew she had to give in. She signaled him she couldn't breathe, so he let go.

"Don't get any funny ideas, bitch. Suck."

She did. After he achieved a full erection, he instructed

Heather to remove her slacks. By the time the tight slacks were off, he was unable to complete penetration. He made repeated efforts to enter her vaginally, but could not.

"Okay, bitch, you did your best. It's not my fault you're so ugly that I can't get it up long enough." He laughed at his own joke.

Heather asked the man to please take her back to where they met on Ridgewood Avenue. On the drive back they shared a marijuana joint. When they arrived at their original point of meeting, the man let her out. Heather said she notified the Daytona Beach Police. She later said no one followed up on her complaint. If there was a forensic rape exam, it yielded no physical evidence. Confusing as it is, it is unclear whether or not a police report was ever taken. "I saved my life by doing everything his way," Heather said later when interviewed.

―――――――――

By doing painstaking work to locate Abbe Smith's husband, Slim, Detective Gambrell was finally successful in late June 2005. The man was in county jail. In fact, he had turned himself in because he heard Gambrell was looking everywhere for him. Slim had a warrant and needed a place to stay anyway. Gambrell introduced herself and told Slim Smith he might have valuable evidence in a case she was working. She asked him if he remembered a situation over a year ago when a guy in a blue van raped Abbe. Smith shook his head negatively, but didn't do it too convincingly. "Least I don' think I remember."

"Well, I spoke with Abbe," Gambrell said, "And she said she thinks you wrote this guy's license number down when he drove away. You guys were mad at him for raping her, and for not paying her. You couldn't chase him because you were out of gas."

Smith furrowed his brow, looking like he was trying to remember. "Yeah, maybe. We wuz out of gas a lot."

"Abbe said she thinks you put the paper with the license number in your wallet. I know it was a long time ago, but if you still have that license number, it could help a lot. Do I have your permission to look in your wallet? I know you don't have anything bad in there or the deputies would have found it when you were booked."

"I ain't got nothin' bad in it, and I ain't got nothin' of value either. That's one sorry-ass empty wallet. If I let you look, can you get me a break on this case?"

Slim Smith's pending case involved the failure to appear on a misdemeanor warrant and there was nothing Detective Gambrell could do. She did offer to tell the prosecuting and defense attorneys that he was helpful.

The tense scene in the property area of county jail was like the time Geraldo Rivera went into Al Capone's tomb on national television. The result was the same too: nothing. There was no license number. Hours spent looking for Slim Smith and hours negotiating this activity ended up with nothing to show for it.

CHAPTER 19

Detective Gambrell was constantly being reminded that she had a potential blockbuster of a case on her hands. The DNA results and the details of all the rape cases had gone rapidly up the "food chain" in the sheriff's department. One day Captain Dave Hudson summoned Gambrell to his office. Cynthia feared the department was going to take the case from her and give it to some hotshot specialized unit.

Gambrell was now a twenty-year veteran. Police work had not always been on her mind. In her youth, she'd set out to become a veterinarian. That was the plan anyway. In school, the athletic Gambrell joined the swim team. Several police officers worked out at the pool where her team swam. She became friendly with them, listening to entertaining stories of their daily work. She joined the Police Explorer Post sponsored by the department and became "hooked" on police work. Her love of animals would now have to be a hobby. Cindy soon became a Volusia County deputy sheriff.

She had started her career in court services, and then

performed a lengthy assignment in Patrol followed by stints in Warrants/Extraditions and Narcotics. Gambrell believed she had found her niche in Sex Crimes. She had the understanding of a woman, but the hard-nosed realism of a career street cop. You had to have both to succeed. If you had the mentality of a soft-skinned social worker, without the realism of a police officer, you would care only about the well-being of the victim, without factoring in the realization that a criminal must be caught and punished for what he had done to the victim.

While victims have to be treated humanely and protected from abuse by the "system," society must also be protected from sexual predators. Sometimes it was necessary for a victim to get worked over on the witness stand by a defense attorney who was ruthless but stayed within the limits of the law. Often the tactic backfired on an aggressive attorney in the form of an angry jury who felt sorry for the victim being grilled incessantly and unnecessarily but, according to the law, permissibly. It was the way the game was played.

Good sex-crimes detectives and prosecutors know the balance that must be present in a case. By properly educating and nurturing sex-crimes victims, prosecutors and detectives can prepare them to survive a defense attorney's verbal onslaught and character attack.

The Volusia County Sheriff's Department had over 450 sworn deputies and at least three times that many support personnel. They policed the airport and had specialty units such as Canine, Marine, and a narcotics task force. The department was fairly bursting with up-and-comers who could become media darlings and wrest the case from Detective Gambrell.

Contrary to her fears, Captain Hudson assured Gambrell immediately that the case would remain with her. Gambrell had no ax to grind with the department. She had always been treated fairly. But her initial fear of losing the case to someone else had been well grounded.

With that out of the way, a plan of attack was formulated. Gambrell would herself recontact every police agency in Volusia County. She would give out more bulletins containing the composite drawing and the vehicle description. Then she hoped someone would find the guy.

—————

On July 5, 2005, Ida Jones* was in familiar territory, the beach area of Volusia County Florida. Ida's very best years were behind her, but she could still get out there and hustle with the best, or rather, the rest of the other prostitutes.

Ida had been arrested for solicitation for prostitution a few times and believed she knew the ropes. She knew the laws of entrapment as well as anyone in the public defender's office, and she knew Vice cops sometimes fudged a little on their reports to make it sound like the prostitute made the initial overture, when in fact the cop actually did the deal making. She didn't like that part of the life, but it was the way of the street.

Ida didn't like the men who stopped to get her services either. For the most part, they were stupid, demanding, and often foul. It was no wonder they couldn't get a regular date. The men tried to be charming at first. When the sex act was over, they wanted Ida out of the car, and out of their lives. She never received a "tip" for extraordinary service. But then she rarely gave extraordinary service. That too was the way of the street.

On this humid July night around 3:30 a.m. a man driving a dark van pulled to the curb on North Street, near Segrave Avenue, waiting for Ida to walk up to where he had stopped. A good long look convinced the experienced Ida that this slob wasn't a cop. After getting in the van, she and the man didn't waste any time.

"You dating?"

"Yes."

"How's forty sound?"

"For what?"

"A regular screw."

"You wear a rubber?"

"Yup."

"Deal."

They found an isolated area of a local park. Ida crawled to the back of the van. The man knelt in front of where she was sitting, on top of a spare tire. "I need the money, and I don't see no rubbers."

"The money's in the front, on the visor in front of the driver's seat."

"Get it. Don't forget the rubber either."

"Hey look, don't worry about the damn money. I'm good for it."

"I'm sure you are. I just don't want you to forget. That's why you're getting it now."

"I told you, you'll get it. Take your pants off."

"What about the condom?"

"Ah, don't worry about that either. Let's get going."

"Bullshit. No money and no condom. What the hell's going on?"

The man showed her what was going on. He punched Ida on the left side of the head with his right fist. He lunged at her, gripping her neck with both hands. He threw her to the floor of the van. The harder Ida resisted, the tighter this madman squeezed. She could feel his thumbs crushing her throat. She choked, fearful she was going to pass out or die.

Somehow Ida was able to stop struggling and convince this guy she would give in. "Okay, okay. I will."

"You damned right you will," he said. He took off his pants and instructed Ida in street language to fellate him. She did so until he ejaculated in her mouth.

She emptied her mouth on the floor of the van, gagging and choking in the process. "Quit fakin', bitch. I ain't that big." Then he laughed. "Maybe I am. That wasn't the best I've had, but it wasn't the worst. Get out, bitch. Get lost."

Since she was so far away from anywhere, Ida convinced the man to give her a ride back to town. He drove her to Martin Luther King Boulevard, where he told her again to, "Get lost."

That night the street had been tough on her. For whatever reasons a prostitute has, Ida did not call the police. She dusted herself off and her life went on.

———————

Detective Gambrell's life went on too. She wasn't happy knowing that a murdering rapist was operating with apparent impunity in her jurisdiction and neighboring jurisdictions. Gambrell would have been even unhappier if she knew Ida Jones had been raped but did not report it. If she had known that Ida was the ninth woman raped by the guy in the blue van, she would have been frantic. So far, only Debbie Farris had reported the crime immediately after it happened.

A couple of other women later said they had reported the crimes to other jurisdictions, but no reports ever came across Gambrell's desk when she put out the information on the blue van with the angry potbellied man. It was probably better, for Detective Gambrell's sanity at least, that she knew of only one at this time, plus the few others who told her about the rapes after they were in jail.

Ida Jones managed to get herself arrested, in spite of her self-proclaimed expertise in spotting Vice cops. While in county jail, she came across Debbie Farris, who told her of Detective Gambrell's interest in the rapist in the dark van. Ida bristled when she heard about the guy, having been a victim of his just a few days before. Debbie explained that her rape had happened the previous November.

"Damn, that guy's been raising a fuss for a long time. I better talk to that lady cop you talked to."

Detective Cindy Gambrell went to the Volusia County Jail to speak with Ida Jones. Always skeptical of copycats and someone who merely wanted to jump on the band-wagon, Gambrell subjected her to a thorough interview. While remaining understanding and gentle, she made sure Jones was not running a game on her. When she notified Jones that there was nothing the sheriff's department could do about the charge for which she was currently in jail, Jones didn't object. Gambrell had been fearful Jones wanted to "buy" her way out of a charge by supplying information on the rapes, whether the information was true or not.

Since no suspect was in custody, Gambrell honestly told Jones they were still looking for the guy. Jones was grateful that someone in authority believed she had been a rape victim.

CHAPTER 20

Daytona Beach police officer Jason Kilker grew up in Pleasant Hill, California, in the San Francisco Bay Area. He'd spent a lot of time alone, entertaining himself. He lived on North Main Street, with houses on one side only. On the other side was a twenty-foot wall erected to block out the sounds of I-680.

Jason was a dark-haired young fellow, tall for his age, who didn't mind talking to people. On many days he would sit in his front yard and gab with a Pleasant Hill motorcycle police officer who would set up shop there with his hand-held radar gun, tracking motorists speeding off the freeway ramp. Jason's yard sported a large ivy bush that provided perfect concealment for a motorcycle cop.

Everyone called Officer Chilimedes "Big Chili." He was a large African-American with a deep voice and a gentle manner—gentle most of the time anyway. Young Jason often thought if you looked like Big Chili you didn't really need to carry a gun. For hours he would watch Officer Chilimedes aim his radar at cars that were exiting I-680 in excess of the speed limit. Once the motor cop had a "radar lock," and the driver was classified as a speeder, he would put the radar gun in its holder, start up his Kawasaki motorcycle, and take off after the car, emergency lights flashing the uneven rhythm that attracted attention several blocks away.

Soon Officer Chilimedes would return to his unofficial post in Jason's yard. Jason would ask how fast the driver had been going. Big Chili would tell him. Jason would spend hours with Chilimedes passing the time, begging the large cop to tell him stories about police work.

Jason Kilker was only about five years old when he formed his friendship with Big Chili. His mother didn't mind that he was out there. After all, she had a free babysitter, a large black man who carried a gun. She thought Jason would be safe.

The fallout from Jason's experience with Big Chili was predictable. He became enthralled with motorcycles and cops. He became an avid viewer of *ChiPs* with John and Ponch hotdogging their way through crime-ridden Los Angeles, breaking up auto-theft and robbery rings while presenting a positive image of the state traffic officers. That program did for motorcycle cops and highway-patrol officers what *Dragnet* and *Adam 12* did for all city police departments. The shows were the best recruitment tool on the block.

As Jason grew older, he developed a fascination with speed, action, and adventure. He watched *Dukes of Hazzard,* featuring the "General Lee" car that went airborne on almost every episode without ever sustaining any frame damage or even a flat tire. Jason loved to go fast on his bicycle. He fantasized about going fast in cars when he got older. Jason thought he wanted to be a police officer. Then he saw Stanley Kubrick's *Full Metal Jacket* and decided he wanted to be a United States Marine.

Jason didn't go to college before the Marine Corps, but he was more intelligent than most of the other boots in his recruit unit. He was also smarter than most of his immediate superiors in the corps.

Jason stood well over six feet tall. His vision was excellent. His grip was strong and his confidence was superb. He wanted to be a sniper, just like the guys he had seen in *Full Metal Jacket*. Although he was a crack shot who exhibited good judgment, did the Marines give him a variety of rifles and let him loose as a sniper? No, they made him an instructor. Jason knew his stuff well enough to be chosen for the job. He was an excellent communicator, patient with the recruits. His units won competition after competition within the corps, much to the joy of his superiors. But this success didn't thrill Jason much.

Initially, Jason Kilker wanted to be a career Marine. But being stuck in a classroom most of the time, and on the shooting range only a fraction of the time, didn't sit well with him. When his four years were up, he left the Marines.

Jason stayed in Twentynine Palms, California, home of the large Marine base, trying to decide what to do with his life. There wasn't much of a market for snipers in the civilian world, at least not legally. And, Jason lived by a strong moral code, instilled in him by his family.

One day, on a whim, he and a buddy rented a Ryder truck and moved to the Atlantic coast of Florida. Jason kicked around for a while, trying to find himself.

Finally he again decided he wanted to be a police officer. Using money he was entitled to through the GI Bill, Jason put himself through the police academy. Given his intelligence, good judgment, and physical presence and attributes, the Daytona Beach Police Department snatched him up before he even graduated. Officer Kilker had found a home. He started work for the department on December 2, 2002.

———

Officer Kilker became an aggressive patrol cop who knew his beat area inside and out. He knew the bad guys. He knew the good guys, few as they were, on the graveyard shift. He candidly said, "I work in a shithole, and I love it. The bad guys hate me and I love that too." In spite of the colorful description of his work area, Kilker was not cynical. He retained a cop's sense of humor, a must for survival in the law enforcement profession. The crooks didn't love having Kilker in the area, though. Every time they turned around, there was the six-foot-four, 225-plus-pounder breathing down their necks. While few, if any, decided to go straight, many of the bad guys decided to move on to other parts of the city.

Kilker's regular beat was thirteen blocks long and five blocks wide. The activity never stopped. Newcomers to the underbelly of nighttime Daytona Beach soon learned they were being watched. They were accountable for their actions to one Jason Kilker.

Kilker was big, strong, tough, and fair, just like Big Chili had been. Never brutal, sometimes even gentle, Jason did his job in fine fashion. His powers of information retention were impressive. He didn't forget license numbers of stolen cars. He remembered minute details given out on suspicious activity during roll call. He knew the law and the elements of crimes. When Jason Kilker made an arrest, it stuck. The assistant state's attorneys didn't have to do extra work to make Kilker's cases. They were nearly always ready to go into a courtroom with what he had done.

———

It was Detective Gambrell's good fortune to have given the information on the rapist in the blue van with no windows to Jason Kilker back in April 2005. The officer on the adjoining beat, Robert Carter, was just like Kilker. They had joined the Daytona Beach department on the same day in December of 2002. Both were good-sized cops. One can only imagine some loudmouth trying to intimidate these two.

Gambrell's meeting with them was in April. Some officers would have looked until the end of the shift, or maybe a few days more. Kilker and Carter were on a mission. There was a rapist operating in their "shithole" beats and they didn't like that.

Kilker stopped many prostitutes during the course of a shift. If they had warrants, they went to jail. If they jaywalked and maybe had some information on a crime or a crook, they might catch a break. If they had nothing to offer Officer Kilker, they more than likely received a ticket for their pedestrian transgression. If they ignored the summons, Jason would arrest them in a month or two when the ticket turned into a warrant. That's how he did his job.

One night around 2 a.m., Kilker spotted a dark van with no windows cruising the area frequented by prostitutes. He watched it for several blocks, noting the driver did all of the telltale things that a john did. He drove by the girls as they walked slowly down the street, or sat on bus benches, or on the short walls in front of businesses. Sometimes the driver stopped to engage the girls in conversation. Jason moved closer and noted the color of the van was green not blue. The key word was *dark*.

The van was dark. Under the streetlights, one person's version of blue might be another's green or black. The van Jason was watching certainly wasn't pastel. Close enough for government work. If this was the rapist's vehicle, some defense attorney would work on Jason's powers of observation and perception of color, but it would be to no avail. To an impartial judge, under the Florida streetlights, dark green would be as good as dark blue from a half block away.

Jason followed the van until the driver committed a traffic violation. When he got out of the vehicle, Jason noted he was not in his late forties, but rather in his late twenties. And he was slender and not potbellied like the rapist in Florida who had committed the murder in California. Looking closer, Jason decided the driver had probably been five or six years old when the California murder happened. He was still worth checking out, at least to find out if anyone else occasionally drove the van. And Jason planned to tell him to get off the avenue where the hookers worked.

Jason questioned the driver about who else might drive the vehicle. When the driver said he was the only one who drove it, Jason took down all of the information on the vehicle and driver. He looked inside the van. Detective Gambrell had told the patrol cops that work implements were in the back, possibly carpet-laying equipment.

Officer Kilker told the young man he was asking for trouble by messing with the street hookers. "For your own good, you ought to get out of here and go home. There's nothing but problems waiting for you if you stick around here. If I see you again, I'll be your problem."

The young fellow craned his neck to look up at the behemoth cop. "Yes, Officer, thank you. Thanks for the warning too."

Officers Carter and Kilker laughed after the driver left the area. While the traffic stop was technically a valid one, it would have been a chickenshit ticket if Kilker had actually written it. He didn't write tickets like that, not usually anyway.

Another traffic stop a month later was a closer match. The guy seemed too young, but he was still a possible viable suspect. The van was closer in appearance to the one they were looking for, this one being black. Maybe Kilker was onto something.

Officer Kilker took his time writing the ticket. The driver lit a filtered cigarette and smoked the entire thing while Kilker scratched out the summons. After receiving the ticket, he flipped the cigarette butt into the gutter. Keeping his eye on the finished smoke, Kilker carefully picked it up, flicked off the burning end, and put it in an evidence bag. He logged it in and notified Detective Gambrell the next day. He told her he didn't think he had the guy, but he had something for the chemists to look at. The butt was examined and DNA was extracted.

Officer Kilker never heard back from Detective Gambrell on that submission. He correctly assumed the butt didn't come from the rapist. Kilker never stopped looking.

CHAPTER 21

On July 9, 2005, at 1:16 a.m., four days after Ida Jones was raped, Officer Kilker saw a dark blue van cruising the beach area where the prostitutes hung out. The van had no side or back windows. Although it had been over three months since Detective Gambrell had given Kilker and Officer Robert Carter the information on the rapist, it was still fresh in Kilker's mind. He held no affinity for prostitutes, but at the same time believed they did not deserve to be rape victims.

Kilker had forwarded the information on the other two drivers and vehicles to Detective Gambrell. When he did not hear back, the young patrol officer assumed neither of these two guys was the rapist.

The dark blue Ford van Kilker was following now gave him a different feeling. The feeling was right in the gut where cops have intuitions that are not admissible in court, but are as real as the crescent moon that was faintly glimmering on this hot, sticky night. By the driver's actions, Kilker knew this guy was definitely cruising for girls. And the van was definitely dark blue, not green or black. Edging behind the vehicle, Kilker radioed his adjoining beat partner, Robert Carter, that he might have a "possible" on the info from Volusia County. Knowing what he meant, Carter began driving toward Kilker's location.

Officer Kilker did a rolling registration check on the van. He could see that the sticker in the corner of the license plate was still current. However, the dispatcher soon informed him that the license plate came back as expired. This was strange. The sticker was up-to-date, but the plate was not. The van's rear bumper bore a bumper sticker that had REAL MEN LOVE JESUS. *Okay, maybe so,* he thought.

The expired plate was the "probable cause" Kilker was waiting for. He activated his lights and the van pulled to the curb. Officer Carter was there by the time the van had stopped.

The driver was in his late forties, about five-foot-eight and close to two hundred pounds. He had dark, greasy hair and a potbelly. Kilker's internal calculator was adding up similarities to the information Detective Gambrell had supplied.

"What's the trouble, Officer?"

"Your vehicle license plate. May I see your driver's license and vehicle registration?"

"Sure. There ain't nothin', wrong with my registration."

The driver's license identified the man as Mark Elder of nearby Orange City. Elder accompanied Kilker to the back of the van. In Florida, the number of the license plate is on the validation sticker in the corner of the plate in small print. Kilker shined his flashlight on the sticker and said, "See? That identifying number on the sticker is not the number on the plate. Both numbers should be the same. This sticker shouldn't be on this plate. It should be on another plate."

"Oh shit. You're right. I got two vans. I put the wrong sticker on this plate. It's okay. You're not going to give me a ticket, are you?"

"Well, the almighty computer says your plate is expired. Do you have anything illegal inside your van?"

The driver, Mark Elder, was getting fidgety now. He pulled a pack of generic cigarettes from his pocket and lit one. "Naw, I ain't got nothin' illegal."

"No? Is it okay if I look around?"

"Okay, but make it quick."

While Officer Carter stayed with Elder, Kilker opened the driver's door to look inside. In the space between the bucket seats he saw two pairs of soiled women's underwear. Above the visor was a length of connected condoms, still in the wrappers. He pulled the visor down and the condoms fell onto the seat. Without counting them, Kilker estimated there were about twenty. This guy must buy his rubbers by the gross.

The interior of the front of the van was a mess. Food wrappers, dirt, papers, and more condoms were on the front seats and floor. Kilker shined his flashlight in the back and felt a rush of excitement. The back was full of carpet-laying equipment. There were knee kickers and a six-foot straight edge. Kilker knew this was carpet equipment because he had worked as an apprentice for a time at a carpet-installation business. He had done everything except the actual carpet laying. He was familiar with all of the equipment, including the gluing apparatus, straight edge, and cutting implements. Things were adding up.

Kilker climbed back farther into the van and found a small battery-operated video-recording device. There was a tape inside. He hit the rewind button, then the play button.

The image on the camera was Mark Elder. He was holding the camera in front of himself with the lens pointing toward him, essentially filming himself. He looked like he was adjusting settings on the camera. It appeared that he had set the device on something at almost eye level, like a bookcase. Then he walked out of the room. In a short time he returned with a woman. Elder moved out of the sight line of the camera. The woman began to disrobe. The battery went dead. Shit. If he had more probable cause, Kilker could have taken the tape and player. At this point he did not have enough. The tape had to stay. This guy definitely had a thing for women.

Kilker looked around the interior of the back. The van was a mess, but there was nothing more of interest. As he was climbing out the front, he saw a marijuana cigarette butt, a "roach," in a cup holder near the front console. While not the biggest bust of Officer Kilker's career, Elder's possessing the roach was a violation of the law.

Kilker approached Elder and turned him around. While putting handcuffs on him, he told him of the marijuana. "Oh, that," said Elder. "Shit, that's been there a long time."

Kilker pulled Carter off to the side and told him of the contents of the van, including the huge supply of condoms, carpet-installing equipment, and the strange videotape. It looked like they had a hot one. They put Elder in the backseat of the patrol car and turned off the police radio.

When Officer Kilker had picked up the discarded cigarette butt from the young guy in the dark van weeks before, he really didn't think he had the killer/rapist. That's why he waited until the next morning to notify Detective Gambrell. This time his heart was beating more noticeably. He thought he had the guy, and he didn't want to make a mistake.

Kilker stepped away from the patrol car and phoned Cindy Gambrell at home. She responded groggily that she was awake "now," and asked what he had. Jason Kilker told her he thought he had her guy, really had him, and asked her what he should do. "I think this guy's the one," he said. "I really do. Everything fits, including the carpet equipment. How do you want me to handle it?"

Gambrell, experienced in the way of the courts, collected her thoughts. She went over what Kilker had explained. It would be a shame to have the right guy, but have something go wrong with the stop.

"Tell me again about the marijuana," Gambrell told him.

"It's only a roach. Barely anything in it."

"What would you normally do with a roach?"

In reality, most of the time, any cop in the Western world who had ever spent hours writing reports and sitting in the hallway of the courthouse on his or her day off would have crumbed the roach between the thumb and forefinger and said, "What roach?"

Kilker told her he normally would confiscate the roach, write the man a citation for possession of marijuana under a certain amount, and send the offender on his way. That is what most department policy manuals instructed officers to do.

Gambrell said, "That's what you should do. Write him a cite and let him go. Do what you normally would."

"I think he's your guy."

"He might be. Just do things as you normally would. Don't question him about the rapes. Don't let him know we even suspect him."

"Okay. I'll take the roach for possible DNA. I'll write him a ticket for the expired plate, one for the marijuana, and let him go. What should I do with the roach?"

"Put it in an evidence bag and secure it at your police station. I'll get it in the morning. It sounds good so far, but we don't want to spook him, if he's the guy. And thanks."

CHAPTER 22

The next morning, after reviewing the facts, Detective Gambrell decided that Mark Elder was a "keeper." She drove to the Daytona Beach Police Department and picked up the marijuana roach in the evidence bag.

Gambrell checked with the forensic division of the sheriff's department to ask about the turnaround time for getting a DNA reading on the roach back to her. The answer was disheartening. The roach would have to be sent to the state lab. It would take a few months. Gambrell was incredulous. This was a murder they were talking about, a cold murder and an active rapist. The best they could do was a "few months"? The institutional answer was, "Yes. It's the best we can do. Everyone's cases are big." Gambrell had to get in line, murder or not. This did not make her any less upset.

She phoned Ron Thill and asked if San Diego could do any better in the speed department. Since the San Diego police had its own forensic section headed up by Dr. Patrick O'Connell, Thill said they could analyze the roach in a matter of days.

Detective Gambrell called the state attorney's office to check on any issues of chain of custody and contamination of evidence. It would be permissible to overnight the evidence with one of the well-known private mail services. The evidence could be tracked electronically from the time it left the detective's hands until it came into the custody of the San Diego Police Laboratory.

Arrangements were made to ship the roach to San Diego on July 25, 2005. Gambrell was under the impression her lab would overnight the package to San Diego. She supplied the San Diego police address and David Cornacchia's name to her lab and phoned Ron Thill to give him the good news that the contraband was on its way. After the evidence had been taken care of, Cindy Gambrell tried to find out more about Mark Elder. She believed he was their man. Who was he?

Elder's criminal record was not that of a seemingly dangerous man. He had a few trespassing beefs that resulted in probation. In 1988, he was arrested for fraud and pleaded no contest, which is the same as a guilty plea. The court gave him one year of house arrest and two years of probation, hardly the stuff of a public enemy. She also learned some files on Elder had been deleted or lost. That was disheartening.

Gambrell found no violence in his record, or any rape convictions. Mark Elder was a mystery. If he was their guy, the one who killed a woman in 1988, what had he been doing since then? He hadn't been in jail or prison. What had he been doing? It did not seem logical that a guy could kill someone in 1988 the way Janet Moore had been killed, be a good citizen for seventeen years, and then start raping in 2004 like there was no tomorrow. There was nothing for Detective Gambrell to do but wait.

Back in San Diego, some "weeping and gnashing of teeth" had been going on. Detective Gambrell told San Diego her department would be overnighting the package to them. When it didn't show up the next day, prosecutor Andrea Freshwater phoned Florida to find out the tracking number. She was dismayed to learn the evidence had not been "overnighted" as promised, but put on a truck and was traveling across the United States with the speed of a caterpillar. The roach was on a damned truck merrily rolling along the highway. Freshwater hoped no drug-sniffing dogs checked the truck shipments.

When the package finally arrived four days later, David Cornacchia opened up the cardboard envelope from Florida. He looked at the small piece of browned cigarette paper in the envelope. Cornacchia looked deeper into the envelope hoping to find more. That was it. His disappointment was real. He wondered if the people submitting the tiny cigarette paper had thought he was some kind of miracle worker.

An hour later Cornacchia was overjoyed to learn that it was possible to get a full DNA profile from the small piece of cigarette paper. After getting the reading, he submitted it to CODIS.

August 4, 2005, was possibly the most hectic, important, action-filled, yet blurry day in the professional life of Detective Cynthia Gambrell. It was on this day that the San Diego Police Department Forensics Division phoned her to say the DNA of Mark Elder from the marijuana roach was the same DNA as had been found in the blood on the washcloth in Janet Moore's bathroom, and the same DNA as had been found in the semen taken from Janet Moore's vaginal cavity. He was their guy, the killer and the rapist. Gambrell's head spun. She knew she'd heard him correctly. "He is your guy," he'd said.

Ever the cautious person, Gambrell asked what the numbers were that implicated Mark Elder. "A lot of zeroes" was the initial answer. A preliminary calculation revealed the chances that the blood on the washcloth in the bathroom was someone else's was one in 3.4 trillion. That latter number would become larger by the time they went to court.

There were about 3.4 trillion things for Detective Gambrell to do on the day she learned Elder was both the cross-country rapist in Florida and the California killer. Because she was an organized detective, Gambrell lined up what needed to be done first. And, because she was a team player, she began seeking help. No one detective could handle this case alone.

The first order of the day was to get an arrest warrant for Mark Elder for sexual assault into the system. The assault in question was that of Debbie Farris. Back in San Diego, a detective would draw up an arrest warrant for Elder for the murder of Janet Moore. Ron Thill was out of town attending a training session. When he heard the news he left the school and headed for San Diego. His wife had a suitcase waiting for him. Thill's coworkers had made travel arrangements for him to fly into Daytona Beach.

The Volusia County Sheriff's Department assigned teams of detectives, including several from Homicide, to begin twenty-four-hour surveillance on Elder. (The A&E Network's television program *Cold Case Files* indicated that Elder was put under twenty-four-hour surveillance immediately after Jason Kilker stopped him and confiscated the marijuana roach. The program is in error.) Out of professional courtesy and common sense, the Volusia County cops knew that Ron Thill should be the one to interview Elder regarding the murder. Thill knew all about the case, having been at the crime scene so many years before.

The second order of the day was to get search warrants for Elder's residence and vehicle. Detective Greg Seymour took care of the search warrants, no small undertaking. The arrest and search warrants eventually were done. The job now was to watch Mark Elder and wait for Ron Thill.

Above:
Entryway into Janet Moore's apartment.

Courtesy of San Diego Police Department

Left:
Bloody washcloth on top of toilet tank in bathroom. Was the killer's blood on it?

Courtesy of San Diego Police Department

Right:
Janet Moore. Too young to die.

Courtesy of San Diego District Attorney's Office

Below:
Apartment building where a brutal killing happened.

Courtesy of San Diego Police Department

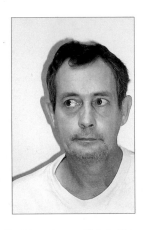

Booking photo of Mark Elder.

Courtesy of Volusia County Sheriff's Department

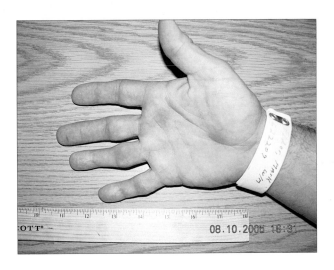

Right hand of killer. Note the deformity on little and ring fingers.

Courtesy of Volusia County Sheriff's Department

Left:
Sergeant Ed Petrick. He said, "We won't be judged on what we did, but by what we didn't do." He was right.

Courtesy of Ed Petrick

Right:
Officer Jason Kilker was inspired at an early age to be a good cop. No one knew he would be so good, so young.

Tom Basinski

Officer Robert Carter (left) and Jason Kilker. These two beat partners never gave up looking for a rapist-killer.

Tom Basinski

Right:
Sergeant Cindy Gambrell knew she had a killer in her area and he had to be found.

Tom Basinski

Left:
Forensic chemist David Cornacchia extracted DNA from two sources and came up with one killer.

Tom Basinski

Cornacchia.

Tom Basinski

Front gate to Donovan Prison, where the cross-country rapist calls "home."

Tom Basinski

Prosecutor Andrea Freshwater made sure the rapist-killer remained where he belonged—behind bars.

Tom Basinski

Left:
Public Defender Robert Ford faced overwhelming odds in the defendant he had.

Tom Basinski

Above:
Detective Ron Thill worked the case as a detective in 1988, and when it closed in 2005.

Tom Basinski

Left:
Mark Elder as a teenager.

Courtesy of Rita Elder

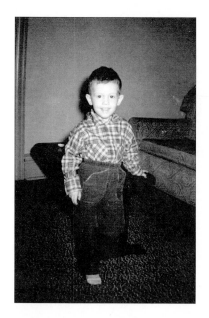

Mark Elder at age three. What did the future hold for him?

Courtesy of Rita Elder

Detective James Bordine. He wasn't around to see justice, but he did a lot of work to make sure it was achieved.

Courtesy of Marcia Bordine

Ron Thill jokes that while Homeland Security and the Transportation Safety Administration have photos of subversives and terrorists at their posts to detain and arrest, his picture, he is convinced, is on a special list called "Delay This Traveler." Perhaps it is his imagination, but Thill says every time he flies, the plane he is on is invariably late. Something always goes wrong. One time, over a year before, a single lightbulb above an exit seat had burned out on a plane Thill was boarding. One would think the technician would reach in the pocket of his coveralls, pull a bulb out, and replace the defective one.

On that flight, when Thill walked down the ramp to his eventual seat, he saw four workers hovering over a blueprint. When everyone was seated, the pilot announced that a lightbulb was out but had been ordered. Thill mused to himself, *Four guys looking at a blueprint of the plane all because of a lightbulb?* Very strange indeed. Ron laughed to himself.

He wasn't laughing forty-five minutes later when the pilot announced that the ordered bulb would "be here shortly." Ron turned to the passenger next to him and said, "If they want, I can run down to Home Depot and get one for 'em."

No reason was given for the delay of the flight Ron was taking to Daytona Beach in August 2005. It was just late. Ron boarded in the morning, hoping to get across the country by five o'clock.

———————

Meanwhile, the cops were poised to either wait Mark Elder out or pounce on him if needed. They didn't think he was aware he was being followed. After all, Jason Kilker had stopped him almost a month before, on July 9. It was now August 5 and the cops had not made a move on Elder. Elder would undoubtedly think he was home free and there was no reason to worry.

The surveillance team followed him to work, and followed him home. His blue van was easy to tail. About an

hour after he arrived home, a woman drove to his house.
She did not get out of the car. Instead, a teenage boy walked
up to the door and entered without knocking. The police
knew Elder was recently divorced. It was likely the woman
was his ex-wife and the boy was his son.

When the woman drove away, one unit followed her.
Elder soon walked out of the house, got into his van, and
took off. This exit caused some flurry of activity among
the police surveilling him. What to do? Was he escaping?
Was he going to the store for milk? It was too early for him
to go out raping. The tailing units did not want to take any
chances. They put out the word to take Elder down.

There are several ways to make an arrest of a moving
suspect. There is the television and movie way, with squeal-
ing tires, shouting, screaming of unintelligible commands,
pointing of guns, and general pandemonium. It makes for
great theater, but is seldom helpful in getting a confused
suspect to follow directions, and eventually to talk, which
is what the police wanted Mark Elder to do before the night
was over.

The lead officer summoned a marked car to make the
stop. Once the patrol cop activated the emergency lights,
Elder pulled over into a gas station. Several unmarked police cars converged on the area. Everyone was calm. The
lead detective informed Mark Elder that they had a warrant
for his arrest and he had to come with them.

The most common response to this information is, "There
must be some mistake. I don't have any warrants. Not a
ticket. Not anything. You guys are wrong. You'll be sorry."

Mark Elder shrugged, saying nothing.

The unit tailing the woman who had dropped off the boy at
Elder's house signaled her to pull over. An officer explained
that she had to return to the house to pick up the boy. The
woman was indeed Elder's ex-wife. She was quiet, shy, and

scared. She asked what the trouble was. The officer could not tell her. He said only, "We're in the middle of an investigation. We'll be doing some things at the house and it is best that the boy not be there. Can you pick him up and find someplace for him?"

The woman said, "Of course. He is my son. What is going on?"

"I'm sorry, ma'am. We're in the middle of an investigation. That's all I can tell you." Elder's ex-wife did as the officer requested.

The police radioed for a tow truck to pick up Elder's van and take it to the sheriff's department, where a detective would oversee the service of the search warrant and collection of evidence by a criminalist. Included in the "things to be seized" portion of the warrant was the videotape of Mark Elder placing the recorder in a bookcase and the woman beginning to disrobe. That is the tape Jason Kilker saw before the battery went dead. The tape and tape player were not inside the van. They did find several pairs of women's underwear and many more condoms.

Back at Elder's residence, with the boy safely gone, the police executed the search warrant for that location. They also looked for the videotape, thinking the female might be a hooker whose rape had been videotaped and kept as a trophy by Elder. They did not find it. Officer Jason Kilker was correct in not seizing the tape because he lacked probable cause to take it. Unfortunately, no one ever found the tape. It is missing to this day.

CHAPTER 23

The police took Elder to the sheriff's office on Indian Lake Road. They let him sit alone for a short while, hoping to buy some time before the arrival of the perennially delayed traveler, Ron Thill. The flight did not arrive on time, with the airlines giving no reason. When they could wait no longer, Detectives Cindy Gambrell and Greg Seymour went into the interview room to begin talking to Elder. As usual, the interview was videotaped from a not-so-surreptitious camera mounted in the upper corner. The camera wasn't hidden. Accused murderers usually have too much on their minds to look around for one. What is on their minds is trying to keep their lies straight so they don't look completely befuddled by the probing questions the cops are asking in several different ways.

Detective Greg Seymour told Elder they wanted to talk to him about some rapes. Elder shrugged. Seymour advised Elder of his constitutional right to have an attorney present before any questioning. He also told Elder that if he could not afford an attorney, one would be appointed for him at no cost.

Seymour read these rights from a printed card in case the exact wording became an issue in the future. When Seymour was done he asked Mark Elder if he understood his rights.

Almost arrogantly, Elder answered, "Sure."

Seymour asked if Elder wanted to talk to them.

"Yeah. Why not?" Elder said, this time with more perceptible arrogance.

Later, Cindy Gambrell, remembering the situation, said it seemed like Elder was their superior, at least in his mind. Even though he was the one who'd been wearing the handcuffs only a few minutes before, he acted almost nonchalant about the proceedings. He appeared not to be worried. He crossed his legs and assumed a position of comfort, given the spartan surroundings.

As the questioning went on, Elder's response to various questions and scenarios was, "I don't know what you're talking about. I never picked up no hookers. I never hit no hookers. You got the wrong guy. What you pickin' on me for? This is all a big mistake. You're wrong."

The detectives went over the rapes slowly and carefully, trying to be thorough and patient while hoping Ron Thill would show up soon. They weren't getting anywhere with Elder. They had a good case on him for the rape of Debbie Farris, but did not mention that medical personnel had removed his DNA from Debbie Farris. They didn't have any physical evidence other than what was taken from Farris, and only some mediocre circumstantial evidence against him from a couple of the other girls. Gambrell actually doubted the story of one of the prostitutes, believing she just wanted to "get in the game" with the other girls. The detectives were patient, though. They knew Elder's problems were bigger than the rape of a prostitute.

———

Ron Thill entered the interview room around nine-thirty. The district attorney's office usually had him rent a vehicle when he went out of town on a case. There'd been no time tonight. A uniformed deputy was waiting for him when he alighted from the plane. The young deputy made it to the sheriff's office in record time, although Thill would swear, if necessary, that the deputy obeyed all traffic laws.

When Thill made his entrance, he introduced himself as a San Diego police officer. Later he and Gambrell said they didn't think it registered with Elder exactly what Thill had said. Both were under the impression that Elder thought he was a Florida cop who maybe used to be a San Diego officer. Thill expected an expression of "Oh shit" to come over his face at the mention of San Diego. None came. Elder kept an impassive countenance.

Making small talk, Thill asked, "What happened to your hand?" pointing to Elder's right hand. The ring and little fingers did not bend.

"Uh, I cut it on a carpet knife at work."

Then, clearly on the videotape, Elder actually put his deformed right hand under his right thigh and sat on it, in what some might say was a futile maneuver to conceal the old injury.

"Do you know this girl?" Thill asked as he plopped down a photo of Janet Moore.

Elder barely looked at it. "Nah, never seen her." He seemed bored.

"How about now?" Thill dropped another picture of Janet Moore, this one taken on the table at the coroner's office just before the start of the autopsy. One must remember that Detective Thill had been at the murder scene of Janet Moore on June 11, 1988. He had seen and smelled Elder's handiwork firsthand, saw the slashed body and bloody walls, and picked up Janet's broken tooth off the floor and fished the tooth chip out of her blood-matted hair on the autopsy table. Thill wasn't in any mood to play games. He had attended the autopsy that told the story of the early end of the life of Janet Moore, and he had actually taken the

Polaroid photo he was showing. He knew Elder had killed Moore, and he believed he had enough proof to hang a conviction on this arrogant bastard, no matter what Elder said, or didn't say.

Elder studied the autopsy photo a little longer than he had looked at Janet's high school picture. He scrunched up his face. "Is she dead?"

"Deader'n a doornail, buddy," offered Thill, his contempt for Elder becoming more evident. "Do you remember doing that to her?"

"What are you accusing me of, sir?"

Ron Thill is not one given to drama. Yet he paused for several seconds, staring a hole right between Elder's eyes before enunciating, *"Murder."*

"Sir, this is ridiculous."

"Ridiculous, is it? Maybe you can tell me how your DNA was found inside of her."

"I don't know what to tell you, sir. This conversation is over."

Under his breath Thill mumbled, "I thought it would be."

The questioning stopped. The police officers got up and walked out of the room, leaving Elder by himself. The tape continued running. A short time later the videotape reveals Elder saying to himself, "Damn, I guess this is it."

PART III

CHAPTER 24

Mark Elder's final official words to law enforcement were: "Damn. I guess this is it." Detectives Ron Thill's and Cindy Gambrell's next words were, "Now this is *really* it." The next chapter was about to begin. While it was true that both law enforcement officers were certain that the real killer and rapist was behind bars, they also knew from over forty-five years of collective law enforcement experience they had a lot of work to do before the case was over. Catching a killer was one thing. Making sure they had a locked-up-tight, no-acquittal court case that would result in a conviction against him was another.

First, the district attorney's office in San Diego needed to prepare extradition papers for Elder. The murder of Janet Moore happened in California and the case would have to be prosecuted in California. Elder would have the opportunity to waive extradition and agree to let the San Diego authorities take him back to the West Coast right away without any legal wrangling. Deputy District Attorney Robert Locke in San Diego was the resident expert on extraditions.

He had supplied training on that subject to prosecutors all over the state. Locke knew the ins and outs of this process. If Elder decided to fight extradition, it would only be a matter of time before Locke had him "locked up," so to speak, in California.

The state's attorney in Volusia County would have to decide what to do about the rape cases against Elder. From an evidentiary standpoint, even though several girls would eventually claim victim status at the hands of Elder, only Debbie Farris's case was solidly backed up by physical evidence.

———

The detectives who executed the search warrants on Elder's residence and vehicle reported back to Gambrell. Elder had some pornography and enough condoms to open up a condom store, but they never found any real evidence of the rapes, no souvenirs of the crimes, or a calendar documenting every time he committed one.

Cindy Gambrell's phone started ringing soon after Elder's photo was published in the local newspaper. The calls were from county jail. Counting Debbie Farris, a total of nine women were now claiming to have been raped by Mark Elder. Over the next few days Gambrell conducted several interviews of women at the jail. If these new tales were taken to trial, defense attorneys and jurors would view them with skepticism. The logical question would be, "If you were raped, why did you wait until now to report it?" This question would be followed up by an accusatory question: "Isn't it true you never heard of Mark Elder or saw a likeness of him until his picture appeared in the paper?" Those were tough questions and a prosecutor would have difficulty overcoming them.

The sad truth was that some of the prostitutes *had* reported the crime to the various police agencies in the county. Sometimes the patrol officers heard the story and reportedly didn't do anything. After all, the complainant was a street hooker. Some cynical officers, even in this so-called age of sensitivity, still viewed a rape of a hooker as a civil dispute, more of a "failure to pay." It was like ordering a remodel job at your house and not being satisfied with the workmanship. The common remedy is not to pay until you are satisfied. It is not criminal to refuse to pay. It is a civil dispute that must be worked out between the parties, or decided by an arbitrator or judge in court. As time went on, Detective Gambrell never received reports from any other agencies regarding the rapes. That is a sad commentary on law enforcement in Volusia County.

The state's attorney in Florida decided to file Debbie Farris's sexual-battery charge against Elder to be used as a "safety net" in case something went awry with the California murder. Because murder carried a longer penalty, Florida would defer to California's legal system. Florida could always bring rape charges in the event that a problem arose with the murder case.

Ron Thill was in constant contact with his superiors in San Diego. The support staff in San Diego made notifications of Mark Elder's arrest to the family of Janet Moore. The members of the latter had moved all over the country in the last seventeen years. Some were incredulous because they thought the case would never be solved. Others nodded solemnly and said they knew an arrest would happen because they'd never given up hope. The family believed in Ron Thill and Jaime Bordine. The D.A.'s office cautioned Moore's family that the case was a long way from being over. The family had been patient for seventeen years. They had to remain patient a little longer.

To be perfectly blunt, Ron Thill asked no one in particular, "I wonder what this asshole has been doing for the past seventeen years?" The police didn't believe he'd killed someone a long time ago and only started raping within the last year. The detectives began to reconstruct his actions. The best way to do this was to contact Elder's family.

To start with, Elder's parents were still alive and living in nearby Orange City, Florida. They were understandably shocked beyond description. After some initial prodding, the parents did admit that Mark had experienced problems with the law in the past. He had served a few short stints behind bars, but nothing serious, according to them. Even though he was outside the law from time to time, Mark was never what one could call a "hardened criminal." Thill thought to himself, *He is now.*

By this time, Cindy Gambrell had completed her duties interviewing the parade of hookers at county jail. Years later she would admit that while she believed most of the girls claiming victim status, she also believed at least one was lying, for whatever reason. If the Florida rapes were ever prosecuted, those suspected of fabricating the stories would undergo thorough scrutiny.

Thill asked Elder's parents if Mark had ever been in San Diego, specifically in June of 1988. They said he met his ex-wife there, and lived in San Diego, but they were not sure when that was. Thill was satisfied to learn that Elder had been in San Diego. He now had to be able to prove he was in town when Janet Moore was murdered.

The parents painted a nice picture of Mark as a youth. Because he liked to ride motorcycles, the father bought several off-road bikes for him, his brother, and his sister. Mark had only a few friends. He didn't participate in any activities in high school. He had occasional brushes with the law. The parents were mystified at the murder charge. They did admit Mark claimed to have been abused as a child, an allegation they said was not true. They added that Mark blamed them (his parents) for his divorce. Mark's father said that allegation was ridiculous. Of all the untrue things Mark said, his blaming of the parents for his divorce seemed the most painful to them.

They admitted they had not spoken with Mark in over a year. After more questioning, the parents said Mark did not like his sister because he claimed she pushed his face in the snow when she was eight and he was six, while they were living in Pennsylvania. They did buy Mark a bus ticket to San Diego sometime in the late 1980s, but they could not remember exactly when.

Upon more questioning, the answers of the parents became shorter and contained fewer details. Detective Thill, sensing that they were putting up a wall, decided to move on and try talking to Elder's ex-wife.

On August 9, 2005, four days after Elder's arrest, Thill and Gambrell interviewed the ex-wife. She was a slight, shy, soft-spoken Filipina who was clearly ill at ease talking to the two officers who were accusing her ex-husband of rape, and worse. Mary* Elder explained that she had emigrated from the Philippines to San Diego. She met Mark in San Diego at a local church both attended. After a brief court-ship they married in August 1991. They had a son, Eric*, born in 1992. Mark worked for a local flooring company. He installed carpets and did various kinds of work on residential floors.

Thill asked Mary about the injury to Mark's hand. She explained that the hand was deformed, but fully healed, when they met in 1991. Thill nodded and wrote the information in his notebook. If Elder cut his hand in 1988 when his hand slid down the knife while he hacked and stabbed Janet Moore, it stood to reason that the actual exterior cut would be healed by 1991. So far, so good.

Mary continued her story, saying that they moved to Florida, where the rest of Mark's family lived, in 1993. They had resided in various places in Volusia County since then. When they moved to Florida they lived in a rental house owned by Mark's sister. Mary added that the sister,

Cathy Byrne, is a Florida Highway Patrol officer. Thill and Gambrell looked at each other, not saying anything. Mary supplied Byrne's address and phone number.

Mark and Mary divorced in 2004 after twelve years of marriage. Mary was reluctant to give details of why they divorced. She was shocked and had trouble believing the murder charge. The interview lasted seventy-eight minutes.

CHAPTER 25

Gambrell recalled that eight of the nine girls claiming to have been raped said the rapist drove a dark blue van. One of them, Gemma Johnson, said the rapist was driving a white Lincoln when he picked her up. The white Lincoln posed a major inconsistency to the detectives.

The inconsistency was cleared up the following day when Rodney Miller[*], a coworker of Elder's, phoned Detective Gambrell to volunteer information. Thill and Gambrell drove to his house in nearby DeLand, Florida.

Miller's wife sat in on the interview and made insightful contributions. She said Mark Elder always made her feel uncomfortable. Unfortunately, an "uncomfortable feeling" did not have enough evidentiary value to stand up in court. Rodney Miller told them that Elder treated his female flooring customers horribly. Thill asked for examples.

"Well," Miller said, "if the women were home alone, Mark would be very rude. He would call them 'cunts' and 'bitches' and 'stupid.' A lot of complaints about his work started coming in."

"You mean he would actually call a female customer who had hired him to do work in the house a cunt or a bitch to her face?" Thill couldn't believe his ears.

"Yes, he would. The quality of Mark's work was getting increasingly poor too. If there was a man in the house, Mark wouldn't be rude to the women, only if it was a woman alone. I had to go out to a lot of houses afterward and do damage control. I had to clean up Mark's messes. I'm surprised the business didn't go right down the tubes."

Miller said he sometimes rode to jobs with Mark. "I'd get in the van in the morning and see women's underwear. I'd ask him what the hell the underwear was doing there. He'd laugh and say something like, 'I got kinda freaky with this bitch last night. I had a hot one.' Then he'd laugh about it. Mark really creeped me out."

Thill and Gambrell were temporarily silent. Miller continued. "One morning Mark had a cut on his face. I asked where that came from. Mark just laughed and said things got freaky with some whore last night. It was really weird. He referred to all women as 'cunts,' 'bitches,' and 'whores.' He talked awful about women. I ain't no saint, but Mark was something else."

Miller told them when Mark ordered the purchase of his work van he insisted the van have no side or back windows. When Miller asked Elder why, Elder told him it was "for privacy."

"It was a work van, for Christ's sake. Why did he need privacy to carry a roll of carpet?" Miller asked rhetorically.

Miller also said Mark had ordered some work done on his van. During the time the van was gone, Elder borrowed a large white car from someone. Miller wasn't sure what kind, but thought it might have been a Lincoln. That bit of information gave credence to Gemma Johnson's claim.

As the conversation went on, it became clear that Rodney Miller did not want to testify. He had experienced problems of his own with law enforcement in the past. He said he would be embarrassed on the witness stand by Elder's defense attorney, who would have access to Miller's criminal record. Thill told him there were no guarantees about his testifying or not testifying. The prosecuting attorney would decide if what Miller had to say was important enough to the case. If the prosecutor opted for him to testify, the prosecutor could protect him somewhat, but the thing he had on his side was the truth.

"I sure hope I don't have to [testify]. I believe Mark was awful. But I don't want any defense attorney getting on my case either."

———————

Mark Elder, in spite of the evidence of the rape and murder against him, still posed a mystery. Why was he like he was? The detectives had interviewed his parents and ex-wife. The detectives didn't think any of them had been completely candid with them. Sometimes an ex-wife is an excellent source to "get the dirt" on someone. Especially in police work, "a woman scorned" scenario was valuable. In fact, ex-spouses frequently embellished a person's misdeeds and characterized them as worse than they were just for spite or revenge. The detectives believed that if Elder's parents and ex-wife weren't completely protecting him, they were not revealing their true feelings toward him and were protecting him, to a degree. Or maybe they were just embarrassed.

Mark Elder's sister was a law enforcement officer. His brother lived nearby in central Florida. It was time to talk with them.

Cathy Byrne, Mark's sister, had wanted to be a forest ranger and earned a degree in biology. Jobs for women in the ranger field, in the Florida area, were scarce. Cathy then became a dispatcher for the highway patrol. Later she entered the police academy and joined the Florida Highway Patrol as a trooper in 1983. During her career she had worked at several duty stations throughout the state. Cathy said that she was a year and a half older than Mark. The family started out in New Kensington, Pennsylvania, about thirty miles northeast of Pittsburgh.

The detectives asked her to comment on the parents' statement that Mark claimed he had been abused as a child, a claim the parents denied.

Byrne shook her head in exasperation. Her voice took on a sharp edge. "Mark thinking he was abused is such a load of crap. I've heard him say that before. He must be trying to put some kind of guilt trip on my parents. That's ridiculous."

Cathy Byrne said her father worked as a laborer in Pennsylvania. Their grandparents lived on the top floor of the family home. She said their family life was great. The parents were loving and generous. "Our life was like a Norman Rockwell painting," she said. "After Memorial Day there were constant picnics and family outings and camping, all the way to Labor Day. It was so much fun. Our house had a flurry of activity always. It was a gathering place for the neighborhood kids. We were together all the time. We got along great. Our life was idyllic. When we were in Pennsylvania and he was younger, Mark was generally okay. Just before his teen years he started changing. He had it in for me, though. I never quite figured out why."

What about the abuse claims? Byrne had no hesitation in calling Mark a liar. There was no abuse at all. She said her parents had always been good to her, Mark, and their younger brother, Matthew. When their father learned one of them had an interest in something, he would buy things to develop their interest.

For example, Mark expressed an interest in motorcycles. Cathy and Matthew also liked the bikes. Soon there were ten motorcycles in the garage of the home. All the kids rode the cycles. Their father encouraged them to learn about the machines and become proficient in fixing them. That didn't sound like abuse to the detectives.

Cathy said that Mark was just plain mean. His meanness went way beyond sibling rivalry. Cathy said one day when she was sitting alone in the family room reading a book, Mark walked by, stopped, and punched her right in the head. She had not spoken to Mark, or even looked at him. The blindside hit came out of nowhere and for no ostensible reason.

Cathy said when she told her parents about the unprovoked punching, they dismissed it, saying something like, "Come on, you two. Try to get along."

She said Mark eventually fabricated a scenario to explain why he didn't like her. She said he accused her of pushing his face in the snow one day when they were very young. Cathy said she never did this. Even if she had, that act would not have been enough to engender Mark's lifelong hatred of her.

In 1972, when Mark was fourteen, the family moved to Florida. The steel mill where the senior Elder worked closed and he took a job selling tools used by the National Aeronautics and Space Administration. Thill noted that this was high school age for Mark. He asked if Mark had participated in any school activities. Byrne said he didn't.

"What were his friends like?" Gambrell asked.

"He really didn't have what you would call friends. He had some guys he did drugs with, but I never thought of them as his friends. Mark might have thought they were friends. They were just a bunch of losers. Mark was never in any clubs at school, or sports. He never attended any games. He wasn't a part of anything except the drug stuff."

Detective Gambrell asked what kind of drugs he used. "Everything. He used marijuana and LSD when he was a kid. Later he went on to cocaine." For some reason Mark showed Cathy his private stash locations within the house. He would hide marijuana in the family's freezer.

Mark ridiculed his parents to Cathy. He told her they were so stupid that they couldn't figure out he used drugs and had hidden them inside the house, right under their noses. Cathy was repulsed by what Mark was doing and by his callous attitude. She was angry that Mark denigrated the parents. But since she was a teenager too, she didn't tattle on him. She said, "I probably should have told them. But you know how kids are. At that age there's a kind of an 'us against them' attitude. I never felt I was against my parents, but I kept Mark's drug involvement to myself. If I would have told them what Mark said about them, they wouldn't have believed me anyway and would have thought I was being spiteful."

Byrne said Elder was always an outsider. He had a mean streak that manifested itself in the way he talked about people. Mark believed he was smarter than everyone. Byrne said he didn't do well in school because he didn't think he needed to know anything those "idiots" were teaching him. Elder's language was foul. He called women "bitches" and "whores." Everyone else was a "loser" or an "asshole." Mark dropped out of school before graduating.

Regarding meanness, Gambrell asked if he was mean to animals. Cathy, the career police officer, knew where this was going. Many killers start off their lives of gratuitous violence by mutilating pets in the neighborhood. "Nope," she said. "As bad as he was, I never knew him to hurt any animals."

Cathy Byrne laughed once during her recounting of life with Mark. She said, "When we were younger we would play cops and robbers. Mark *always* wanted to be the robber. I always had to be the cop. I guess it was kind of prophetic."

The police were starting to form a picture of Mark Elder. Most of what Cathy Byrne told them would not be admissible in court, at least not during the prosecution's initial case. But the prosecutor needed to know the information she was giving. The prosecution needed to know everything there was to know about Elder. They didn't know what the defense might say about him. If the defense attorney tried to portray Elder as a good kid, active in youth organizations and helping the community, the information Cathy Byrne supplied could then be introduced to rebut the portrayal.

"The murder in San Diego happened in 1988," Ron Thill said to Byrne. "Since his DNA was at the crime scene, and we know he was there, we need to prove by even stronger evidence, and other means, he actually was in San Diego at that time. Your parents said he took the bus to San Diego around that general time, but they couldn't narrow it down to place his body there with certainty. Can you?"

"I sure can," Byrne offered. "This story gets kind of long." She said that Mark's use of drugs continued well after high school. He had minor arrests and spent short stints in jail. It came to light that Mark had a warrant for his arrest on a felony theft or fraud charge. Mark was around thirty years old and not living with his parents. The neighbors knew Mark had warrants. When they saw him around the family home, they would call the police. The police would come by looking for him. By the time they arrived, he was always gone.

Mark's parents didn't like the police knocking on their door all the time. Cathy told them they had to convince Mark to turn himself in to get the warrants cleared. That was the only way the police would stop bothering them. How hard the parents tried to convince Mark to give himself up was not clear.

Cathy tried to make her position stronger. She told her parents that they were subject to arrest for harboring a fugitive. They were putting themselves in jeopardy by allowing Mark to hang around the house. She couldn't help adding that Mark was not worth going to jail for.

In early June 1988, Cathy was on her way to a mandated

law enforcement training seminar. When she stopped by her parents' house, Mark was there. They had a family meeting, during which Cathy laid the facts out to all of them, Mark included. She chided Mark for putting the parents at risk. "How can you put your own parents through this?" she asked. Mark merely shrugged and smirked at her when the parents were not looking. Cathy told him he had to leave or she was going to personally see to it that he was arrested.

The parents asked Mark, if he could go anywhere in the entire United States, where he would like to go? After thinking about it awhile, he said he wanted to go to San Diego. The parents said they would give him a hundred dollars. But they had done that before and Mark didn't go where he said he was going. He'd simply cash in the bus ticket and keep the rest of the money for drugs.

This time the parents said they would buy him a bus ticket to San Diego and make sure he was aboard when the bus left the station. Once he was in San Diego, he would contact them and they would wire him the rest of the money. This way they would be absolutely certain he was in San Diego.

Cathy consulted her training certificates to verify the date. She said Mark climbed on the bus to San Diego on a Monday or Tuesday, around the fifth or sixth of June. Mark arrived in San Diego on a Thursday or Friday. Janet Moore was murdered on June 11, a Saturday. The detectives took note that they could now put Mark Elder in San Diego at the time Janet Moore was murdered. If they had to, the parents could testify that they wired him the money after he landed in San Diego. Cathy could testify about the date when her class was held, and verify the date when her brother got on the bus. Things were looking better for the detectives.

The detectives wondered what Mark did after the murder. Cathy said she thought he hitchhiked to Long Beach, where he was promptly arrested. "Arrested for what?" Gambrell asked.

Byrne explained that she didn't know the exact truth because you could never get the exact truth from Mark. She thought the arrest was for extortion. Mark claimed to have "found" a wallet. He called the owner and offered to return the wallet in exchange for a hundred dollars. "Ever the Good Samaritan," Thill said. Byrne smiled and continued her story.

The man who had lost his wallet called the police and related Mark's phone call. Undercover officers concealed themselves in the vicinity of the wallet exchange. Instead of meeting the owner of the lost wallet, Mark met a cop, and was arrested. After the police took him into custody, a record check revealed the warrant that had caused him to leave Florida in the first place. Mark fought extradition back to Florida, but eventually had to return. Cathy thought he had done a little time in jail before going to a halfway house.

Once his debts to society were paid, Mark decided to return to California sometime in 1989. He continued to live in that state, where he learned skills in the flooring trade. He met and married Mary in August 1991. Their son was born about a year later. In 1993, Mark, Mary, and their son, Eric, moved back to Florida.

———

Cathy recounted how tragedy struck her personally. Her son had been killed in the aftermath of a tornado. She was working as a highway patrol officer and trying to deal with her personal grief. When she heard Mark and Mary and the baby were moving to Florida, she offered to rent them a home she owned. She wanted to give them a bargain because of Mary and the baby, but not because of Mark.

While waiting for Mark and his family to arrive, Cathy spent her free time fixing up the house in Deltona. She said she painted the exterior a pretty green and yellow. When Mark first saw the house he asked, "Where the hell did you get that ugly green paint, at the army-surplus store?" Cathy said Mary seemed embarrassed by his attitude and lack of class.

———————

Shortly after Mark's family arrived in Florida, Mark told his mother that he didn't want Cathy and her giving Mary any of their "women's lib ideas." He wanted to keep Mary pliable and subservient. Mark's mother was hardly a women's libber. Given her profession, Cathy might be called one, but only to the extent that she stood up for herself.

The family thought very highly of Mary and Eric. They cringed when Mark abused Mary verbally. Cathy said, "I knew exactly what Mark was thinking when he married Mary. He wanted a subservient foreign-born wife he could order around and do anything he wanted without consequence. He wanted a wife who would be afraid to stand up to him and make him accountable for what he did. Mary was nice, sweet, and shy. She was exactly what he wanted. We all tried to look out for her."

After Mark moved back to Florida, Cathy saw him frequently at family gatherings. He continued to verbally abuse everyone, including her. She said she learned that Mark used the services of street prostitutes. Mary just kept taking it and taking it. While Mary did not like his actions, she accepted them, apparently as her lot in life.

Cathy said one time Mark picked up a prostitute. For some inexplicable reason he drove her to a remote road near a local jail, or maybe it was a prison. An off-duty guard was leaving the facility in his private vehicle. He heard the woman in Mark's van hollering. When the guard approached, Mark took off at a high rate of speed. The officer gave chase while giving details to the police from his cell phone. He pursued Mark through the Daytona Beach area, involving several cities. Finally Mark stopped the car when he was surrounded by police officers in marked cars.

When a Florida Highway Patrol officer approached him, Mark said, "Do you know my sister, Cathy?"

When the officer phoned Cathy, she told him to do whatever he needed to do to Mark. She said, "If you're accusing him of something, he's probably guilty."

The woman, a previously convicted, and obvious prostitute, had signs of physical abuse. She refused to make a criminal complaint against Mark. Neither Mark nor the hooker knew the other's name, but they told the police they were friends. Because the corrections officer had a jacket over his uniform, and was in his private vehicle, the authorities could not charge Mark with evading a police officer. Mark would merely say he was trying to get away from someone who was attempting to harm him. Cathy said this was just one more instance when Mark thwarted the law and got away with it.

———————

Cathy said she was the only one in the family who was willing to confront Mark. She didn't do it constantly, only when she couldn't take his antics any longer, or when his antics were over the top. It was as if everyone was scared of him. Mark was short and heavy, not athletic or very strong. He was not an accomplished fighter, more of a bully of the weak. He had a mean, lying mouth and a nasty personality. Cathy tried to avoid him as much as possible. More than once when the family was together, and the others were distracted, Mark would get up close to Cathy and whisper, "I hate you."

Cathy would smile and say back, "And the same for you."

One time at a family gathering, Mark said, "Cathy, everyone forgives me except you. Why can't you ever forgive me for things?"

Cathy said, "Don't mistake the family's reaction to what you do as forgiveness. It isn't. They're just putting up with you."

"I need *everyone* behind me for forgiveness."

"You need more than to be forgiven," Cathy said.

The truth was an unknown commodity for Mark, according to Cathy. Once, when his parents were out of town, he brought a prostitute over to their house. He tied her up and had his way with her. During the "festivities" he broke an antique end table. Mark even invited some friends over to the house to go at it with the woman. A few did, but even most of Mark's low-life friends were too repulsed to participate.

When the parents came home days later, they asked what had happened to the valuable table. With a straight face Mark told them, "I tripped over it in the dark. Sorry."

The truth came to light accidentally when Mark's mother had an appointment to get some work done. The woman who was going to help her had a son about Mark's age, and the son had told his mother about the tied-up hooker and the broken table. The son had declined to participate in the gang bang of the woman. When Mark's mother heard what really happened to the table and the surrounding circumstances, she said only, "Oh dear."

If she did confront Mark with the story she had heard, no one ever knew. Cathy Byrne said Mark's reaction to an accusation was predictable. He would always deny it, the denial accompanied by a profanity-laced accusation of the unreliability of the "asshole" who told his mother the story. The denial would be followed up with, "I don't know what the hell you're talking about, and neither do you."

No one knows if the hooker reported the incident. No one believes she was ever paid for what she went through, or if she had agreed to be tied up when she made the deal with Mark.

CHAPTER 26

According to his sister, Cathy, Mark could do whatever he wanted in his marriage. She said Mark planned it that way. Mary was subservient nearly all the time. Maybe her attitude was cultural, or maybe it was part of her shy and accommodating personality. Mark often left in the middle of the night and did not come home until early morning. No one knew where he went, or what he did.

No one knows what *really* went on behind closed doors in the Mark and Mary Elder household. Mary wasn't one to complain, but others just knew life was not good for her. Friends and visitors saw how Mark demeaned his wife all the time. They could only imagine how he treated her with no witnesses around.

After Mark was involved in the police chase that wasn't really a police chase—because the authorities couldn't prove in court that the corrections officer wearing the jacket over his uniform really was a law enforcement officer—Mary put her foot down and made Mark move from the house.

This arrangement was somewhat tricky and awkward

because Mark and Mary were living directly across the street from Mark's parents. While the parents often appeared to overlook Mark's faults, they never took his side when it came to Mark and Mary's relationship. They never abandoned Mary either. They always supported her emotionally when anything went wrong, and things were always going wrong. During the time Mark was out of the home, the family helped Mary out.

Although Mark managed to beg his way back home within a short time. Mary, in a surprising show of strength, insisted he live in another portion of the house. She was empowered by her newfound resilience and made sure Mark stayed away from her, even though he was still within their four walls.

Mark tried to worm his way back into Mary's life. He was, at least temporarily, kind, thoughtful, and didn't display any of the antagonistic behavior that had become his trademark.

One day Mark's model behavior changed. Maybe he was getting tired of being restricted within his own house. Maybe he didn't like having his actions dictated by a *woman,* and a Filipina at that.

Mary returned from a morning shopping trip. The couple exchanged words about an unknown subject. He grabbed her by the shoulders. No one knew what was said because Mary never told. Mark turned her around so her back was to him. He maneuvered her into a corner, pushing himself against her into the wall. His arms encircled her head and neck. The crushing pressure caused her to try to free herself. When her strength was insufficient to break his hold, she bit him on the arm. Mark let her loose, probably calling her the usual string of profanities he regularly applied to women.

A short time later his father came to the house and had Mary and Eric come across the street to stay with them. The parents knew something was not right, but, as was their custom, they did not pry. In their hearts they knew if there was trouble between Mark and Mary, it was Mark's fault. If Mary wanted to let them know what had happened, she would tell them in due time. The day proceeded without further incident. Mary and Eric were quieter than usual. Mark stayed home across the street and Mary remained at her in-laws' house.

About six hours after the physical confrontation, there was a knock on the door of the parents' house. Mark was polite and charming. He asked Mary to come home and cook his dinner. Later Mary would acknowledge that this was a big mistake on her part. Her words were, "Fool, me. I went and prepared his dinner." She also said she was expecting some family members to stay at their house. She told Mark that after her family concluded their visit, she was filing for divorce.

Mark left the room. Within the hour, two Orange City police officers stood shoulder to shoulder at the front door. They spoke briefly with Mark, then handcuffed Mary and took her to jail. Mark had decided to press charges for domestic violence. It is not known what he told the officers. But he had a single bite mark on the back of his arm. Although the bite did not break the skin, there was still a visible mark.

Of course Mary was bewildered and speechless with shame. People who knew her doubted she had ever even committed a traffic violation, certainly not wittingly. For her to be booked into county jail on a domestic-violence charge was unthinkable.

The court appointed a public defender to represent her. Mark showed up at Mary's arraignment carrying a Bible. Fortunately, the deputy state's attorney was a woman who was familiar with domestic violence. After a quick conference with the public defender, the prosecutor dismissed the charges. She knew that when a woman delivers a single bite at that particular angle on a man's arm, it is more often than not in an effort to escape from a choke hold.

Mary was now a free woman. Mark would laugh at her and ridicule her for getting arrested. Mary never brought up the fact that the charges had been dismissed because the authorities believed her and not him.

Mark began staying home from work and eventually lost his job. This meant the loss of his health insurance. Cathy said Mary didn't feel well much of the time and began exhibiting signs of serious illness. She developed a tumor that kept growing. As a housewife, she had no health insurance independent of her husband. Without treatment, Cathy said Mary's condition continued to worsen. The rest of the family watched her deteriorate.

Mark would work occasionally. But he never worked enough to qualify for benefits. The money he earned was just sufficient to keep the family off public assistance. Mary couldn't even show up at the hospital and claim to be a ward of the county.

After several months of wrangling within the house, Mary finally decided she had to do something or risk dying. She calculated their assets again and found she was eligible for public assistance. She presented herself at the county hospital for examination. Within a few days the tumor was removed and she eventually regained her health. Mark immediately went back to work full-time. Some family members believed that he was indirectly trying to kill Mary by not qualifying for health insurance. As long as they kept her from getting the care she needed, the tumor would continue to grow and Mary's health would continue to deteriorate. The family's theory was that Mark expected her to die and then he'd be free of her.

Cathy knew that Mark's use of street prostitutes posed a health problem for everyone in the family. She insisted that

Mary and Mark be tested for sexually transmitted diseases and hepatitis. She wanted Mary, Mark, Eric, and even her parents to be tested for hepatitis. A major argument ensued, and Mark eventually consented to be tested. The results were that Mark and Mary were positive for hepatitis.

Later Cathy said, "I was sure that Mark was harming lots of women. I suspected he had even killed someone. His behavior was so violent. I was trying to figure out what to do. I even thought of going to the local police and giving them my DNA. I knew that siblings had similar DNA. Even though the DNA wouldn't be exact, it would be close enough to at least point back to me if there were a positive DNA on an open homicide. If my DNA was close to the killer in an open case, I could direct them to Mark. I never did it, though. I guess I was too embarrassed. I didn't know for sure he had killed anyone, but I figured he probably had. I just didn't have any proof. I was embarrassed and frustrated."

Cathy Byrne had it out with Mark several times. She told him she did not want to associate with him. She said she would put up with him at family gatherings for the sake of the family, but she wanted him to stay away from her within the house.

Her last contact with Mark had occurred in 1999. She told him, "I'm a ghost to you."

Mark's brother, Matthew, was slightly younger. They were close enough in age to hang with some of the same friends. Matthew admitted to smoking marijuana with Mark and his friends. He said Mark used harder drugs too.

Matthew said Mark's nickname in high school had been "Microdot." The term referred to hits of the drug LSD, which was sold on sheets of paper dotted with the drug.

Mark took so much LSD that the stoners who hung around with him gave him that name. He seemed to be proud of his drug use and nickname.

Matthew said something had happened that made him decide early on not to use hard drugs. He said one of Mark's friends was loaded on drugs one day. The friend wanted a marijuana joint that Matthew had. He offered to trade Matthew a motorcycle in exchange for the joint. According to Matthew, the bike was worth about $300. Matthew gave the guy the joint and the guy gave him the bike. Matthew said, "Right then and there I decided that if hard drugs did that to your mind"—that is, caused you to make such bad decisions—"I didn't want any part of it. I never did hard drugs. I quit marijuana a little while after that too."

Another time Matthew said the family was missing one of their ten motorcycles. "It just disappeared. Someone stole it." He said the bike had a distinctive gas tank. There was an oval advertising sticker on the tank. A short time later Matthew saw an identical tank on one of Mark's friends' motorcycles. There was an adhesive design on the tank in the shape of the missing sticker. It looked like someone had removed the sticker. When Matthew told Mark about the tank, Mark said he was mistaken, that it wasn't their motorcycle.

Matt said, "I know Mark sold him the motorcycle, probably for drugs, and then said someone stole it. Mark denied the bike was ours too quickly. It was too close of a match for him to say right away that it wasn't ours. It was our bike."

Another time Matthew said someone stole several items from their parents. The thief took coins and guns and food. Mark's dad visited several pawnshops in the area. Matthew said his dad found the guns at the pawnshop. The owner showed him that Mark had pawned the items. In spite of this overwhelming evidence, Mark denied taking the items, or pawning them. "You're just spaced out," he said to his dad. Surprisingly, the parents never had a serious confrontation with Mark over the theft. Matthew is convinced Mark pawned the items to get money for drugs.

———————

Matthew confirmed that Mark used the services of prostitutes. He sheepishly admitted that he was with Mark a couple of times when they both picked up the same prostitute.

It was a good thing that Matthew was along—good for the prostitutes, anyway. He said Mark used to make a deal with the hookers, have sex with them, not pay them, sometimes beat them, and usually throw them out of the vehicle without clothes. Matthew told Mark, "Why do you have to do that, Mark? Don't hit them. Give them their money and clothes." He said Mark told him all the women were bitches. When Matthew was with him, Mark did not hit them or toss them out of the vehicle naked. But he still didn't pay them.

One time Mark and Matthew picked up a street hooker. They took her up to a property where a private water company was located. It was a weekend and no workers were there. There was a small pavilion with a few picnic tables on the grounds. Workers often took their lunch breaks in the pavilion during the week.

Some of Mark's friends knew he would be going up there with a woman. While he was there, several of the men joined him and had sex with the woman. After they were done, Mark put the woman back in the van and took off. Matthew said Mark planned to beat her and toss her out without her clothes. Matthew said, "Mark, don't do that. She didn't do anything to you. Give her the clothes." Matthew's intervention saved the woman a beating, and allowed her to retain her clothing. Matthew said he didn't think the woman was paid.

Matthew said Mark would say, "Those stupid bitches won't report anything [like beatings or not being paid]. They're nothing but cunts. No one will believe them." Then he would laugh. Matthew said that was the final time he accompanied Mark to get a woman.

One time Mark's son, Eric, was doing homework at the kitchen table. The study session was not going well. He was avoiding completing his assignment. Mary was quizzing Eric on what he had read. For whatever reason, Eric was not retaining the contents of the chapter. Becoming short on patience, Mary tossed the book back to Eric, telling him to read the chapter again and to remember what was in it. Eric wasn't looking, and the book struck him in the upper lip, leaving a small mark.

Mark came into the room and saw the discoloration on Eric's upper lip. When asked, Eric said his mom had tossed a book at him. Mark smiled and left the room. Soon the police knocked on their door. The police looked at the lip, spoke with Eric and Mary, then left without doing anything. They said it was not child abuse. They told Eric to read the chapter more closely. Mark's attempt to portray Mary as an abuser failed just like the contrived domestic-violence case he manufactured.

Eventually, Mary found the strength to divorce Mark. No one knows where the strength came from, but the family was happy when she filed and followed through.

After the divorce Mark had the audacity to take young Eric around the neighborhood with him. He presented the neighbors with a petition saying that Mary was an unfit mother and that a family-court judge should award custody of Eric to Mark. It is believed that not one person signed the petition. The neighbors knew what Mark was like, and assumed the petition was an attempt to avoid paying child support.

Although the family members were upset when Mark and Mary divorced, they also felt some measure of relief. The parents hated that Mark and Mary had admitted defeat, yet an end to Mary's sufferings was welcomed. She would no longer have to worry about Mark demeaning her. She wouldn't have to worry about his midnight forays, the unexplained scratches on his face. She wouldn't ask questions of Mark only to be told, "None of your business."

The divorce became final in December 2004. Family members were especially grateful that neither Mary nor Eric was living in the house when it was searched by the police after Mark became a murder suspect. Having officers invade one's house and meticulously go over every inch is very unsettling, even when they are legally entitled to perform the search.

What Mary didn't know about before the divorce was the $50,000-plus credit card debt Mark had accumulated during the marriage. He hadn't paid off any of it at the time of his August 2005 arrest.

The family did not pry into Mary's finances. She subsequently obtained training and landed a steady job in a professional field. It is unknown if the credit card company forgave any part of the debt, or how much of it accrued after the divorce. Mary is now gainfully employed and seems to be happy.

Young Eric became a normal teenager, if that was possible given his childhood. He enjoys the usual activities associated with a boy his age. Both Mary and Eric carry the knowledge of the crimes perpetrated by the man who lived with them for so many years. While it is necessary to forget most of Mark's misdeeds, it is also important to learn from them and try somehow to turn them into an advantage, if that is also possible.

San Diego authorities extradited Mark Elder back to San Diego shortly after his arrest. Florida prosecutors filed charges of sexual battery but later held them in abeyance pending the outcome of California's legal dealings with Elder.

CHAPTER 27

While the citizens, especially the street prostitutes, of Volusia County, Florida, could rest easier because a serial rapist was securely housed in jail, there was no rest in store for California prosecutor Andrea Freshwater. The mystery of "who did it" was solved. What remained to be done was the most important part: making sure the case was proven beyond a reasonable doubt, and a dangerous person was eliminated from society for as long as legally possible.

Freshwater went over the thick casebook documenting all the work the San Diego police had done in 1988 and the years that followed. She studied the police reports that had been generated in Florida. Strangely, the only rape reported to the authorities immediately after it happened was that of Debbie Farris. One of the other girls claimed she had contacted police, but the report had not surfaced.

In looking over the case, Freshwater did what all good prosecutors and cops do when conducting an in-depth assessment of the facts: she looked at the possible dangers, weaknesses, and pitfalls instead of the strong points. There is no point in dwelling on the pluses. They are self-evident. You must be able to recognize where your case is vulnerable. Once you know the weaknesses in your case, you can deal with them.

Andrea Freshwater was born in Sacramento, California. Her father worked as an aeronautical engineer. Following declines in the industry, her family moved to the central valley of California and took over a family farm. Andrea had worked all her life. She enrolled at California State University Stanislaus, in Turlock, just north of Fresno off of Interstate 99. When she earned her Bachelor of Science degree in sociology and criminal justice, her goal was to be a probation officer. She'd always had an interest in law enforcement. Andrea's father was adamant and vocal in his position that Andrea not work as a police officer.

Andrea is a slim, attractive woman who would probably have made an excellent investigator, but did not have the physical size or presence to become a patrol officer. (The concept of physical attributes required to be an effective patrol officer can be debated, but not here.) When Andrea consulted Stanislaus County job information sources about joining the probation department, she learned she would have to serve as a volunteer for two years. She couldn't handle the financial implications of that. "I was born with a plastic spoon in my mouth, not a silver spoon," Andrea was fond of saying. "I needed a job that paid."

So she enrolled in the McGeorge School of Law at the University of the Pacific in Sacramento. Upon graduation and while awaiting results of the California Bar, Andrea worked for the Riverside County District Attorney's Office. When she learned she had passed the bar exam, she applied for a job with, and was hired in February 1990 by, the office of Edwin L. Miller Jr., the then San Diego district attorney. Miller is an avuncular gentleman who, although twelve years out of office, still considers people he hired as family.

Years later a writer asked Freshwater what her hobbies were. "I had three children very close together, and I work. Those girls keep me busy." Andrea's husband, Ken, is a supervising investigator for the San Diego district attorney.

As Freshwater continued to pore over the case before her, she looked at the facts the same way a defense attorney would. That is, how would she attack the case if she were on the other side? What openings existed, either provided by mistakes the police made, or inherent in the case itself? She would have to head off problems and plug any openings the defense would exploit.

She had the defendant's blood and semen at Janet Moore's crime scene. She had a right-handed defendant with horribly disfigured fingers on his right hand, probably from his hand sliding down the knife blade when he repeatedly stabbed Janet Moore. In Florida, she had a single prostitute with Elder's semen in her. Together, that evidence was not bad, but how could it be overcome by the defense? She started to construct scenarios in her head.

A good hypothetical story that Elder might tell was that he went to Janet Moore's apartment to have consensual sex (a male defendant seldom admits paying for sex). The scenario would be that "something happened" in the form of some kind of argument in Moore's apartment after the sex and Janet Moore attacked Elder with a knife she had in her apartment. (No one ever found the weapon used to murder Janet Moore.) Elder would say he merely defended himself against the knife-wielding woman, and "just snapped," as they say.

The next thing he knew he was kneeling over her body, frantically plunging the knife into her. When he came to his senses and realized what he was doing, he stopped. When he regained control of himself, he discovered he had been seriously wounded during the ordeal, probably raising his hand trying to deflect one of Janet's knife thrusts. He was afraid the police would never believe he was trying to save his own life. So, in a panic, he fled without notifying anyone.

Not bad, as far as defenses went. A jury, or one juror, *might* buy it. As for the Florida cases, the defense's possible explanations about the so-called rapes by Elder would be easier. They would go like this: He had consensual sex with a woman who never asked for money until it was over. When he refused to pay (probably because he had never paid for it in his life), she got mad and cried rape. Both Mark and the hooker had participated in a mutually enjoyable sexual experience before the greedy woman demanded pay. Elder would look at the woman demanding money from him as a blackmailer, and himself as the victim. Naturally, semen would be left behind. They had consensual sex, remember? Mark would insist there was one victim: Mark Elder, the victim of blackmail.

Freshwater also knew that an additional problem existed that would have to be confronted. The victims had been prostitutes. Andrea had been in town back in the nineties when artists with grants from the National Endowment for the Arts had decried the San Diego police for not caring when harm came to a prostitute. Possessing a degree in sociology, Freshwater knew it was not the police in particular who lacked sympathy for women who get in strangers' cars and have sex for money. It was society in general, the same society whose members would sit on a jury.

From the aspect of physical evidence, Freshwater was in good shape. Prosecutors love to have DNA in the forms of blood and semen. But in terms of potential reasonable defenses and explanations for that evidence, she knew she had a tough fight ahead.

Freshwater painstakingly looked over the crime-scene photos. She noted again the presence of the defendant's blood dripping down the front of the dresser drawers. David Cornacchia, the DNA expert from the San Diego police, went over the photos with her to make sure she was in full possession of the facts. If Elder testified in this case, and it would seem he would have to testify, Freshwater could ask him why he ransacked Moore's apartment after the killing. Elder couldn't say he was looking for something to stop the bleeding because he already had found the washcloth in the bathroom.

Also, the blood smears on Janet's body looked like someone had "finger-painted" on her stomach and breasts. That thought sickened Freshwater. She firmly believed she was dealing with a sick person in Mark Elder.

What do murderers, robbers, thieves, child molesters, panty sniffers, and con artists look like? Cops and prosecutors always wonder before they lay eyes on the people they hunt, arrest, and prosecute. It would be easy if all killers were square-jawed, muscular, stubble-chinned, glowering guys with their hands hanging down almost to their knees.

How convenient for an indecent-exposure specialist to be an emaciated, unshaven, bug-eyed guy wearing the traditional trench coat when he was apprehended at a playground or outside an elementary school.

The con artist, if provided by central casting, would be perfectly coiffed, manicured, and groomed, wearing a suit and an expensive pinkie ring, while sporting a confidence-winning smile.

It doesn't work that way. Crooks come in all shapes and sizes. In Judge David Szumowski's Department 12 Felony Arraignment Court, where Mark Elder was arraigned, you could spend all morning trying to match defendants' physical appearance with their crimes when they walk into the tank. You'd seldom be correct. Anyone is capable of anything, and accused crooks look like regular people, no matter what their alleged offense.

The Office of the Public Defender assigned attorney Robert L. Ford to represent Mark Elder. Ford graduated from the University of San Diego Law School in 1996 and was admitted to the California Bar Association shortly there-after. He had a reputation as a competent, thorough, hard-fighting attorney. His intelligence, imagination, and resourcefulness were valuable to someone who defended people who were usually factually guilty. It was Ford's job to make sure the prosecution proved all the allegations made against his client.

Whether or not Elder was factually guilty was not a con-cern to Ford. His job as a public defender was to make the district attorney prove that all of his clients were *legally* guilty, and there was a big difference between the two. He wanted to make sure the state proved its case based on solid evidence.

Robert Ford came to the practice of law in a circuitous way. He was born in Redding, California, in the northern part of the state, but his family moved to the Sacramento area when he was a youngster. Ford did his undergraduate work, majoring in biology, at the University of California Davis, near Sacramento, one of the top science schools in the state.

The study of law was far from Ford's mind. He began working in the cardiopulmonary field, eventually ending up in San Diego. Soon he became a licensed respiratory-care technician and practitioner. His mother became an attor-ney late in life. His brother and sister were both attorneys. One Thanksgiving, the family was conversing in "lawyer-ese" or "lawyerspeak" and Ford felt left out. His mother told him the best way to get into the loop was to become a lawyer too. She said that Robert seemed to have more apti-tude in the area than his siblings.

Robert didn't make the leap quickly, though. He knew the work he did at hospitals, and with patients, and with research, was valuable. But he also knew that insurance companies were balking at some of the things they had to pay for in the pulmonary business. A team of "management study people" (read "hatchet men") visited the hospital regularly and wrote reports. Ford knew his days were numbered. Even though he was doing good work, he was making too much money in the eyes of the management types. The administration was looking for ways to get the things he worked on done more economically.

So, at the age of thirty-nine, Robert Ford entered law school. His mother turned out to have been right. He did seem to have an aptitude for law. The precision he employed while doing studies on lungs and breathing was the same precision he used to dissect complex legal arguments and theories and put them into practice.

While still in law school, Ford worked for the San Diego public defender, participating in a "clinical rotation." He toiled in all areas of the public defender's office and believed he'd found a home.

After passing the bar, he did misdemeanor trials for about three years. His formal training as a defender of felonies started on the ominous day of September 11, 2001. Soon, Ford was defending all kinds of felonies, mostly auto theft, possession and sale of drugs, and an occasional robbery.

He "second-chaired" a couple of homicide cases. This is a common practice, both in the district attorney's office and the public defender's, where a newcomer sits in on the trial, watches, and learns. He may cross-examine a minor witness or two, and perform some legwork for the first-chair attorney.

Mark Elder was his first solo flight in the world of defending murder. Ford was asked how it came to be that he was picked for the case. He said the case was a difficult one to defend because of the overwhelming evidence. This fact alone suggested the likelihood of a conviction. Because defending Mark Elder was such an uphill battle, Ford would suffer no diminishment of professional stature if the jury convicted Elder. If Ford earned a not-guilty verdict, he would be a hero in the office.

Mark Elder's physical appearance was not that of a vicious killer who stabbed women, or of a nasty rapist who beat, choked, and cursed women before kicking them naked out of his van. If he were standing behind you in line at Home Depot buying a box of nails or some lightbulbs, you wouldn't take a second look at him. He stood about five feet eight inches tall. He had stringy black hair and a pronounced paunch. He did not have a menacing look about him. In fact, he looked rather vulnerable when Judge Szumowski read the charges to him. Because of the seriousness of the charges, no bail was set.

CHAPTER 28

A preliminary hearing was scheduled for November, only three months after authorities brought Elder to California. Fortunately, Freshwater only had to put on a "bare bones" presentation at the hearing. In California, the prosecution has to prove two things at a preliminary hearing:

1. That a crime was committed, and
2. There is probable cause to believe that the defendant committed the offense.

While not being overly confident, Freshwater knew the preliminary hearing would be a "walk-through." She knew the judge would not dismiss the case for a lack of evidence, even though she planned only to put on a portion of it. The defense would get a peek at her case. Because a defense attorney rarely presents a defense at a prelim, she wouldn't have any idea how the public defender would handle Mark Elder. She wished the public defender would plead him guilty. No such luck.

The preliminary hearing was held November 15, 2005, in the courtroom of the Honorable Leo Valentine, himself a well-respected former deputy district attorney. The first order of business was for Judge Valentine to hear a "Marsden motion" from the defendant, Mark Elder.

Simply put, a Marsden motion (*People v. Marsden* (1970) 2 Cal. 3d 118) is a vehicle whereby a defendant can get rid of his court-appointed attorney. The court must give the defendant the opportunity to tell the judge why he wants to relieve the attorney so the judge can make a sensible decision about the matter.

The reasons a defendant may want his or her attorney replaced are many. A defendant may allege improper actions by the attorney. The defendant may believe there is a bias or a conflict, real or perceived, or anything that a judge might think could disqualify a particular attorney from defending someone. No one knows what goes on inside the room during a Marsden hearing, and the deputy district attorney is not allowed in the judge's chambers during it. When the parties emerged from Judge Valentine's chambers, Robert Ford was still the attorney of record for Mark Elder.

While Freshwater didn't know exactly what went on, she did know that if there was a Marsden hearing, there was trouble in the opposition's camp. Trouble for them wouldn't be a bad thing for her—dissension on the opposing team is usually a good thing. Over the years, Freshwater had had victims angry with her for whatever reason, although she tried very hard to get along and communicate with them. Because the conflict was between the accused and his attorney, Freshwater couldn't help but smile, just a little.

The preliminary hearing continued after Elder's failed attempt to have Robert Ford replaced. Andrea Freshwater put on the evidence in a straightforward manner. There was no need to put on her "game face" without a jury present. Judge Valentine and Robert Ford had been through the drill many times before. The prelim was simply for the record, to establish that a crime had been committed and to show reasonable cause that Elder had committed it.

Freshwater put on only two witnesses, Detective Ron Thill and SDPD forensic chemist David Cornacchia. Hearsay is not allowed in trials, but is permitted in preliminary hearings. Because of this, Thill could "speak" for others whose personal testimony would be required at trial.

Ron Thill told about his experience investigating homicides. He described the crime scene and autopsy. Robert Ford made a big deal out of the fact that Deputy Medical Examiner John Eisele did not testify. Thill explained that he had retired from county service and was not available now. Eisele would be there for the trial. Thill's testimony was accepted.

David Cornacchia told briefly about DNA and the astounding numbers that linked Mark Elder to the blood on the washcloth and the semen taken from Janet Moore's vagina.

Ford made an objection here and there, but he knew the judge was going to bind Elder over for a trial. That's when the bare-knuckles fight would begin. To the surprise of no one, Mark Elder was held to stand trial for the June 11, 1988, murder of Janet Moore. The trial was scheduled for June 2006.

Public defender Robert Ford sprang into action almost immediately. He scheduled an evidentiary hearing for February 9, 2006. Ford's strategy was clear. He wanted to attack the validity of the traffic stop of Mark Elder by Officer Jason Kilker back in July, a few weeks before Elder's arrest. Because Elder's DNA was found on the marijuana cigarette butt, and the DNA subsequently tied Elder to the California murder, if Ford could get the traffic stop thrown out, a significant part of the prosecution's case would be gone, at least temporarily. The legal proceedings, called a 1538.5 Evidence Code Hearing, was held in front of the Honorable Kerry Wells, herself a well-respected former prosecutor. Now she was a well-respected, knowledgeable, and fair jurist.

Officer Jason Kilker flew in from Daytona Beach to participate in the questioning by Andrea Freshwater and the subsequent grilling from Robert Ford. Prosecutor Freshwater walked Kilker through the initial building-block procedure. Kilker, at the time of the stop, had been a police officer for three years. In step-by-step fashion Kilker laid out the chronology of events. He said Detective Cindy Gambrell contacted him a few months before the July traffic stop. Gambrell related that a man driving a blue van was an active rapist of prostitutes in the beach area. Not only that, but the DNA of the unknown rapist was tied to an old California homicide. Kilker said Gambrell had told him the guy might have tools in the back of the van associated with carpet installation.

Kilker related that he saw a blue van in a high-prostitution area in the very early morning hours. The van seemed to be meandering instead of actually going to a destination. Kilker pulled in behind the vehicle and relayed the license plate to the dispatcher, asking for an ownership record on the plate, and if the registration was current. Within moments the dispatcher informed him that the plate had expired. That was step one in having probable cause.

Kilker pulled the van over and spoke to the driver, Mark Elder. Elder was able to tell him he had inadvertently switched plates with one of his other vehicles. Kilker pointed out the annual tag did not belong on the plate, no matter if the fees had been paid or not. Judge Wells listened attentively from the bench. Kilker pointed out that the numbers on the stick-on tag did not coincide with those on the license plate.

Next, Kilker *asked* Elder if he could search his vehicle. Kilker did the asking in such a way that caused Ford to get his weapons ready for his turn at questioning the young police officer. Kilker said, "You don't have anything illegal in there, do you?"

When Elder said no, Kilker asked, "Is it okay to search?" Elder then said, "Okay, but make it quick."

After Kilker related that verbal exchange, he told the court what he found in the van, including the marijuana roach. He confiscated the roach, then wrote Elder citations for expired license plates and the marijuana. End of story. He turned the roach over to Detective Gambrell and she had it analyzed.

Robert Ford tried to find holes in Kilker's testimony. The young officer's story held up under questioning. Ford tried to ascribe some shady motives to Detective Gambrell and Officer Kilker. He tried to befuddle Kilker regarding the license-plate situation.

Kilker had removed the license plate from his own vehicle in Florida and brought it with him to California. He removed the plate from his briefcase and showed how the numbers on the plate are the same as the numbers on the validation sticker. Ford moved on to other things.

Ford hinted that once it was learned that Elder had actually paid for the license plate, but put in on the wrong vehicle, Kilker should have apologized for detaining him and driven away. Ford made a big deal out of the fact that Kilker wrote an additional report a few months later and asked why it took him two months to write the "extra" report.

The large officer looked at Ford almost with disdain. Kilker testified that he wrote the additional report to clarify something he'd seen in the van during the stop. Kilker didn't make anything up. He did not add to the facts, or subtract from them. He explained a fact that was not readily apparent at the time he wrote the first report.

Ford implied that Kilker had coerced Elder into consenting to the search. No, the truth was simply that Kilker asked if he could search and Elder said he could. There were no threats, real or implied, about the circumstances of the search. Kilker did not promise leniency if he would let him search. He did not promise that he would not physically take Elder into custody, but would only cite him if he found something. In short, Robert Ford had nothing. Because Ford had nothing, he did the only thing he could: he attacked the credibility of Jason Kilker. That was all he had to work with.

While the phrase "It is what it is" is in danger of being overused in the first decade of 2000, in the case of Jason Kilker's testimony, that's what it was. Kilker's findings were what they were. The truth never changes. A phrase from the Talmud reads, "When you add to the truth you subtract from it." The truth remains the same always. Ford couldn't shake Kilker, because his testimony was the truth.

Every time Ford attacked Kilker's credibility, Prosecutor Andrea Freshwater objected. Judge Kerry Wells would sustain the objection and Officer Kilker would not have to answer the inflammatory question.

Ford was becoming increasingly irate with Judge Wells because he believed the judge was protecting Kilker. "Your Honor seems to be sustaining every question that I bring that attacks the officer's credibility," he said.

The judge said, "I disagree,"

"Are you interested in knowing—" began Ford.

Judge Wells apparently had had enough and uncharacteristically cut Ford off. "I'm sustaining objections that are brought and I need to make a call on that [the objections]. Ask your next question. I'm not prohibiting in any way the attacking of the officer's credibility if you have evidence to attack his credibility."

If Ford had had evidence to attack Officer Kilker's credibility, he would have unloaded it. Judge Wells would have allowed the questions. But Ford had no evidence against Kilker's credibility.

"No further questions," Robert Ford said.

The evidentiary hearing was concluded with all of the evidence allowed into the record. The traffic stop was good. The seizure of the cigarette was good, and the eventual obtaining of the DNA was good.

Although Robert Ford failed in his quest, he at least established that he was putting up a vigorous fight for his client.

CHAPTER 29

Andrea Freshwater began her preparation for the courtroom right away. Even though "showtime" was a few months away, there was much to do. The reality shows on Court TV or even the Arts and Entertainment Network crime shows don't present the full, tedious picture of how a case is put together. Hours go into formulating a battle plan, with the prosecution mapping out its case, anticipating objections and strategy from the defense. Prosecutors also formulate plans to weaken or thwart the defense's presentation once they know what it is.

In short, the prosecution wants to lay every bit of information that is helpful to its case out for the jury to see. Conversely, the defense wants to keep everything out that is harmful to its client, which is mostly everything the prosecution wants to put in. By the same token, the prosecution will strive to block any information that weakens the case. Given the laws of discovery that allow the defense to see everything the prosecution has in its arsenal, and vice versa, almost nothing is left out these days.

Attorneys on both sides continually accuse each other of "hiding the ball" and not revealing evidence until it is too late to attack it. In spite of the improved laws of discovery, legal bickering will continue as long as there are attorneys breathing the air of this world.

In the case of Mark Elder, accused of killing a San Diego prostitute, Freshwater wanted to bring in a representative number of the Florida prostitutes to show what Mark Elder was like when he was alone with a woman, or rather, a prostitute. More specifically, she wanted to show his propensity for violence toward hookers, how he beat and choked them before forcing sex on them, or beat them after having sex with them when they demanded payment. She wanted to show how he booted them from his van, leaving them stranded and lost. Her image of what happened to Janet Moore was that Elder made a deal for sex, much as he did with the Florida prostitutes. The presence of semen in Moore's body showed they had sex, either forced or with the promise of eventual payment. When Janet asked for money and Elder refused, Elder hit or choked her like he did the Florida women. Janet did something the women in Florida didn't do: she fought back. It cost her her life.

Freshwater was confident that Officer Jason Kilker's rendition of the events of the traffic stop and subsequent seizure of the marijuana cigarette that yielded the incriminating DNA was straightforward and simple. A jury would believe him. The young officer's actions were logical and appropriate. First, he made sure he had a reason to stop the vehicle (expired plate). Second, he asked permission to search. (Elder freely gave him that.) Third, he found the roach in plain sight. Fourth, Officer Kilker cited Elder for the initial license-plate violation for which he was stopped. Fifth, he cited Elder for the marijuana roach and collected the evidence.

Andrea Freshwater filed a motion to have four of the Florida prostitutes testify in Elder's murder trial. This was a sticky situation because Elder wasn't being charged with anything he'd done in Florida. There is a section in the California evidence code that says "evidence of a person's character or a trait of his or her character (whether in the form of an opinion, evidence of reputation, or evidence of specific instances of his or her conduct) is inadmissible when offered to prove his or her conduct on a specified occasion" (Evidence Code 1101[a]).

The section right after that, 1102(b), does allow some latitude, permitting the prosecution to admit evidence that a person committed a crime when the admission of that evidence is relevant to prove a fact such as motive, opportunity, intent, or whether a defendant in a prosecution for an *unlawful sexual act* (author's italics) did not reasonably and in good faith believe the victim consented.

To further confuse the layman, Evidence Code 1108 (a) allows that: "In a criminal action in which the defendant is accused of a sexual offense, evidence of the defendant's commission of another sexual offense or offenses is not made inadmissible by Section 1101."

These sections were relevant to Andrea Freshwater because she wanted to prove that Elder's perverse sexual acts in Florida were comparable, if not identical, to what happened to Janet Moore, with the exception that the Florida women acquiesced to Elder's violence and submitted to being raped, choked, and hit. Janet Moore fought back.

While Evidence Code Section 1101 appeared to limit what Freshwater could bring up about Elder, Section 1108 appeared to allow that testimony because the acts were of a sexual nature.

To further muddy the legal waters, Elder was not charged with the rape of Janet Moore. While she might have been raped, and probably was raped, there was no way to prove rape. Although it is unlikely, Moore may have consented to be paid *after* the sex act. When Elder refused to pay and Moore emphatically demanded payment, the violence may have started. The only two who knew what really happened were Mark Elder and the forever-silenced Janet Moore.

Needless to say, a legal battle loomed on the horizon. The locale of the horizon was to be in the courtroom of the Honorable William Kennedy, Department 54, San Diego Superior Court.

————————

Some judges in San Diego have mixed reputations among the prosecution and defense bar. That is, many defense attorneys favor certain judges while prosecutors cringe when assigned to these same judges. Conversely, there are other judges whom prosecutors seem to favor. When a case is assigned to the latter, the defense attorneys shake their collective heads and pray for better days.

Judge William H. Kennedy is neither favored nor loathed by members of the local bar. He goes by the book in all matters. Kennedy knows the law and follows the law. Even if a crime is despicable to mankind, He will give his rulings according to the law, not according to emotions.

A former lieutenant commander in the United States Navy, Kennedy brought a military bearing and evenhanded approach to his duties when he joined the San Diego District Attorney's Office in the late 1960s. He toiled as a regular deputy district attorney under the sitting D.A., James Don Keller.

In 1970, Edwin L. Miller, a Democrat recently fired as the United States attorney in San Diego, ran for the nonpartisan county district-attorney job. An election battle ensued that tested loyalties within the D.A.'s office. The "old guard" deputy district attorneys didn't want Miller in. They wanted Assistant D.A. Bob Thomas to succeed Keller. When Miller won the hard-fought election, he brought over hard-charging Richard L. Huffman, an outsider from the California Department of Justice, to be his top assistant. (Huffman is now a state appellate-court judge.) Miller elevated Kennedy to fill out the triumvirate at the top of the organization chart. The move to promote Kennedy was done to assuage the feelings of the attorneys who did not want Miller in office.

Kennedy was a logical choice. Although he had a political side to him, Bill Kennedy was more interested in bringing justice to the citizens of San Diego and peace to the district attorney's office. Everyone in the office liked and respected him. Miller theorized that if he could win Kennedy over, the others might follow.

It worked. Kennedy served as a valuable cog in the district attorney's machine. He could be counted on to make the right call even if the call was a painful one. Kennedy always did the right thing, no matter the consequences. He was principled, honest, and ethical, exactly what Miller wanted.

After about a dozen years, the president of the United States appointed William H. Kennedy to be the U.S. attorney in San Diego, prosecuting federal crimes in the area. Kennedy continued to work as the U.S. attorney in the same fashion he had performed every one of his tasks over the years.

Eventually Kennedy became a political casualty. He opted to prosecute some federal officers he deemed to have overstepped their authority. This did not sit well with other members of the Justice Department. When Kennedy decided to follow his principles and refused to back down, he was "invited" to leave office. More bluntly, he was fired.

Ed Miller didn't take even a full minute to rehire Kennedy as one of his top assistants. Kennedy toiled in that position until he was appointed as a San Diego Superior Court judge in the 1980s.

On May 11, 2006, Andrea Freshwater filed a motion to allow the testimony of Florida prostitutes Ida Jones, Carrie Bell, Debbie Farris, and Ellen Graham. She argued that Elder's sexual activity with the Florida women was similar enough to what happened to Janet Moore to warrant the jury's consideration.

On May 18, 2006, Robert Ford asked for a continuance on the matter. He said he was trying to locate witnesses the prosecution had interviewed many years before whose testimony would shed light on Janet Moore's life and actions. Ford also indicated that Janet Moore was *not* a prostitute.

Not a prostitute? Ms. Freshwater wondered where this was going.

———————

Prosecutor Freshwater resisted the continuance. She said the logistical problems of getting the four prostitute/witnesses to San Diego from Florida at the same time were numerous. One of them was in jail, and one of them had no available child care. That meant the woman had to bring her child to San Diego with her. Freshwater said the prosecution needed to get the women here all at the same time, and get things done in an orderly fashion. The logistics of airline travel was a nightmare in itself.

Regarding Ford's assertion that Janet was not a prostitute, Freshwater figured he had to be grasping at some kind of a straw, hoping to salvage whatever he could from the case. Many people knew Janet Moore had engaged in prostitution, her family included. If the family would admit this embarrassing fact, it had to be true. Ford's strategy was to ask why the prosecution was bringing in prostitutes to show his client's guilt when the woman his client was accused of killing wasn't even a prostitute.

There was another reason for Elder's request for a continuance. At first, Elder told his attorney he had never been in Janet Moore's apartment. He was now changing his story and bringing a defense of "third-party culpability." When Ms. Freshwater saw this tactic, she wondered who would be accused of the murder.

Judge Kennedy denied the motion for a continuance. He allowed the four women to come to San Diego. If things were not complicated enough already, he would hear their testimony before it could be presented to the jury. After evaluating the women, he would rule on the relevance of their testimony. This tricky legal maneuver is allowed under Evidence Code 402 (b), which says, "The court may hear and determine the question of the admissibility of evidence out of the presence or hearing of the jury."

Judge Kennedy was treading on potentially shaky legal ground, and was certainly inviting an appeal in the event of a conviction for Elder. Nonetheless, he believed he had to hear what the women had to say. If he allowed their testimony, his ruling would undoubtedly be grounds for an appeal. Never one to avoid a hard choice, Kennedy said it was time to get on with the case.

———————

One week before the case started, Freshwater received word that Deputy Medical Examiner John Eisele would not be testifying, but not because he had retired and was out of the area. He would not be testifying because he had died. The deputy district attorney would have to find another pathologist in the M.E.'s office to testify as to Eisele's report. It could be done. It just made things more difficult.

Jury selection took place June 1 and 2. Once the jury and alternates had been selected, the jury was told to sit tight because the attorneys and judge had to argue about and sort out several evidentiary matters.

On June 5 and 6, the women from Florida testified. Their testimony was consistent with what they had told Cindy Gambrell many months before. By now, Gambrell was a sergeant, having been recently promoted. When asked, she humbly said her work on the case had nothing to do with the promotion. This was the first time she had decided to compete, and the results had been good for her.

The four women on the witness stand related their ordeals with Elder. All identified him by pointing to him at the defendant's table and describing the clothing he was wearing, the common method of identification used by court personnel. The direct testimony went smoothly. Defense attorney Robert Ford took notes furiously while the women testified. When it was time to cross-examine them, he had a fertile field in which to operate. First, the profession of the women was illegal in itself. Every night when they stepped out they committed crimes by selling their bodies. Some explained they had resorted to prostitution to feed a narcotic habit. This testimony was all the better for Ford. They not only performed illegal sex acts, they ingested illegal drugs. Hopefully it was strike one and strike two to their credibility.

Ford also made a big deal out of the fact that the women, except for Debbie Farris, did not report the so-called rapes in a timely fashion. Some waited until they heard about Elder while they were in jail. One prostitute claimed she had reported the crime to the police. Detective Cindy Gambrell could not locate the report at the police department where the woman said she complained. Some of the other women waited to come forward until they saw Elder's picture in the paper. In short, Ford implied they were making their stories up just to get a free trip to San Diego or to gain some kind of notoriety.

The women stuck to their stories, and the stories didn't change. Freshwater had no choice but to sit there while Ford attacked their character and honesty. Oddly enough, their honesty was evident. When they said they didn't report the rapes because they didn't think the police would believe them, their testimony rang true. Law enforcement in Florida is somewhat different than it is in San Diego.

For the female witnesses, it was no picnic getting hammered and ridiculed by a defense attorney. Because the truth doesn't change, neither did the girls' stories change. Judge Kennedy ruled they could testify at trial. Robert Ford probably began thinking about appealing the case if he lost shortly after Judge Kennedy allowed them to testify.

The actual trial started with opening statements on June 7, 2006. Andrea Freshwater's presentation was predictable. She cited the DNA of the defendant found at a murder scene. She promised to prove that Mark Elder left the DNA when he killed Janet Moore. She promised to show by his repeated violence toward prostitutes in Florida that he committed violence on prostitute Janet Moore that resulted in her death. She didn't want the jury to make any leaps of faith, only to rely on common sense.

The veteran prosecutor did have one "oops" moment during her opening statement. Immediately after making the comment, she knew she had made a mistake. While recounting Elder's conversation with Detective Thill in the interview room in Florida, she alluded to Elder saying, "This conversation is over."

In the nitpicky concept of a suspect's rights, if a prosecutor says that a defendant indicated a conversation is over, it means he is claiming his right against self-incrimination guaranteed by the Fifth Amendment. And, prosecutors can't say a defendant claimed that privilege. Robert Ford jumped to his feet immediately and objected. Even though Elder had said the conversation was over, Judge Kennedy ruled that Freshwater's statement merely be stricken, and disregarded by the jury.

Kennedy believed the error was harmless. But he knew by not calling for a mistrial, he was opening himself up for an appeal. The rule Andrea Freshwater violated is called a "Griffin error." (*Griffin v. California* 380 U.S. 609) Freshwater admitted she shouldn't have mentioned Elder's termination of the interview. But a jury would have to be stupid not to wonder why a thorough, hardworking detective like Ron Thill would have ended the conversation so quickly, and at the moment when he was starting to show Elder some damaging evidence, the photographs of Janet Moore. Judge Kennedy allowed Freshwater to continue.

When Freshwater finished her opening, Robert Ford stood up and trumpeted his client's innocence. He promised the jury that they would hear from Elder himself, that the accused would testify as to what really happened and why. When Elder was done testifying, everything would be clear, and the jury would find him not guilty.

Ford dropped a hint of what the defense would be. Apparently, the Asian doctor Henry Tan had killed the woman. Ford told the jury Mark Elder met Janet Moore by the Broadway pier in downtown San Diego. Within hours they were hitting it off famously. They went to Janet's apartment, ingested some street drugs, had sex a few times, and were enjoying each other. Suddenly a jealous Henry Tan broke into the apartment, confronted Janet, and hit Mark Elder with his fist, rendering him unconscious. While Elder was out cold, Tan stabbed Janet to death. For good measure, being a medical doctor, Tan skillfully cut Elder's fingers while Elder was unconscious. Ford proclaimed that Henry Tan was the murderer. This would have been a pretty good Perry Mason–like TV ending, but Robert Ford wasn't Perry Mason and this wasn't television. And Perry Mason has never defended a client who was, in fact, guilty.

Andrea Freshwater sat there feeling relief. The self-defense scenario she made up, and was afraid Mark Elder would present, was a lot better than the line of baloney Robert Ford had just spouted. Anticipating the self-defense story Elder would come up with, Freshwater had been afraid Elder would say Janet had come at him with a knife. He deflected the blows, thus cutting his hand. After disarming her, he fought back more than he should have and killed her.

Freshwater's was not a bad story. The version Elder planned to tell was ludicrous. Mark Elder had only learned of the existence of Henry Tan by reading the police reports that documented Tan as Janet's "sugar daddy." When given the opportunity in Florida to tell Ron Thill about Henry Tan, Elder didn't. The reason was simple: Mark Elder didn't know about Henry Tan until he read the reports of the police interviews with Tan. Freshwater felt a lot better. She could handle Mark Elder on cross-examination. That would be a fun day in the trial.

CHAPTER 30

Andrea Freshwater began the testimony in chronological order. Detective Ron Thill described the crime scene. Criminalist Randy Gibson displayed and commented on the photos he took and the fingerprints he lifted. He pointed out the bloody washcloth in the bathroom and the bloody finger marks on the dresser. Brian Burritt and David Cornacchia from the San Diego Police Forensic Laboratory led the jury through a lengthy explanation of the DNA samples they extracted from the washcloth and from various points around Janet's apartment. They explained that there had been two donors of blood, one being Janet Moore, and the other the individual who had remained unidentified for so many years.

This could have been tricky. DNA testimony is not very action-packed. But Cornacchia has an engaging and entertaining way of presenting information. The tall, thin scientist looks like he is going to break into a smile at any moment. His eyes focus on whomever he is talking to, tracking whether the audience is absorbing what he is saying.

He explained that in 1988 the technology regarding DNA had not been developed well enough to make cases. Fortunately, the homicide team had preserved the evidence so that when forensic science developed sufficiently, scientists could test it. Cornacchia went through the actual physical steps he and Brian Burritt performed to extract the DNA and put the readings into the database. He said, as a scientist, the odds were one in 82 quadrillion that the DNA belonged to someone other than Mark Elder.

A few people in the courtroom, jurors included, sat there with a glazed look in their eyes, undoubtedly wondering how much a "quadrillion" was. Cornacchia said he would have to find 90 billion planets like Earth and check all the inhabitants of the 90 billion planets before he could find someone with the same DNA as Mark Elder. Cornacchia got through to the jurors. They could relate to that explanation. Ninety billion planets was something to think about. The truth was that it was Mark Elder's DNA, and only Mark Elder's, in Janet Moore's apartment, and in her body.

Cornacchia explained that the San Diego Police Department does not use the word *match* when describing DNA and its association with people. He said the department uses a more conservative approach. This explains the use of the staggering numbers instead of saying "we had a match." But one way or another, a match was what they had. The blood and semen came from Mark Elder.

––––––––––

Dr. Glenn Wagner took the witness stand. San Diego's chief medical examiner took the long road to his present position. Just as prosecutor Andrea Freshwater was born, with a plastic rather than a silver spoon in her mouth, Wagner had started out as a police officer in Philadelphia, worked as a criminal investigator and homicide detective for many years, and finally enrolled in medical school.

Wagner detailed his path through school, and his efforts

to obtain his medical license while carrying a badge and gun. He eventually specialized in pathology. Wagner's track record included performing or supervising over eleven thousand autopsies. This litany of his experiences was presented for a reason: Dr. Glenn Wagner had not performed the autopsy on Janet Moore. Dr. John Eisele had, but Eisele was now dead.

Wagner went over the report prepared by Eisele and gave his opinions. The testimony was straightforward and uncomplicated. The autopsy report of someone who died of thirty-nine stab wounds would not necessarily be complicated. Wagner did show the many wounds on Janet's hands and forearms that resulted from trying to deflect the knife thrusts. Some of the cuts went right to the bone. Her resistance to the attack was well noted. Wagner also commented on the severity of the wounds, including the one on the very top of her head. Janet had fought furiously but was no match for her attacker. After hearing Wagner's testimony, onlookers agreed that it was true that a victim could "speak from the grave," as Janet's autopsy report indicated how hard she had fought before death.

Robert Ford tried to attack Wagner. There were some peculiarities in Dr. Eisele's report that were different from one that Wagner would have prepared if he had performed the postmortem exam on Moore. But any discrepancies could be explained by the fact that different people go about their jobs in different ways.

Another prosecutor would have prepared the case differently than Andrea Freshwater. Robert Ford's colleagues at the public defender's office would have prepared and presented Elder's defense differently than Ford had. The discrepancy pointed to nothing more than the differences in human nature. The end result was the same: Janet Moore had died of thirty-nine stabbing and incise wounds. Her body showed the presence of illegal drugs. End of story. Ford could attack all he wanted. The truth was the truth.

The jury appeared to buy into Wagner's testimony. After all, it wasn't a suicide. Wagner never said Mark Elder killed Janet Moore. He only said how she died and what caused her to die. Ford could question the autopsy report all he wanted. His questions would change nothing.

The next witness was Adam Dutrà, a blood expert criminalist. He commented on the gruesome photos of the nude Janet Moore. Dutra pointed out the markings in blood on her stomach and chest. The blood configurations were different from those of a person who bled out after being stabbed. Dutra had not seen a body with bloody markings like this before. Asked to give his opinion, he said it looked like someone had moved his or her hands around on the nude, bloody body of Janet Moore. Or perhaps someone had lain on top of her after she had been bleeding. His description of the possible causes of the markings was bizarre. Dutra had no exact explanation. Freshwater's theory was that Mark Elder had "played with" the body at the time of death, or shortly after. That thought raised disgusting images in the minds of people listening to Dutra's testimony.

Robert Ford attacked Dutra's theories. But given the condition of Janet Moore's body, there was nothing definitive Ford could do to get Dutra to change his theory. The photographs spoke for themselves.

Having gone through the case from the time of the discovery of Janet Moore's body up until the arrest of Mark Elder, including the complicated, but staggering DNA information, Andrea Freshwater was confident she had proven her case. On June 13, 2006, she announced, "The People rest."

Robert Ford had done all he could to attack the prosecution's case when he cross-examined Andrea Freshwater's witnesses. Courtroom veterans generally agreed that the prosecution's case was very strong, and Ford had done little or no damage to the testimony of the witnesses. Even the prostitutes, including the one who'd come from Florida still in handcuffs, were generally perceived as having told the truth. Their stories of the pain and humiliation suffered at the hands of Mark Elder rang true. Why would anyone want to travel several thousand miles to get in front of a jury and relate that embarrassing information? Robert Ford said they agreed to testify to get a free trip to San Diego.

On June 14, Ford called Detective Sergeant Cynthia Gambrell from Volusia County as a defense witness. Gambrell had been the prosecution's "Most Valuable Player" on the Atlantic coast, even though she did not testify for the prosecution. She had done an excellent job of staying on top of the often frustrating investigation. Back in the 1990s, when the San Diego artists decried the callous attitude of the police toward prostitutes, they could hardly have known about the likes of Gambrell. Her actions represented another side of the relationship between law enforcement and prostitutes. The cops really did care, most of them at least.

Because she did not testify for the prosecution, Gambrell never had the chance to talk about her efforts to track down and stay in contact with Debbie Farris, the young hooker who didn't care whether she cooperated with the police or not. Several months after everything was over, Farris appeared on a true-crime television show, with her face shown, and using her real name. Farris admitted that she ignored Cindy Gambrell's effort to keep track of her. Apparently clean and sober at the time of the television show and subsequent court appearance, Farris said the drugs had such a hold on her during that period that she didn't really care whether her attacker was caught or not. Finally she'd come to her senses and straightened out.

Robert Ford wasn't interested in Gambrell's heroic efforts to find a vicious rapist. He was more interested in the fact that Volusia County was not prosecuting Elder for the alleged rapes in Florida. Gambrell's explanation was honest.

California's case was stronger. It was true that any sexual-assault charges against Elder in Florida would be rife with problems for the prosecution.

The problems were twofold. First, not all of the girls reported the crimes right away. Some waited until Elder was in custody. Second, some of the girls reported the sexual assaults, but the Florida police did not take their accusations seriously. That black eye of police indifference would be a problem if a trial were held in Florida.

Ford expounded on many topics while Gambrell was on the stand. Finally, Judge Kennedy had to say, "Mr. Ford, this [line of questioning] isn't relevant to anything in this case. Let's get down to something that's pertinent." Gambrell was excused.

———————

When Mark Elder took the oath to tell the truth, the whole truth, and nothing but the truth before testifying, it's a good thing his sister, Cathy, wasn't in the audience. If she had been there when Elder said, "I do," the bailiff would have had to remove her for creating a disturbance by laughing out loud. Cathy often said, "There's the truth, and there's Mark's version of the truth."

As Ford fed him questions, Elder readily admitted he was in San Diego on June 11, 1988. He said he got on the bus from Florida to San Diego on June 5, arriving June 8. Elder appeared comfortable and at ease while relating his testimony. He said even though the events happened a long time ago, he remembered meeting Janet while she sat on a bench at the end of Broadway on the pier. Those familiar with San Diego knew that location was, and is, a popular place on San Diego Bay. Many tourists go there to board the various one- or two-hour harbor cruises. That area along Harbor Drive has a few small but good restaurants. The long stretch is ideal for casual walks too.

Elder said he and Janet hung out for a while, talking

and getting to know each other. At some point during their conversation they realized they were both drug users. Elder said at the time he was heavy into drugs and weighed only approximately 130 pounds. One can envision the jurors mentally trying to remove 70 pounds from the five-foot-eight-inch man seated in the witness stand.

Elder continued his testimony, saying that Janet told him she knew where they could score some rock cocaine and asked if he wanted to share. To Mark Elder, that question was like asking a starving man if he wanted a steak sandwich with fries. Of course he did. They walked about sixteen blocks near Eleventh Avenue and Island Street. This is a well-known area where a local detoxification center is located. Instead of taking cooperative drunks to jail, the police take them to detox, where they sober up, go home, and avoid incurring a police arrest record.

Because the area around Eleventh and Island is full of the homeless and disenfranchised, several people who have drugs to sell hang out there. Maybe Mark Elder remembered that geographical and sociological fact independently, or maybe a few days before he testified, a cellmate in county jail answered the question "If I wanted to score some rock in the downtown area in 1988, where would I go?"

Elder continued to testify that he and Janet pooled their money, bought cocaine, and went to Janet's apartment on Seventeenth Street. They ingested the drugs. They wanted another jolt. Janet gave Mark money and he went back to the same area by himself. They shared the cocaine pipe when he returned. Still hungry for a high, Mark went back a third time. After several hours of smoking crack cocaine, the two decided to have sex in Janet's apartment. There was no discussion of money. Mark didn't think she was a prostitute. She wanted to have sex with him just because she wanted to have sex with him.

Shortly after they were finished with the sex, a man burst

into the apartment. Mark and Janet were still naked. The intruder was a slight Asian man. He did not break the door down. Mark didn't know, but thought maybe he had a key because Mark had locked the door when he returned with the cocaine.

"What's going on?" the man screamed.

While Mark was taken off guard and feeling like he had been caught doing something he shouldn't have, Janet was defiant. She appeared to know the man. "You don't own me," she said. "It doesn't matter that you pay for things. We aren't married."

Mark said he now realized he had been having sex with someone else's girlfriend. But he hadn't known she was attached when they'd hooked up earlier in the day. Elder said the man looked at him menacingly while he tried to put his underwear on.

"Who is this?" the man demanded of Janet, pointing to Elder. "Is this your boyfriend?" He was furious.

Elder testified that he told the man he was sorry, that he didn't know she had a boyfriend. He continued putting his underwear on. He fumbled to find his pants and shoes.

Robert Ford asked Elder to describe the man. He was Asian, about five-foot-eight, and weighing about 140 pounds. He was in his forties. Elder paused theatrically, apparently thinking. He said he believed the man's name was maybe Henry.

Henry's anger grew, Elder testified. He picked up the crack pipe Elder and Janet had been smoking. Henry waved the pipe and screamed, "You promised me you were through with this pipe." Before Janet could reply, Henry pointed at Elder and asked Janet, "I guess this is the type of animal you choose to be with?"

Before Elder could react, Henry struck him with one punch, knocking him unconscious. The term Elder used on the witness stand was that the man "coldcocked" him and he "saw stars." Elder said he thought the guy hit him in the nose.

Elder woke up a short time later. As his eyes began to focus he looked around the room. Henry was gone. Janet's body lay nearby on the floor. Blood was all over the apartment. Someone, probably Henry, had stabbed Janet repeatedly. Elder looked at his right hand and noticed the pinkie and ring fingers had been cut severely. He was losing blood rapidly. He had a substantial cut on his right middle finger too, but not as severe as the other two. Elder believed he had suffered major damage to his fingers because he couldn't move them.

Elder said he was in a panic. He looked at Janet, but did not touch her. She didn't move, or breathe. He feared she was dead. A pool of blood formed beneath his dripping right hand during the few moments he studied Janet's body. Mark said he tried to quell the flow of blood. He went into the bathroom, first finding tissue paper. That did nothing. Then he opened the cabinet and found a washcloth.

He told Robert Ford that at the time he feared he would be blamed for the girl's death. Still in panic mode, he was also afraid he was going to pass out from loss of blood. He found a towel, wrapped his fingers tightly, got dressed, took the knife, and left the apartment. Elder said he went to Huntington Beach, then later returned to Florida.

As Andrea Freshwater sat taking notes while Elder spoke, she was filled with the anticipation that she would soon have her chance at this guy. She was glad that Elder had tried the "SODDI" defense (Some Other Dude Did It). She had a good plan of attack ready. Fortunately Elder didn't use the scenario Freshwater had envisioned as a defense, because hers was more believable than the one he had told. If Elder had said he and Janet had argued over money or something after the sex and she attacked him with a knife, it had a possible ring of truth to it. He could have said she slashed his hand and he disarmed her. He thrashed around, fearing for his own life, and the next thing he knew he had stabbed her repeatedly until she quit fighting. Thinking no one would believe that it was self-defense, he left the area, too scared to get medical attention.

Elder had made Andrea Freshwater's job a little easier. It was obvious he was trying to blame Janet's death on Henry Tan, Janet's former "sugar daddy." It was also true that Tan had died in April 2004 and wouldn't be around to clarify his relationship with her. Elder had learned of Tan's death and conveniently chosen to accuse a man who couldn't refute anything that was said about him.

He also said he believed Henry Tan smeared Elder's blood around the dresser drawers and on Janet's purse to make it look even more like Elder had killed her.

Freshwater walked Elder through his previous testimony, locking his story in permanently. She asked him what he did with the knife. He said he threw it in a Dumpster somewhere around the apartment building. He said he thought he was unconscious for five to ten minutes. He said he stayed in San Diego for about three more days before hitchhiking to Florida.

Elder said he didn't call the police because he "always had bad luck with the police." When the prosecutor heard him say this, she looked at the jury with her eyes very wide open. She shook her head up and down as if to ask, "You want me to believe this?"

She repeated it back to him. "You say you had BAD LUCK with the police?"

"Yes, ma'am."

"So, somebody killed a girl you had just met and the killer seriously cut your fingers and you didn't call the police because you had *bad luck* with the police." It wasn't a question. She repeated "bad luck" for emphasis so it was locked in the mind of each juror. Elder had failed to report a murder because he was unlucky with the police.

She asked Elder where the mysterious Asian man had punched him with such force that it knocked him unconscious for five or ten minutes. Elder said he thought it was in the nose. He said he "just saw stars." Freshwater asked him if he had a broken nose as a result. He didn't know.

Prosecutor Freshwater asked Mark Elder what many thought was the million-dollar question: "If it's true that this Asian man killed Janet Moore, why didn't you tell Ron Thill when he interviewed you in Florida?"

"I don't know."

"It wasn't because you had never even heard of Henry Tan, was it?"

"No."

"The truth is that you never heard of Henry Tan until you came into possession of the San Diego Police Department's follow-up reports on their investigation that you're allowed to read as part of your defense. Isn't that true?"

"No, ma'am."

Upon questioning, Elder said he thought about Janet Moore "every single day" since she was killed.

"But you didn't think enough about her to recognize her when Detective Thill showed you a picture of her, did you?"

The question went unanswered. Freshwater didn't press him.

Andrea Freshwater let the jury chew on Elder's testimony for a while. She announced that the People were done with the cross-examination of Mark Elder.

When asked later, Freshwater said she thought the jury followed her closely during her questioning of Elder. She had watched them throughout and was impressed with their attention and note taking. She hoped the jury was on the same wavelength she was. Her impression of Elder's testimony was that it was contrived, rehearsed, and simply not true. And, she didn't think Mark Elder was a very convincing actor. She hoped the jury shared her impressions.

It was now time for the ever-important closing arguments. This is the summation of the case. The closing arguments bring together everything each side has said. Ms. Freshwater reminded the jury that Mark Elder's DNA was everywhere in Janet's apartment. She said after he killed Janet Moore, he went through her purse looking for something to steal. His blood was all over the purse, and inside it. His blood was smeared on the dresser drawers, where he had also searched for things to steal.

Mark Elder had not sought medical attention for his severely cut fingers because he did not want to let anyone know he had killed Janet. His fingers were so damaged that Elder couldn't use them, even to this day. His ring and pinkie fingers couldn't bend because the tendons were cut and never repaired. They were cut when his hand slid down the knife blade while he was stabbing Janet Moore, Freshwater reminded the jury. According to Elder, he didn't call the police to report someone had been killed and he had been severely assaulted because he had "bad luck" with the police. Bad luck indeed.

She reminded the jurors of the peculiar blood patterns on Janet's body. She said they resembled finger painting. She accused Elder of "playing with" the dead body of Janet Moore, an unsettling thought.

Freshwater reminded the jurors that four hookers in Florida who didn't know one another reported similar stories about what Mark Elder had done to them. How could that be? What would their motivation be for retelling their stories and setting themselves up to be cross-examined and ridiculed? The motivation was that they were telling the truth and wanted justice done.

She related how the prostitutes said Mark Elder had been very nice when they got into his van, only to turn into a monster when it came time to pay. "Janet Moore started out with a charming Dr. Jekyll and ended up with a homicidal Mr. Hyde."

She said that a reasonable interpretation of Mark Elder's story about what happened would only have been possible if his story had started out with "Once upon a time . . ." When he learned of the existence of Henry Tan from police reports, he concocted his story about Janet's death.

———————

Robert Ford delivered his closing. The veteran defense attorney knew he had a tough road ahead of him. He ridiculed the Florida prostitutes. He said Elder never raped them. He just didn't pay them, and that was the entire problem—that's why they were angry. Ford said the prostitutes would never allege that a man simply didn't pay them. Instead, they would say the man raped them. Ford further said the prostitutes thought the Florida police would give them breaks in the future for cooperating with the California authorities. And, he added, they got a free trip to California for telling their stories. Ford made a big deal out of the fact that one day they'd even gone to the San Diego Zoo. Freshwater could not help but give a suppressed smile at that ploy. Now a trip to the zoo was a good reason to travel thousands of miles and submit to ridicule and scorn in order to falsely accuse a man of rape.

Robert Ford continued to blame Henry Tan. He said Tan smeared the unconscious Mark Elder's blood around the apartment after he had sliced open Elder's hand. He also said the autopsy report on Janet Moore showed no evidence of choking, but all of the Florida girls said Elder choked them. Ford tried to show inconsistency in the prosecution's case.

During the closing argument, Freshwater had to object five times because Ford was telling the jury "facts not in evidence." All of the objections were sustained. This means Ford, and Elder, wanted the jury to accept as fact something that was only a theory. Judge Kennedy did not allow their theories. He only allowed facts.

When the jury went out, Andrea Freshwater had the same funny feeling in the pit of her stomach she always had at that moment. She knew she had done everything she could to put on a compelling case. She had covered everything both legally and emotionally for the jury to consider. There was no denying that a courtroom is partly a theater and part legal forum.

In the past, juries had come up with some very strange decisions for a variety of reasons. Defense attorneys have said to juries, "You may not like me and the things I do on this case, but do not hold it against my client." What the attorney meant was that if he vigorously went after a witness on cross-examination, the jury should not vote to convict his client just because they did not like the defense attorney or his style.

Conversely, the prosecution hopes zealous questioning and grilling of a defendant will not result in the jury feeling sorry for the defendant.

Freshwater was confident she had not done anything to offend the jury. And she believed Mark Elder had hurt himself with his weak version of what happened. But still, strange things happen in criminal cases. It takes only one juror to hang up a case. In California, verdicts must be unanimous. If there is not total agreement among the twelve jurors in a criminal case, a mistrial is called and they start over from square one, with a new jury.

During deliberations in one San Diego case from the 1980s, a juror said, "I simply cannot judge someone enough to find that person guilty." The unasked question from the judge then became, "If you couldn't find someone guilty, why didn't you bring that up before you were seated on the jury? Your job was to make a call."

After a few hours of deliberation the jury returned with a guilty verdict for first-degree murder, and an additional enhancement of murder with a deadly weapon, the knife.

CHAPTER 31

Sentencing for Mark Elder was on August 24, 2006, in Department 54 of the San Diego Superior Court. The room was full, mostly with Janet Moore's relatives. Janet's mother, Rusty Sabor, who was living in the southern part of the country, told Andrea Freshwater she didn't think she was strong enough emotionally to attend. Janet's brother, sisters, aunts, uncles, and cousins attended, about twenty-five in all. After the sentencing the family would go upstairs to the D.A.'s office to make statements for the Arts and Entertainment Network's *Cold Case Files* television show. After that, the family would make a videotape for the D.A.'s "Lifer Unit" to be played at future parole hearings for Mark Elder. That taping meant their feelings and beliefs about the case would be memorialized for consideration by the parole board at future parole hearings.

Mark Elder's sister, Cathy Byrne, and her husband were in the audience. They were not there to support Mark, but to witness what was happening. Cathy's presence was welcomed by almost all of Janet's family.

For the first order of business, the formality of a probation report had to be put into the record. Probation Officer
Laura Thomas presented the findings. In Thomas's report,
Mark Elder did not admit responsibility for Janet's death.
When Thomas interviewed Elder he declined to talk about
his family or his fractured relationship with his sister. He
said the family dynamic was "a long story." Elder said
he didn't care what his family thought of his conviction. He
didn't say anything about being sorry for any hurt or embarrassment he had caused his family.

The probation report allows space for possible mitigation
of the offense. If there are facts that tend to lessen anything
about the crime, or give possible excuses for the conduct of
the guilty defendant, these circumstances are brought out
then. There was nothing to mitigate the crime or make Mark
Elder appear in any better light. Because of the nature of the
crime, no probation would be recommended. The probation
report was only a formality. No probation can ever be
granted for first-degree murder.

At each sentencing in California, victims, family, and
friends are allowed to give "impact statements" about how
the loss has affected them. This is a free-for-all, figuratively
speaking, that allows the family members to get all the
deep feelings they harbor out in the open. The family is allowed to address the convicted person directly. Sometimes
people who are not present send letters for the judge to read
and include in the record. Occasionally people who don't
trust their talent to speak extemporaneously read from prepared statements. Profanity is not allowed. Neither are
physical attacks, although bailiffs occasionally have to in-
tervene. Just about anything else is fair game.

The family of the convicted defendant might object vo-
cally to what the victim's family says about their relative
seated at the defendant's table. The defendant's family can
be removed from the courtroom if they object demonstra-
bly to what the victim's family is saying.

In this case, Cathy Byrne was Mark Elder's only family member present, and she agreed with what Janet Moore's family had to say about him.

———————

The first person to speak was Dale Allen Moore, Janet's half brother, and a Baptist minister, who had made the trip from Indiana. He said even though Janet was a long time gone, it was difficult to clear her out of his mind. She still occupied his thoughts. Reverend Moore said it is good to forgive, but there also needed to be punishment for the crime. He said it would bring peace to his family for Mark Elder to receive the maximum penalty. The minister said Mark Elder should not ever be released on parole. He said Elder had been free for eighteen years after killing Janet and the minister wanted the punishment to be four times eighteen years.

Janet's sister Sheri Lynn Moore also spoke. She tearfully said she could not spend time with her sister. This loss was a result of the "cruelty of a single remorseless man." She also said she wanted Elder never to be released on parole.

Robert "Uncle Bob" Moore, the brother of Janet's late father, spoke in colorful, down-home, simple language. Moore was a crusty, rumpled guy with a lined face, raspy voice, and strong, gnarled hands. He also had a twinkle in his eye. Alcohol had not passed over his lips in a long time. It wasn't always that way, though. Moore had served time not only in jail, but in prison. He was never in for violence. He had been knocked around in his life and had learned from the knocks. He knew what Elder could look forward to while locked up.

While Janet's brother and sister spoke about their feelings at the loss of Janet and asked Judge Kennedy to punish Elder, Uncle Bob spoke to Mark Elder directly. With a decidedly Southern twang Uncle Bob said his words slowly and with great deliberation without benefit of notes.

He said he hoped Elder had a real tough time in prison. "I hope them guys are mean to you in the joint. I hope they take your candy from you. I hope they take your cigarettes from you." (Because he had not been in prison recently, Uncle Bob was not aware that no tobacco products are allowed in any of California's prisons. But the tobacco ban didn't matter. Bob's words sounded good.) "I hope they rape you." Uncle Bob smirked contemptuously at Elder then sat down.

Sandra Moore, the fill-in matriarch and sister of Janet, spoke. She urged Judge Kennedy never to let Mark Elder out.

Defense attorney Robert Ford attempted to have Judge Kennedy strike the remarks of Uncle Bob about the hoped-for rape of Mark Elder. Kennedy refused. The Victim Impact Statement is an unfettered opportunity for the family of the victim to vent their feelings. If Janet's family hoped Mark Elder would get raped in prison, let them hope that. It was okay to hope that. Ford knew Judge Kennedy wouldn't strike the words. He wanted his objection noted for the record.

Mark Elder had a chance to address the court and/or Janet's family. He declined. Defendants often don't say anything at sentencing. Their statements are part of the record that the parole board will consider when the defendant comes up for parole. If the defendant plans to appeal, the court of appeal will also consider what he said at sentencing. For example, if Mark Elder had stood up and apologized for killing Janet Moore, he couldn't very well say at a later date that he hadn't killed Janet Moore and Henry Tan really had.

Judge Kennedy had the final word. He said even if he had the discretion to grant probation to Elder, he would not do so. He pointed out the criminal sophistication involved in the murder, a sophistication that posed a danger to society. He also said he had no discretion on the twenty-five-years-to-life-plus-one-year sentence. That sentence was prescribed by law and out of his control. He could not impose life without parole.

Kennedy continued that Janet Moore was twenty-seven when Elder took her life, and Elder was thirty. "You managed to avoid detection for eighteen years. The best years of her life were taken from her, and you were able to live your best years. There is a distasteful irony in that."

Kennedy reminded Robert Ford and Mark Elder that the People [police] found a horrendous crime scene. The defense wounds on Janet and the blood were awful. He told Elder that his blood was everywhere at the scene because he injured his hand. He reminded Elder that his semen was found in Janet. The semen was deposited just before, and/or maybe even just after, the killing. "You tried to blame Henry Tan based on what you learned from the prosecution. You almost pulled it off. Justice long delayed has finally endured. I will recommend the parole board never release you."

With that, Kennedy sentenced Mark Elder to prison for twenty-five years to life, plus one more year for the use of a deadly weapon. He also fined Elder $10,000 in restitution, standard in California homicides.

Elder was never linked to any other San Diego cases through DNA or other means. He could not be included in any of the murders the Homicide Task Force investigated during their time in existence.

Florida authorities presented a court order at the time of Elder's sentencing to obtain hair samples from Mark Elder. It seems they were investigating an old case that involved someone dumping a prostitute's body in a ditch near a place where Elder used to live in Florida. As of this writing, no resolution has been made. Florida authorities would not comment on the status of the case.

CHAPTER 32

As expected, Mark Elder appealed the verdict. His appellate attorney, who did not return calls for comment, claimed the court had made mistakes in four areas:

1. Judge Kennedy erred by denying Elder's request for a continuance following Kennedy's ruling allowing testimony from the prostitutes for the uncharged offenses (the Florida rapes). The appellate attorney said the trial attorney needed more time to prepare for what the prostitutes might say.
2. Kennedy erred by subsequently admitting the evidence from the prostitutes for the uncharged crimes into the record.
3. Kennedy should have called for a mistrial based on the prosecutor's statements to the jury about Elder's silence during the interview in Florida after being given his Miranda rights.
4. Kennedy should not have imposed a restitution fine against Elder. Fining him violated a constitutional

prohibition against ex post facto laws. (The law under which Judge Kennedy allowed the restitution fine was not in existence when Elder killed Janet Moore. Therefore, Elder should not be subject to the restitution fine.)

The Fourth District Court of Appeal ruled on the issues on February 15, 2008, in an unpublished decision. The fact that it is "unpublished" means no other courts or parties can cite or rely on the opinions contained in the decision except as specified by Rule 8.115(b) of the rules of evidence. Also, the ruling in the case is not binding as a precedent in other cases.

The thirty-one-page decision denied the first three grounds for appeal and allowed Elder's conviction to stand. The appellate justices overturned the provision that Elder should pay the restitution fine because the law mandating the payment was not in existence at the time of the crime.

When Judge Kennedy sentenced Elder, Kennedy commented that Elder had taken the best years of Janet's life while he was able to live the best years of his life. Kennedy said for Elder to be free during those years was a "distasteful irony."

What might be viewed as a reverse irony is that the three justices who ruled on the issues were Presiding Judge Judith McConnell, Judge Judith Haller, and Judge Joan Irion, all women. Of the ten judges on the court, five are men and five are women. The cases are assigned randomly for the justices to review. How ironic that three of the justices who decided Elder's appellate fate were women when Elder committed the atrocities he did on women. Mark Elder got on the prison bus, not to experience freedom for a long time, if ever.

Few areas in overcrowded, bustling San Diego can be called "out in the middle of nowhere." The location of the

Richard J. Donovan Correction Facility, about one mile north of the Mexican border and ten miles inland from the Pacific Ocean, is about as close as you can get to "nowhere." When this state prison was built in on 780 acres in 1987, nothing really stood between it and Mexico except for the U.S. Customs commercial truck crossing, the site of many large seizures of smuggled contraband and humans. Since 1987, the area immediately around the border has grown. But the prison today still remains isolated on barren land past the newly populated regions. Since the prison's construction, industry has cut a parallel swath along the border through the dirt and scrub brush, causing the relocation of multitudes of jackrabbits, rattlesnakes, and coyotes, hardly endangered species in that area. Near the border, strip malls have popped up virtually overnight, featuring fast-food restaurants and several gas stations. Storefronts that converted dollars into pesos, and vice versa, dot the strip malls, along with cut-rate clothing stores. The immediate border area is booming now.

The prison was built to handle 2,208 inmates. As of July 2007, the latest figures from the department of corrections Web site show that 962 corrections officers guard the 4,770 inmates, over double the optimum population. Some of the inmates are doing short stints for parole violation. Others are in for the long haul, many doing impressive stretches such as twenty-five years to life for first-degree murder.

The prison is not accessible by commercial or mass-transit bus, only by taxicab and private vehicle. Taxi drivers are wary of picking up fares near the prison. In the early 1990s, an inmate managed to walk away from a work detail, drop a dime (remember, it was a long time ago) into a pay phone, and have a taxi at his service in a matter of minutes. Local newspapers and other media had a field day with that one. As a result of the publicity, red-faced prison administrators made sure taxi pickups near the prison were few and far between.

Road workers have improved part of the two-lane road connecting to the path that leads to the prison. Small factories are popping up along the roadway. A sign advertising HAPPY HOUR 3–6 for a small restaurant/bar arouses curiosity in passersby. Who can attend a happy hour there? Corrections officers heading home to the south in their vehicles and undocumented immigrants heading north on foot are the only people out there. And besides, what is there to be happy about on that stretch except to leave it? Along with the state prison, the area is home to three other detention facilities, the George Bailey County Jail, the Wackenhut private jail, used for selected misdemeanor offenders, and a recently constructed county juvenile detention facility.

Donovan Prison is what Mark Elder has called home since his conviction in 2006. In keeping with Department of Corrections policy, Elder will probably be moved every few years unless he has special needs such as medical or behavioral issues.

THROUGH THE EYES OF A KILLER:
A Sunday Chat with Mark Elder

In early July 2007, I decided to attempt to interview Elder in prison. All he could do was say no.

I sent Elder a letter telling him I was writing a book about the case and asked to speak to him to get his side of the story. I also asked what he thought of his defense attorney, the prosecutor, the judge, and the jury. If he wanted to confess to other old murders and tell me where he buried the bodies, I was there for that too, although I never mentioned the latter possibility.

He answered back on July 26, 2007, saying he would speak with me. Elder wrote that he was glad someone wanted to write about his "incarcaration" (sic). I thought it unusual that he assumed he was going to be the focal point of the book and I was going to feature his incarceration. He was not my main interest. The focal point was the entire police investigation, including the trial, and the lives of those involved. Later, I learned that the response from him was consistent with his personality. He would have a part in the book, but only the part pertaining to his role as killer, and his role in the legal proceedings.

He sent me a visitor application to be filled out and approved before a visit could happen. Curiously enough, for the letter's closing, he wrote: "In Christ, Mark Elder." In Christ indeed. I did remember that the bumper sticker on his blue "rapemobile" van read, REAL MEN LOVE JESUS. Maybe we would get into his theological views during the visit.

I had been assigned to the South Bay Branch in Chula Vista for seven of my seventeen years as a district-attorney investigator. This office handled the prosecution of all the crimes inside Donovan Prison that the corrections officers brought to our attention. The state penal system has its own way of handling most transgressions that occur within the walls. That is, if a guy is caught with some minor contraband in his "house" [cell], the prison deals with it internally. The guy will get some form of restriction of privileges or extra confinement.

Even the discovery of weapons is not always grounds for formal criminal prosecution. The prison has a thing called a "115 Hearing." This is an in-house method of discipline. The inmates call it a "kangaroo court." No rules of evidence are present. No cross-examination of witnesses is held. A corrections officer will say, "I tossed Inmate Jones's cell and found a shank [makeshift prison knife] made from a toothbrush handle hidden under his mattress."

End of case. Jones gets some prison discipline, and a letter in his file to be reviewed at his next parole hearing.

If something more serious should happen, the prison staff can refer the case to the district attorney for prosecution. Those cases are difficult for the district attorney. First, most corrections officers are not in the business of writing reports and testifying in court. Writing and testifying are acquired skills that city cops and sheriff deputies employ daily. A trial in superior court is not a Prison 115 hearing. A courtroom contains a defense attorney who is accustomed to giving blistering cross-examinations of witness testimony. Because the COs (they don't like to be called "guards") don't usually deal with penal-code violations, they tend not to be familiar with evidence regulations and the chain of custody required in the state courts. Before sending cases to the D.A., corrections officers' reports don't receive the scrutiny from a supervisor that a regular cop's does.

As a D.A. investigator, it was my job to help the deputy district attorney get a criminal case ready for court. Among the more serious cases we handled was the attempted rape of a prison nurse (female) by an inmate on a quiet Sunday morning. We also handled several violent fights in the yard, including a stabbing captured on videotape. The cases were difficult because the COs were not at ease expressing themselves verbally in court, and they did not, as a rule, have the organizational skills associated with collecting evidence or writing detailed, chronological reports.

An additional problem for the prosecution was that almost everyone involved in the case presented a very fierce picture to the jurors. That is, a tattooed, muscular, brooding man would be seated at the defense table glowering at everyone. He was the defendant. The victim, also a tattooed, muscular, brooding man, who had had a prison-made knife shoved between his ribs, would be sitting in the witness box, alternately glaring at the defendant and the jurors. There were usually two or three corrections officers assigned to both the victim and defendant. Often the victim would not be cooperative.

I remember one case involving an inmate who had stabbed another in the yard of the Administrative Segregation Unit. (This is the latest euphemism for "solitary confinement," where the guys are let out of their cells into the recreation yard an hour a day.) The entire violent incident was memorialized on several videotapes from various angles in the yard. There was no doubt who the stabber and the stabbee were. It was right there for all to see, much like instant replay on a football game. The victim, after being sworn to tell the truth, the whole truth, and nothing but the truth, told the jury he didn't know who stabbed him. The deputy D.A. asked him if he recognized the man at the defense table. "I seen him around, I guess," was his answer.

"Did he stab you?"

"I dunno."

There was no conviction. The jury hung (could not reach a verdict), 6–6, probably because they were afraid of the victim, the defendant, and were most likely also afraid of the six corrections officers in the courtroom. The victim would usually settle the score in much the way it had all begun, at a different time, or have someone else do it.

In an effort to help the prosecution of these cases, I went to Donovan Prison on numerous occasions to give classes on how to testify in court. I also talked about the importance of writing accurate reports and doing proper interviews. Not much changed, however. I interviewed many inmates over the years for a variety of reasons.

What was nice was that if I wanted to come to the prison to interview an inmate, I would pick up the phone, call my contact at the Security Squad, and tell him what I wanted and when I would be coming. When I drove up, the gate guard would wave me through. The freshly scrubbed inmate would be waiting for me in an interview room. I would conduct my business and be on my way.

Because I retired as a police officer in January 2005, I was now nothing more than a regular citizen in my quest to interview Mark Elder. So I had to jump through all the hoops that a regular citizen does.

My first step was to fill out the multipage application Elder sent me, which contained all my vital information. The prison conducted a criminal record check on me. This takes about six weeks. The inmate would contact me to let me know if I had been approved.

When Elder sent my application, he said he did want to read my first book, *No Good Deed*. This was another true-crime book set in San Diego. I tried to mail him a copy, but the prison sent it back to me, saying books had to come from a publisher or a vendor. My editor at Berkley Books indicated she would mail him a book.

I looked at the numerous visitor rules on the California Department of Corrections Web site. I knew enough not to wear anything with denim, because the inmates wore denim. I knew enough not to bring firearms or alcohol or handcuff keys or a cake with a hacksaw inside. I wasn't quite ready for the whole experience, though. Visiting was allowed only on Saturdays and Sundays and selected holidays between 8 a.m. and 3 p.m.

I phoned the prison in the middle of the week to see if there had been any changes. I gave Elder's Department of Corrections number. I waited while the clerk clicked the numbers into the computer. "Inmate's name?" she asked.

"Mark Elder."

"Yes, he's here."

"Do I need an appointment?"

"Let's see. No, he doesn't have any restrictions. You can come anytime during visiting hours."

"Uh, I noticed on the rules that I can't bring paper or writing materials or a tape recorder. I'm writing a book about the murder this guy did. Is there anything I can bring to help me?"

The clerk was not sarcastic, and was quite pleasant as she said, "Bring a good memory."

Sunday, November 4, 2007, was a perfect day to visit a prison. The early fog was more reminiscent of Alcatraz in San Francisco than Donovan Prison in San Diego. The air was still damp, cold, thick, and heavy as I made my way to the parking lot. I couldn't help thinking of and pining for the "old days" when I would drive up, show my badge, meet the subject of the interview, and be gone in a hour or two.

The first thing you have to do is go to the visitors' trailer and sign in, picking up a numbered pass. My number was 314. There were about fifty people standing huddled in the dampness. I wondered what to do next. Within a few minutes a minibus pulled up. A uniformed corrections officer holding a clipboard got out. He hollered, "Number 230." And so it went until the fifteen seats were full. Then he took off.

About one hour and many pickups later, number 314 was called. We took the two-minute drive to the reception center. Inside, the people I had seen standing in line at the visitors' trailer were now standing in line in the reception center. A lighted sign like in a bakery or ice-cream store displaying changing "Now Serving" numbers hung on the wall above the two officers. I had no idea what to do. A very young woman with a toddler and a two-week-old infant told me when the number on my pass showed up I should go to one of the officers.

Within a minute "314" flashed. I presented my driver's license to an officer and sheepishly said, "This is my first time." I think he took pity on me because he actually offered some help, the only time a staff member did so all day. None of the staff ever exhibited any anger. They were expressionless when dealing with the public, kind of like the Pod People from *Invasion of the Body Snatchers*. I did see them laugh and joke among themselves. They sure flatlined us, though.

The officer pointed to two lines, a really long one, and a shorter one next to it, and said, "Get in that line."

"The long one?" I asked.

"Afraid so. When you get to the front, you'll have to take your shoes off and it'll be like just like the airport."

I got in line and stood there for about forty-five minutes as I inched my way to the next station. A lady with two young girls was next to me. We were going to the same place, the 3-Yard. The lady pointed out several people in front of me who were going to be rejected by the staff for improper dress. About 90 percent of the visitors were female. The rejections most often came because of clothing that was too tight, too revealing, or the wrong color. I knew about the color restrictions, but became confused about tightness. One woman left the room in tears. My companion in line said, "I knew it. The blouse is too tight." The expelled woman had on a blouse that I wouldn't have given a second look on the outside.

My new friend said, "I wear the exact same clothes every week. That way I know it's okay." She had on a pair of baggy cotton slacks, a baggy blouse, and a baggy jacket. The operative word was *baggy*.

I was saddened at the sight of so many young children visiting the prison. On the one hand, I realized that fathers should be allowed to see their kids. On the other, I was disturbed because the kids were learning at a very early age that prison was just a way of life. It was kind of like going to see Dad "at work," only he was in state prison. The kids accepted prison as a normal part of life. "Dad's in prison. He gets out in two years." They accept it, and the acceptance is not right. Who am I to deprive a family of not seeing one another? I don't know. I just don't like seeing all those young children view state prison as a regular part of life.

When I was back at the visitors' center, I noticed a handwritten sign saying gray T-shirts were forbidden, even though the Web site had said nothing about that. I was wearing gray cotton slacks, a plaid flannel shirt, and a gray T-shirt as an undershirt to protect against the morning chill. Once I saw the sign I buttoned my shirt all the way to the top.

I had left everything except my driver's license and car keys back at the car. When my turn finally came I walked up to the corrections officer. She looked me over and I apparently passed the visual. I removed my shoes, wrist-watch, belt, and even my glasses. My car keys had a remote locking device. Not good. I thought I was going to be banished. She did give me a lock and told me to put the key and remote in one of the lockers against the wall and scoldingly warned me never to bring the remote lock again. After securing my key and remote, I walked through the metal detector without incident then took a seat waiting for the bus to the 3-Yard. Soon an officer appeared who told everyone, "Anyone going to Four?" Half the people at the center got up and left.

The room filled up again. When all the chairs were taken, I stood up to let a woman who just passed through the metal detector sit down. A roomful of eyes collectively looked at me with what seemed like disbelief. No one apparently had ever offered his seat to an older woman. Soon an officer appeared asking for those going to 3. I verified it on my slip and stood up. A skinny, almost attractive girl who couldn't have been more than twenty said to me, "I hope we get there before count."

"What's count?" I asked.

"At eleven o'clock they have a head count. If we don't get there before, then we have to wait until one o'clock. I missed it yesterday and went home."

I looked at my watch. It was 10:48. Damn. I didn't want to wait, and I sure didn't want to go home and come back just to go through all this again. The girl asked the officer if we would make it.

"Dunno. It's gonna be close," was all he said without expression or inflection. I love it when a man hates his job.

"If you're with me, we aren't going to make it," I told the young girl. "It's always my luck." She laughed. I saw nothing to laugh about. Bad luck follows me like airline delays follow Ron Thill.

As things turned out, we did make it. Once inside the visitors' room, I looked around. It looked like a dining room. There were probably twenty-five square tables for four. Another woman with two young kids seemed to take pity on me. I don't know if it was the look on my face, like I'd just landed on another planet, or just plain bewilderment.

"Is it your first time?" she asked.

"Yes."

"Well, you can sit with us. We're waiting for my husband. They want everyone to be sitting down."

I looked around the room and saw that every table was occupied. I was grateful for the woman's hospitality, but wondered how long it would take for her husband to find his prison shank and ventilate my spleen for sitting with his woman.

She introduced herself and her daughters. "Who are you meeting?" she asked.

"Well, it's a guy who doesn't know me, but I know what he looks like."

She seemed confused. I told her I was there to interview a guy because I was writing a book about his case. She looked puzzled. "He's in for murder," I said.

She seemed to think writing a book about murder was quite cool. She offered her hand and said her name was Debbie. I told her my name, all the while looking for her husband, who might decide to stab me in the back or possibly in the kidney. Debbie was in her forties, and was by far the best-looking woman in the room.

Soon her husband—Tony—came up and shook my hand. While I was trying to look for an escape route in case he attacked me, or another place to sit, I saw Mark Elder enter the room. He stood just inside the entry looking around for his visitor. I thanked Debbie and Tony and excused myself.

———————

Mark stood just inside the doorway. Since I had been at his sentencing, I knew what he looked like, but he had never met me. I offered my hand and told him my name. Although the room was noisy and crowded, an outside patio was equipped with benches. "Can we go out there?" I asked.

"I don't know. I've never been here." Mark later told me he had not had a visitor since he had been in prison.

We sat out on the patio. I looked at the other inmates, a strange group of men, to be sure. For example, many of the tattoos they sported were "out there." I saw several guys loaded up with tattoos. While I don't have any feelings one way or another about someone having a tattoo, I think it is counterproductive for a career criminal to have a tattoo across his forehead. If you are embarking on a life of crime, why have a ready-made identifier? It made no sense. Some of the guys could probably credit their distinctive visible tattoos for earning them a place in the institution.

I remember when I was a working police officer, we bagged a few that way. Some store clerk who had been a victim of a robbery would describe a distinctive tattoo on the arm or neck or forehead of the person who robbed him. We would call the parole office and send a bulletin describing the strange tattoo. More often than not, we would get a call from a parole officer telling us he or she had our guy for a client. There is a sign in the entryway of county jail that reads LIFE IS TOUGH. IT'S TOUGHER IF YOU'RE STUPID. Ah yes, the tattoos.

There were many guys with shaved heads and elaborate tattoos on their skulls. There were dragons, flames, devil's horns, and a multitude of designs. I suppose if one wanted to conceal the head tattoos, one could grow hair or wear a hat.

———————

Mark looked heavier than he did at sentencing, going well over two hundred pounds with a large stomach. His hair was longer. My eyes kept going to the ring and pinkie fingers of his right hand. The digits were deformed. When he clenched his right hand, I noticed the fingers did not bend. I tried to make my fingers do that when I made a fist, but the ring finger always bent involuntarily.

I gave a brief introduction of myself again. I neglected to tell Elder I was a retired police officer. If he asked, I would have told him. If we had a second interview I would probably let him know then. Besides, I was no longer a sworn police officer, just a regular ink-stained wretch trying to write a book.

I told him I wouldn't ask him if he was guilty or not (because that had already been decided by twelve people). I told him I was interested in his personal background and what he thought of his treatment by the criminal-justice system, including the defense attorney, prosecutor, and judge.

He said, "I can tell you the entire story. Everything. It's bigger than you can imagine. I'll leave nothing out. But we gotta talk about compensation."

I don't usually interrupt. This time I had to in order to save time. "Mark," I said, "there is no compensation. I'm a beginning writer without a name who's only done one other book. Contrary to what you might think, I don't make much money on a book, about a buck an hour, I'd guess. Besides, I don't pay for interviews. Nobody but the supermarket tabloids and sensationalized TV shows pay. I'm writing a true-crime book. That's all. I'd like your input. If you don't want to talk about a specific subject, that's okay. Just tell me. I do have some questions, though."

He mentally chewed on the absence of compensation

for a while, his look going to other prisoners and their guests on the patio. I figured the interview was over, wondering how long I would have to wait for the two bus rides back to my car.

He pointed to a line of vending machines against the wall. "Okay, do you think you can buy me a soda?"

"Damn, Mark, I didn't know what I could bring in here. I left all my money in the car."

"Okay. Next time," he said. "You can bring five bucks in paper money and change in a plastic see-through bag." The interview was apparently back on.

We sat down and started in. Regarding his childhood, Mark said it was okay. He indicated he always had to do a lot of work around the house. His family had purchased a two-story fixer-upper in New Kensington, Pennsylvania. After they moved in, Mark helped his father constantly. He said he wasn't forced to work on the house, but it was "expected" of him. So he worked. He didn't play much with the other kids because of the work.

Mark said he was the middle of three children. His sister was slightly older. She and Mark didn't get along when they were growing up, and still don't to this day. Even though I knew why Mark said he didn't like her, I didn't let on, or ask why. He does like his younger brother. The family moved to Florida when he was fourteen. As a teenager, he was into surfing and motorcycles.

Thinking I was probably pressed for time, I jumped ahead from his adolescent life and time in Florida, asking him how he came to be in San Diego in June of 1988. At first he said he couldn't find work in Florida. He explained there was a recession and recessions start in the East and head west. Because I know as much about national economics as I do about molecular biology, I let him keep talking. He could be telling the truth, except I already knew there had been another reason for him going to California, recession or not.

Elder said his parents told him he could go anywhere in the United States, and they would provide bus fare. He said he knew that San Diego had the best climate of anywhere and he convinced them to send him there.

He didn't say anything about them giving him only half of the money, with the stipulation that they would give him the rest when he actually got to California, information I had learned from his sister.

"How'd you get back to Florida?" I asked.

Elder smiled and said, "It's a long story. I ended up going to Long Beach first."

I recalled Mark's sister's story of Mark finding a wallet and trying to extort money from the guy who lost it. Mark gave a slightly sanitized version of this. He actually admitted that he was doing something dishonest in calling the owner of the wallet and telling him he had the wallet, but it would cost him money to get it back. Mark admitted that the owner of the wallet set him up and the police arrested him. That's when he told me the real reason he left Florida.

"Part of the reason I left Florida was because I had warrants for me there and my parents wanted me to get out of the area." He said the warrants were for some fraud violations. After his arrest in Long Beach, Florida authorities extradited him back to that state to serve a sentence.

After he had paid his debt to the state of Florida, he wanted to go back to California because he liked it so well. (By this time in Mark's life, Janet Moore was dead. She was killed within a few days of Elder's arrival in California. Strangely enough, he said nothing about the dead girl. I kept listening.)

Back then, in 1988, he was thirty years of age. In California, he began working as a floor installer. He attended a local church, where he met his future wife, Mary. Elder couldn't remember the denomination of the church. At first he thought it was Episcopal. He described it as "waving their arms and dancing around."

"Do you mean Pentecostal?"

"Yeah, that's it."

When Elder spoke of his wife, a wistful look passed across his face. He said Mary was a wonderful person. Curiously, he added that he was the best thing that had ever happened to her. Later in the conversation he said his wife had told him, "The last ten years have been heaven." I decided not to ask why, if the last ten years had been so great, did she divorce him? (Author's note: I never interviewed Mary. I believed her burden in being married to Mark Elder was too great. She had been through enough. Had Mary asked, I would have interviewed her. When Cathy Byrne told her later about my conversation with Mark, Mary became angry over some of the things Mark had said. She told Cathy the early years of her marriage had been good, but the last few were awful. She toyed with the idea of talking with me. I told Cathy that Mary would have to call me. I would not call her because it might look like a coercive gesture on my part. And as I said, I believed Mary had suffered enough. She never contacted me.)

Mark said when his and Mary's son was born, he decided it would be best to return to Florida, where family was. So they moved back, Mark found work, and their lives went on.

This was a very nice story of the life of Mark Elder. But I knew there was a dead woman in California and at least ten women in Florida who said Mark Elder was a vicious animal who punched, choked, raped, and spewed profanity at an alarming rate. I needed to steer the conversation to something other than how nice things were, and what a great guy he was.

After all, he was sitting there wearing denim pants that read CDC (California Department of Corrections) in large

yellow letters, up near the belt. Bright letters reading PRIS-
ONER ran vertically down the length of his right leg. He
wasn't dressed like that for nothing.

"Mark, I don't want to talk about whether or not you
killed that girl in San Diego," I said. "But I have to say I
read the transcript of your trial testimony where you said
you had consensual sex with the girl. Then the guy came
in, punched you, killed her, and cut your fingers. It seemed
pretty unusual." I had to choose my words carefully. "I
have to tell you that if I had been on the jury, I wouldn't
have believed you and I would have voted to convict you.
What did you think of the jury?"

Elder smiled his friendly smile, shrugged, and said, "I
guess they didn't believe me." He offered no other explanation at that time.

I had read the Florida police reports, which had mentioned that some of the girls said he had a really nice smile
and was friendly at first (before he started beating, choking, and raping them). Elder said he had sex with the girl in
San Diego. (I never called her Janet, nor did Mark.) Soon
the Asian man burst into the room and started yelling at
both Mark and the girl. With one punch the man knocked
Mark unconscious. When Mark awoke he was bleeding
profusely. He couldn't use his two fingers on his right hand,
and the girl was dead.

"Man, there was blood all over the place," he said. "I
tried to clean up as best I could. I was lucky I didn't pass out
from loss of blood. I just wanted to get out of there."

This was not the time for a confrontation. As a veteran
police officer who had worked ten years in Patrol, and as a
licensed former boxing judge for the state athletic commission, I have seen many punches thrown. For Mark Elder to
say a little Asian man knocked him out with a single punch,
and didn't break his jaw or nose, or cause other facial damage, and that the blow had kept him unconscious while his

assailant killed a woman and disfigured Elder's hand, was just too much swallow. No wonder the jury didn't believe him.

My mind kept involuntarily recalling the words of Mark's sister, Cathy. "There are always two versions of what happened: The truth, and Mark's version."

"Let's talk about drugs," I said, not knowing how he would react.

Again the smile. "I used all of 'em except heroin," he said. "In fact, I love marijuana, always have. If you broke out a joint right now, I'd ask to share."

"Sorry, they searched me just before I came in."

Elder laughed at that. I believed we were bonding. (Good grief.) He continued speaking, saying that he used drugs a lot, and really liked cocaine. It became evident to me that if we were going to get to the meat, I was going to have to start asking pointed questions.

"Mark, you said you had a great marriage with Mary, and her life was 'heaven' with you. But you got divorced. How did that happen?"

Again the smile. He said he really liked Mary. She was a mixture of Filipina and Chinese and very sweet. "But she just didn't go for oral sex, and I liked that [oral sex]." Mark also said he was plagued with insomnia, even today. "I only sleep about an hour or two a night. I got tired of laying awake, so sometimes I would leave in the middle of the night."

Then he related a story about how one night he picked up a girl hitchhiking. As the story went on I realized he was telling me the same story his sister had related about Mark being with a hooker and being chased by an off-duty corrections officer. Only it was a different version—"Mark's version," as Cathy would say.

In Mark's version, he picked up a girl hitchhiking and asked where she was going. She told him her destination was a city farther than Mark was going. He said he could take her to the city right before the one she wanted to go to. She said, "If you take me all the way, I'll give you a blow job." Mark said that because his wife never offered him that benefit, he agreed. After the sex act was completed and they were on their way, the girl held out her hand and said, "Twenty dollars."

Mark said he asked what for and she said, "The blow job." Mark told her that wasn't part of the deal, that he was taking her the extra distance she needed to go. The additional distance was the price of the blow job, not twenty dollars. They argued and she got out at a stoplight. A man in a pickup truck was behind him. She got into the pickup truck and the truck followed Mark. Because he was scared, Mark eventually accelerated and tried to lose them. The "chase" went through several small cities. "Somehow, the cops got involved and a highway-patrol officer pulled me over. When the trooper came up to the car, I asked if he knew my sister, and he did." I began to marvel at the mind of Mark Elder. Again, his sister's words rang in my head. "There's the truth, and there's Mark's version."

Mark's sister had said Mark had been beating a woman and a corrections officer came to see what was going on. Mark fled with the woman in the vehicle. Mark's version was that he picked up a hitchhiker and they had a disagreement over a business deal for oral sex. She left Mark's vehicle and got into a total stranger's truck and the stranger agreed to get into a high-speed pursuit of the man even though he didn't know either Mark or the girl. It was strange indeed.

"What about the divorce?" I asked.

Mark explained that his wife had become very irate with him after the chase incident. They fought a lot. One day Mary came at him with a hammer. He was able to pin her arms to her body and spin her around in order to protect himself. She bit him on the arm. Mark said the police showed up, saw the bite mark on his arm, and arrested Mary.

My mind went to the story Mark's sister told of the biting incident. The versions were similar in some parts, but really quite different in totality. "How did the cops get called?" I asked. I remembered that after the bite, Mary went across the street to her in-laws, and the police didn't get called for six or seven hours. "Oh, the fight went all over the place, even outside. I guess the neighbors called."

"What happened to Mary?"

"She got arrested and taken to jail. I called the state's attorney the next day and had the charges dropped."

Mark's sister said the state's attorney dropped the charges on her own after listening to Mary's story and noticing that the bite mark suggested that Mark had been holding her from behind and was received in an attempt to free herself. Again, there were two versions. I was starting to get a feel for Mark Elder.

Mark said he really believed his parents wanted him to divorce Mary. I asked why. He didn't know. I asked how he came to that conclusion.

"We had been separated for a little while. Mary and me were working things out and I hoped we would be able to get back together. One day I was over at my parents' house. Mary wasn't there. We was watching television. My dad was in a chair, and my mom was laying across the couch. I casually mentioned to them, 'Mary and me might be getting back together.' Well, my mother sat upright and said, 'That's what you say.' To me, that proved they didn't want us back together."

Because I had not been in the room with them when

this conversation took place, I couldn't get a feel for the situation. But to imply that his parents wanted them separated because of those four words by his mother seemed to be a stretch to me. I *really* was starting to get a feel for Mark Elder.

———

Time was moving on in the visiting area of the prison and I needed to get to the nitty-gritty, as best I could.

"Mark, I don't know what happened in San Diego, and I don't know what happened in Florida. I do know about nine or ten women in Florida all said the same thing about you. They said you picked them up, had sex with them, beat them, and threw them out of the vehicle. And one of them, the one who reported it to the police, had your semen in her. Maybe some of them jumped on the bandwagon after you were arrested. But all those women said the same thing. Are they making it up, and what about the semen?"

"Tom, you mentioned ten prostitutes. Try sixtyfold."

Inwardly I was shocked, but tried to maintain an even expression. I told him I wasn't very good in math, but sixty times ten came to about six hundred. I asked if that was correct. He said about six hundred women was correct.

The smile again. "Tom, I hate prostitutes. Really hate them," he said. "I hate prostitutes with a passion."

I nodded in agreement. I had seen crime-scene pictures of Janet Moore. All you could do was agree with Mark Elder on this point. He did hate prostitutes.

He explained that he had his own plan about what to do about prostitutes.

———

Mark said he had often been out late at night because he couldn't sleep. Driving along, he would see the women out on Atlantic Avenue or other places he frequented. He knew the women were prostitutes and he hated prostitutes. Why else would those women be out there at that time dressed in those clothes unless they were prostitutes?

Mark said he would pick up a prostitute. They would make a verbal deal for the sex act and agree on how much the sex would cost. Usually the woman suggested where to go to "do it," either a motel, or someplace off the path, but still in the area of a commercial strip near the beach.

"Even though I'd agree, I would never actually go to a motel, or where they suggested," he said. "As we drove I always told them I knew a better place. Then I'd keep driving and take 'em way out there."

Mark said they would drive several miles to a remote area. "I'd do this because it would be a long way back for them." Once at their destination, he and the woman went to the back of the van.

"This is when they always want their money, before anything happens. They'd ask for the money. I'd tell 'em I had trouble sometimes gettin' it up. And I didn't want to pay for anything I wasn't going to get, in case I had trouble, you know."

Elder said that quite often the girls wouldn't buy his excuse for not paying until the sex was over. They would demand the money up front, no matter what his problems were. "If they insisted on their money I'd throw 'em out of the van and make 'em walk back. They'd be out there in the middle of nowhere." He explained that he would lecture them that they shouldn't be prostitutes while he was booting them out the door.

"Now, sometimes the girls would believe me, and think they were going to get paid after we were done doing our thing."

"What would happen then?" I asked.

"Well, we'd do our thing, either regular sex, or a blow job, whatever I wanted. Then they'd ask for their money." Elder smiled again. He said he would tell them there wasn't going to be any money. They shouldn't be out there prostituting themselves; it was a horrible, nasty job, and it was wrong. Then he'd throw them out and make them walk back to wherever they'd come from.

"I'd tell 'em I didn't want to see them out on the street again. If I did see 'em, they'd be in big trouble."

———

Later, as I was digesting what Mark had said, a few things came clear to me. First, nine different women had accused him of sexual assault. When asked about this, he himself estimated the number was closer to six hundred. But in "The Truth According to Mark," no sexual violence ever took place. If no consensual sex act happened out in the middle of nowhere, he would merely have thrown the woman out of his van. This was not a violation of criminal law. Somewhere in that scenario a criminal solicitation for prostitution took place. There was no way of knowing if the solicitation came from Mark or the woman. So far, given Mark's version of events, he had not committed a criminal violation of the law.

In the scenario where he and the woman did perform a sex act, again there was no violence, according to Mark. He said the woman was stupid enough to believe him when he said he would pay her when it was over. Instead, he would lecture her and throw her out of the van. Again, there was no violence associated with this activity, according to Mark.

Later, in thinking about what Mark said he did, I marveled at how his mind worked. He conveniently removed any criminal responsibility from himself. Instead, he actually believed he was performing a community service in the form of prostitution abatement.

———

I asked Elder about the "Marsden hearing" before the start of his preliminary hearing. I told him I knew those hearings dealt with a defendant "divorcing" the defense attorney.

"Why did you want to get rid of Mr. Ford?"

Elder gave a slight laugh. "That guy," he said. "He told me he thought I was guilty. I just couldn't trust him after that."

"Mark, are you sure he told you he thought you were guilty?" I have been involved with defense attorneys for many years. One of the subjects they almost never broach is whether or not their client actually committed the crime for which they are charged. Most defendants really are factually guilty. That is not the point. The point is whether the prosecution can prove it.

So, I doubt if Ford even asked Elder if he "did it." Defense attorneys, if they say anything, say, "I don't care if you did it. I only care if they can prove you did it." The most logical scenario was that Ford laid out the facts and wondered how he and Mark could overcome the large amount of evidence against Mark.

"What did you tell Judge Valentine?"

"I told him I didn't trust Ford, that he said he thought I was guilty."

"Then what?"

"The judge asked Ford if he said that. Ford said he didn't say he thought I was guilty. He really did say I was guilty, though."

"I guess the judge didn't remove him."

"Nah. He said there wasn't no way to prove that. So, Ford stayed."

"It must have been rough since that trust was gone."

"Yeah."

I reminded Mark that he testified, but the jury found him guilty. "Didn't they believe you?"

"It's hard to say. I made a mistake, or somebody did

anyway. My attorney told me to talk to the jury. You know, look at them when I was talking. Well, I was raised to talk to the person who was talking to me. So, when my attorney and the lady attorney"—Prosecutor Andrea Freshwater— "were asking me questions, I would give my answer to them and not the jury.

"If I would have looked at the jury, it would have been really weird. I would have had to look at the attorney on the other side of the room when they asked the question and then turn to the jury to give the answer. Too awkward, man."

"What did you think of Ms. Freshwater, the prosecutor?"

"She was weird."

"No kidding. How?"

"She was saying that I did things to the body, and that wasn't true. That was sick, man."

"Other than that, what did you think of her?"

"Okay, I guess. She was just doing her job."

Elder's take was interesting. The jury voted to convict him not because he was a sadistic, violent murderer, rapist, and sociopath, but because HE DIDN'T LOOK AT THEM.

While sitting in the patio of the visiting area, I had other questions for Mark. The questions that day were merely of the "softball" variety. That is, I wouldn't question or confront him about anything dicey. I wanted to keep things comfortable. I wanted him to feel at ease with me. If he wanted to believe I was accepting everything he said, that was okay too.

I told him I needed to think about what we had talked about. I said I would come up with additional questions, write them down, and mail them to him. That way, he could think about the answers before I came back. I asked if that was okay. He agreed.

When Mark had written to me the first two times, he closed his letters with "In Christ." Knowing that he'd met his wife at a church, I thought he might be religious, the violent brutal sex acts notwithstanding.

"Mark, is Sunday a good day to come, or should I come on Saturday?" I thought he might go to chapel services on Sunday and the interview today was keeping him from doing so.

"Come on a Saturday next time," he said.

"Oh, do you go to church services?"

"No, NASCAR is on television on Sunday."

While driving home, I continued to think about the interview with Mark Elder. In my mediocre college career I think I took only an introductory psychology class. But I am familiar with the term *narcissism*. Among other things, it means "an excessive interest in one's own importance, abilities, etc." That definition begins to describe Mark Elder. In his mind he is at the center of the universe.

He thought I wanted to write a book about his "incarcaration" (sic). It didn't matter that there had been a massive cross-country police investigation after the brutal murder of a young girl and the rapes of at least nine others. No, he thought I wanted to write about his imprisonment, as if Mark Elder's time in prison was the focal point of everything.

Elder really believed the jury convicted him not because they believed he brutally murdered Janet Moore, but because he didn't look at them while he was testifying. He found a convenient excuse for what had landed him in prison, and it didn't involve anything he did wrong. If he only would have looked at the jury.

At the beginning of our conversation he said he moved to California from Florida because of a recession in the Eastern part of the United States. He didn't mention anything about being wanted by the police. It was only after I directly asked him how he got back to Florida that he said he was extradited by the authorities to answer fraud charges.

Mark said he never raped any hookers. He tried to point them on the path away from prostitution. No matter that they all said they were beaten, choked, and raped. In Elder's description of the events he never broke any laws. He only kicked them out of his vehicle and failed to pay them, if they did have sex. He was doing them a favor by lecturing them to stop being prostitutes.

———————

Six days later I received a letter from Elder. He told me the program officer at the prison called him in to tell him he was going to be transferred to Mule Creek Prison, about a hundred miles north of Sacramento. He said I should come to see him soon. Then came the inevitable: He told me to send him a money order, not for five or ten dollars, but for a hundred dollars. He didn't ask for the money. He *told* me to send it to him. Elder apparently forgot that I said I didn't pay for interviews. I did offer to bring change for him to buy something from the vending machines. He closed with "Thank you" and not "In Christ."

That letter concluded my communication with him. When I mentioned Elder's request for a money order to a cynical relative of mine, the relative said I should have gone to the prison for another interview. I should have told Mark, "I'll pay you, but I want to make sure you've given me enough good information. I won't pay you until AFTER the interview."

If he wouldn't agree, I would get up and leave. If he

agreed to the interview without an up-front payment, I would proceed with it. When it came time to pay, I would have done what he did to the hookers—not paid him, while reminding him I did not pay for interviews.

We never corresponded after that.

AFTERWORD

I write books about murder for a number of reasons. Chief among them is to let readers not involved in homicide investigation know what it is like to work a murder from start to finish. Television doesn't do justice to the effort, although a few "true" shows like *The First 48* do a commendable job.

I want the reader to experience, through my words, the frustrations, the disappointments, and hopefully the exhilaration of finally solving a case and getting a conviction. (Sometimes cops know who did a killing, but through no fault of their own, they can't muster enough evidence to convict.) I want readers to learn about the criminal-justice system and the joys and problems of being a cop.

I don't write true crime to sensationalize or titillate, even though, because of human nature, many interesting murder cases have an erotic component. I write to entertain, and to educate. Sometimes families are reluctant to talk about a family member involved in a murder. A few of Janet's relatives wanted to talk to me. They did talk enough to tell me they were afraid of incurring the wrath of Janet's sister Sandra. So they didn't talk, except to apologize for not talking.

Dale Moore, the minister from Indiana, agreed to send a photograph of Janet for inclusion in the book. In fact, he agreed to send it four times—each time I called him. Dale was always a perfect gentleman, polite and soft-spoken. I never got the photo, though. If I called him any more times, I was afraid he would accuse me of harassment.

I assured Janet's family I was not going to write the story as if it were a supermarket tabloid. I wanted to present a complete picture of Janet—the daughter, sister, artist, and friend. Most family members stayed steadfast in their refusal to cooperate. They believed that if they refused to give information about Janet, I would abandon the project.

Others subsequently agreed to reveal bits of information about Janet if I did not identify them. They realized that prostitution and drug use are facts of life, and an integral part of this particular criminal case. The activities outside the law are a matter of public record. I didn't need anyone from the family to talk about that aspect of Janet's life. I wanted them to tell me the good things about her. For the most part they were afraid to tell me anything. Sandra's influence on them was strong.

When all is said and done about a case such as the Janet Moore murder, is there anything to be learned? What good can result from a story like this? Some might say I am merely a cheerleader for the police, attacking artists who question the motivations of the police and giving short shrift to the many defense attorneys who labor fiercely to defend their clients. While it is true that I worked Homicide for many years, experiencing both the frustration and exhilaration of the job, I also recognize good work done by good cops, and poor work from lazy and insensitive cops.

I was critical of the Florida officers who took lightly the crimes against the prostitutes. It is true that most women who work the streets do not confine their lawbreaking to sexual activities. Most, if not all, are involved in drugs. Many steal from their victims, and also engage in burglary, shoplifting, and various scams. Some even set their johns up to be robbed and/or beaten by male accomplices who act as pimps and bodyguards. Truth be told, many street hookers, in spite of being human beings, are really among the dregs of society. Nevertheless, if a prostitute claims to be a victim of a crime, police officers cannot and should not decide to take, or not take, a crime report depending on the victim's standing in society.

The Florida street cops should have been more receptive to the prostitutes who claimed to have been raped. The police administrators for the local departments should have had better communication when looking for Mark Elder. It's not easy for them to change, but it's not too late either.

Defense attorneys everywhere who are charged with defending people like Mark Elder have their work cut out for them. The conservative media vilify many defense attorneys. "How can they defend that monster?" they ask when someone goes on trial for a particularly gruesome murder. Yet everyone is entitled to a vigorous defense. Ideally, when a guilty "monster" is arrested, he should do the right thing and "plead to the sheet," thus saving the taxpayers time, money, and anguish. But because we live where we do, such malefactors are entitled to the best defense. Dedicated defense attorneys are a necessity in our country, even though we sometimes lose sight of this.

Public defenders get a bad rap, even from those in jail. I have heard many crooks say, "I would have been found not guilty, but I had a public defender." The assumption that a public defender is a second-class attorney is a myth. In my experience, public defenders are often excellent attorneys. Due to time constraints, they often "cut to the chase" and accept reality. If they think they can get a client off, they give it a try. If they know they are doomed by an abundance of evidence against their client, they try to get a plea to the best, most lenient charge they can. Public defenders are pragmatic.

I sent Mark's sister, Cathy Byrne, a message a week after I interviewed her: "After hearing what you and your brother Matthew had to say, it became clear to me that, even though Janet Moore was the victim in this case, Mark has victimized your entire family."

She wrote back, "Janet's family was terrorized on one single, horrible night. Mark has been terrorizing his family for over forty years."

Janet's family also endured eighteen years of uncertainty. They never gave up hope, or at least they said they never did. They continued to have faith in the San Diego Police Department. Even though the investigation and trial are over, the victimization of both families continues, and will continue.

One thing is certain: the death of Janet Moore was "not just another murder."

ACKNOWLEDGMENTS

I could not have written this without the cooperation of several people. Many thanks to San Diego District Attorney Bonnie Dumanis for her encouragement and support. The district attorney's staff also helped immensely, including paralegal Bill Reich, investigator Ron Thill, and Deputy District Attorney Andrea Freshwater.

David Cornacchia from the San Diego Police Department Forensic Laboratory was helpful and patient while explaining the DNA extraction process and how it related to this case. Retired detectives Ed Petrick and Terry Torgersen also provided assistance. Jaime Bordine's widow, Marcia, was helpful and generous.

I am indebted to authorities in Florida, especially Detective (now sergeant) Cynthia Gambrell and Officer Jason Kilker. The San Diego murder would never have been solved without their tenacity and dedication.

Louis Hock from the University of California San Diego Art School allowed me to view material he and his group produced during their "No Humans Involved" project.

Cathy Byrne and Matthew Elder, Mark Elder's siblings, were terrific. They were both painfully candid regarding the past history of Mark Elder. Their information provided at least a beginning of understanding of Mark Elder, although I doubt if total understanding of this man is possible.

Members of Janet Moore's family were reluctant to speak with me for fear of alienating one of Janet's sisters. "Uncle Bob" Moore gave me some short anecdotes about Janet, which were a nice addition.

I would also like to thank Thomas Shess, veteran marketing guy and publicist, for helping me see things through the eyes of a businessman. It's nice to write a book, but it's nicer if people buy the book. Bob Conrad assisted with assembling and producing photographs.

Elder's defense attorney, Robert Ford, while not speaking directly about Mark's case, gave good information about how a defense attorney views his work.

Thank you to my former editor, Katie Day, for taking a chance on me when someone else gave up on me. Best of luck in her new position at Columbia University. My current editor, Andie Avila, had great vision in the final production of this book, providing excellent and helpful ideas. When we conflicted, she was usually right. My agent, Jim Cypher, was a most fortunate find for me. I am greatly indebted to him.

Thanks to Mark Elder for allowing me to interview him in prison. I thought the interview would be entertaining. It was.

Tom Basinski was a police officer for thirty-five years (one year Flint, Michigan, seventeen years Chula Vista, California Police, seventeen years San Diego District Attorney Investigator). He holds a B.A. in English literature from St. Mary's University, San Antonio, Texas.

He has written more than 125 true crime stories for various pulp magazines over the years along with two award-winning stories for *San Diego* magazine. His first book, *No Good Deed*, was published in May 2006.

Tom and his wife, Judy, have two adult sons. They live in Chula Vista, California, and Clio, Michigan.